S0-BND-114

ASIAN HISTORICAL DICTIONARIES
Edited by Jon Woronoff

1. *Vietnam,* by William J. Duiker. 1989
2. *Bangladesh,* by Craig Baxter and Syedur Rahman. 1989
3. *Pakistan,* by Shahid Javed Burki. 1991
4. *Jordan,* by Peter Gubser. 1991
5. *Afghanistan,* by Ludwig W. Adamec. 1991
6. *Laos,* by Martin Stuart-Fox and Mary Kooyman. 1992
7. *Singapore,* by K. Mulliner and Lian The-Mulliner. 1991
8. *Israel,* by Bernard Reich. 1992
9. *Indonesia,* by Robert Cribb. 1992
10. *Hong Kong and Macau,* by Elfed Vaughan Roberts, Sum Ngai Ling, and Peter Bradshaw. 1992
11. *Korea,* by Andrew C. Nahm. 1993
12. *Taiwan,* by John F. Copper. 1993
13. *Malaysia,* by Amarjit Kaur. 1993

Historical Dictionary of the Republic of Korea

by

ANDREW C. NAHM

Asian Historical Dictionaries, No. 11

The Scarecrow Press, Inc.
Metuchen, N.J., & London
1993

Maps 1 to 5 on pages lvi to lx were provided courtesy of Hollym Corporation International in Seoul, South Korea, and Elizabeth, NJ, from its publication *Korea: Tradition and Transformation—A History of the Korean People* (1988), authored by Andrew C. Nahm. Map 6 on page lxi was provided courtesy of the Office of Public Information, the Republic of Korea, publisher of the annual *Handbook of Korea.*

British Library Cataloguing-in-Publication data available

Library of Congress Cataloging-in-Publication Data

Nahm, Andrew C.
Historical dictionary of the Republic of Korea / by Andrew C. Nahm.
p. cm. — (Asian historical dictionaries ; no. 11)
Includes bibliographical references.
ISBN 0-8108-2603-8 (acid-free paper)
1. Korea—History—Dictionaries. 2. Korea (South)—History—Dictionaries. I. Title. II. Series.
DS909.N34 1993
951.9′003—dc20 93-3033

Printed on acid-free paper

This Dictionary is dedicated to the people in the Republic of Korea who struggle for democracy and for the construction of social and economic justice while promoting their culture.

CONTENTS

EDITOR'S FOREWORD

It seems that the Republic of Korea, or more commonly South Korea, is always in the news. You had the Korean War, acts of aggression by the North, peace feelers with the North, etc., or stories of another coup, military intervention, riots and demonstrations, followed by the birth pangs of democracy. Meanwhile, on the economic side, the newspapers were busy writing about mismanagement and corruption, then more positively a transformation, and finally an "economic miracle" with incredible growth rates and vast increases in exports. Good or bad, South Korea has been in the public eye.

But all this coverage has not always guaranteed that foreigners (or Koreans) really knew what was going on. For there was usually a bias in the reports (for or against) as well as a tendency to highlight the more sensational events and downplay everything else. So it is good to pause once in a while to get a balanced and objective view, one that provides a longer perspective, and also covers more aspects of South Korean life. That is the purpose of this Dictionary, one it has accomplished quite nicely through a lengthy introduction, numerous entries and tables, a rather detailed chronology, and a comprehensive bibliography.

This latest addition to the series was written by Andrew C. Nahm, professor of history emeritus at Western Michigan University. A Korean, who knows his country extremely well, Dr. Nahm has been teaching Korean history for three decades. He has also written numerous articles and monographs as well as several books. The most recent one is *Korea: Tradition and Transformation—A History of the Korean People.*

Jon Woronoff
Series Editor

PREFACE

There has been a dire need for a Dictionary of Korean history for students and laypeople. Therefore, I was happy to undertake the task of compiling a Historical Dictionary of the Republic of Korea when I was asked to do so.

This Dictionary covers the history of the Republic of Korea or South Korea, which emerged in 1948. The items included in the book encompass domestic, political and social events, foreign affairs, along with economic and cultural development, together with the men and women who have influenced the multifarious events that make up a country's history. However, the chronology and historical narrative included in this book cover the entire history of Korea for the benefit of users of this Dictionary who have little or no knowledge about the history of the Korean people.

This Dictionary is intended as a reference-companion for those who are interested in the history of the Republic of Korea. The selection of topics for a book of this size is difficult: many individuals and incidents have been omitted only with the greatest reluctance. I have attempted to compile a guide to the state of new nation of South Korea in action.

Biographies of most major political and historical figures are included. Unfortunately, the poets, artists, musicians, scientists and business persons who have made major changes to the cultural and social life of the people in South Korea are not included, mainly because of the lack of space.

In compiling this Dictionary, I have used the best available bibliographies, books, magazines and newspapers, and yearbooks and annuals of various kinds, and have tried to summarize the important historical events that took place up to the year 1992. The alphabetical arrangement of the main body of the book is complemented by a chronology, a year-by-year survey of events of major importance in the entire history of Korea, with more items related to South Korea since 1945.

The Romanization system used in this book is that of the Ministry of Education of the Republic of Korea, which is a modified version of the McCune-Reischauer system, widely used in the United States and Europe. I have adopted this because it represents Korean sounds more accurately. For more information on the Korean writing system and Romanization, see pages xi–xiii.

The Romanized Korean names (personal as well as place names) well-known in the West are not changed according to this system. Thus, such individual names as Syngman Rhee, Park Chung-hee, Kim Dae-jung, Kim Jong-pil, Kim Young-sam, and Roh Tae-woo appear in this book as they are instead of Yi Sŭng-man, Pak Chŏng-hŭi, Kim Tae-jung, Kim Chong-p'il, Kim Yŏng-sam, and No T'ae-u. Incidentally, all Korean given names are preceded by surnames (clan names), and given names are hyphenated, except when the given name has a single Chinese character instead of two. The spelling of names of certain well-known places such as Seoul, Pyongyang, and Panmunjom are not changed, although they should be Romanized as Sŏul, P'yŏngyang, and P'anmunjŏm, respectively. Similarly, names of certain industrial firms and educational institutions are kept as they have been known. They are (correct Romanization in parenthesis): Hyundai (Hyŏndae), Samsung (Samsŏng), and Daewoo (Taeu) corporations, and Yonsei (Yŏnse) and Ewha (Ihwa) universities.

I hope that this Dictionary will provide some help to those wishing to increase their knowledge of Korea in general, its history since 1945 in particular, and also generate further studies in this area. The author wishes to express his appreciation for editorial assistance which his wife, Monica, rendered to him, and his thanks to Opal Ellis and Alberta Cumming, secretaries of the History Department of Western Michigan University, for their manuscript typing.

Andrew C. Nahm
Professor of History Emeritus
Western Michigan University
Kalamazoo, Michigan

THE KOREAN WRITING SYSTEM AND ROMANIZATION—A PRONUNCIATION GUIDE

The Koreans had no written language of their own until the middle of the fifteenth century. From the early seventh century to that time, educated Koreans wrote their books and essays in Chinese, the language which was introducted to Korea some time in the fourth century B.C.

In the seventh century, the Korean scholars adopted a device called *kugyŏl* to read Chinese writing in Korean. Meanwhile, they borrowed certain Chinese characters to represent Korean words, including inflections and postpositions. The systems they used to transliterate Korean words into Chinese characters were *idu* and *hyangch'al.* With these devices they wrote native songs called *saenaenorae* ("new native songs") or *hyangga* ("native songs") of various categories.

It was in 1446 that the Koreans were given a writing system of their own by King Sejong (r. 1418–1450) who is known as Sejong the Great. He commissioned certain members of the academy of scholars called Hall of Worthies (Chiphyŏnjŏn) to create an indigenous alphabet for the Korean language. When the new scripts were created by them, King Sejong adopted the new system and it was promulgated in 1446 in *Hunmin chŏng'ŭm,* or the "Correct Sounds to Instruct the People," commonly known as *han'gŭl,* ("Korean letters") or *ŏnmun* ("vernacular letters").

Originally, *han'gŭl* had eleven single vowels and seventeen single consonants, in addition to seven compound vowels (diphthongs) and a dozen compound consonants. Currently, only ten vowels and fourteen consonants, along with diphthongs and compound consonants, are in use.

The six single vowels (monophthongs) of Korean are: *a, ŏ, o, u, ŭ* and *i,* and they are pronounced as follows:

a as the *a* in father
o as the *o* in Ohio
ŭ as the *e* in De Gaulle
ŏ as the *u* in but
u as the *u* in rule
i as the *i* in India

The four other monophthongs which have two sounds are: *ya, yŏ, yo,* and *yu. Yŏ* is pronounced like the *you* in young.

There are seven compound vowels (diphthongs) in Korean, and some of them are pronounced as single vowels as follows:

ae as the *a* in apple
oe like German ö

Other diphthongs are *yae, ye, ui* and *ŭi.* The last two diphthongs are pronounced as follows:

ui like *wi*
ŭi like ŭ-i

A diphthong which is Romanized as *e* has a single sound like a monophthong, and it is pronounced as the *e* in egg.

Vowels in other cases must be pronounced separately as in the cases of *ai* (a-i) and *oi* (o-i).

The Korean consonants *ch, k, p,* and *t* are generally pronounced as follows:

ch as *j*
p as *b* or *v*
k as *g*
t as *d*

When these consonants are followed by a diacritical mark (apostrophe), the sound of each consonant becomes aspirated and changes as follows:

ch' as the *ch* in chance
p' as the *p* in paper
k' as the *k* in king
t' as the *t* in tank

There are a dozen compound (double) consonants in Korean. Some of them carry hard sounds. They are kk, pp, ss, tt and tch, and they are pronounced as follows:

kk as the *g* in god
ss as the *s* in Sam
tch as the *j* in Jack
pp as the *b* in bat
tt as the *d* in dam

Occasionally, an apostrophe is used to separate the sounds of two consonants in such cases as (*han'gŭl*), Han'guk (Han-guk), and Tan'gun (Tan-gun).

Certain Japanese words that appear in this Dictionary are Romanized according to the Hepburn system. Thus long vowels (ō and ū) have a short bar over the vowel. The distinction between long and short vowels is very important in Japanese.

ABBREVIATIONS AND ACRONYMS

ANSP	Agency for National Security Planning (Kukka Anjŏn Kihoekbu)
ASEAN	Association for Southeast Asian Nations
ASPAC	Asia and Pacific Council
CHAMINT'U	Chauju Minju T'ujaeng (Self-oriented Struggle for Democracy)
CHOKCH'ŎNG	Chosŏn Minjok Ch'ŏngnyŏndan (Korean National Youth Corps)
CHŎN-DAEHYŎP	Chŏn'guk Taehaksaeng Taep'yo Hyŏpŭihoe (National Council of Representatives of University Students)
CHŎN'GUK YŎNHAP	National Alliance for Democracy and Unification
CHŎN'GYOJO	National Teacher's Union
CHŎN-MINYŎN	Chŏn'guk Minjujuŭi Undong Yŏnhaphoe (National Coalition for a People's Democratic Movement)
CHŎN-NOHYŎP	Chŏn'guk Nodong Chohap Hyŏpŭihoe (National Council of Labor Unions)
CHŎN'NONG	Chŏn'guk Nongmin Chohap Ch'ongyŏnmaeng (National Federation of Farmers' Unions)
CHŎNP'YŎNG	Chosŏn Nodong Chohap Chŏn'guk P'yŏngŭihoe (National Council of Korean Labor Unions)

CPD	Council for the Promotion of Democracy (Minjujuŭi Ch'oksŏng Hyŏpŭihoe)
CPNR	Committee for the Preparation of National Reconstruction (Kŏnguk Chunbi Wiwŏnhoe)
DJP	Democratic Justice Party (Minju Chŏng'ŭidang)
DKP	Democratic Korea Party (Minju Han'guk Tang)
DLP	Democratic Liberal Party (Chayu Minjudang)
DMZ	Demilitarized Zone
DP	Democratic Party (Minjudang)
DRP	Democratic Republican Party (Minju Konghwadang)
FKEA	Federation of Korean Education Associations
HAN'GUK NORYŎN	Han'guk Nodong Chohap Ch'ongyŏnmaeng (General Federation of Korean Labor Unions)
HANMINDANG	Han'guk Minjudang (Korean Democratic Party)
IAAF	International Athletic Association Federation
KAIST	Korea Advanced Institute for Science and Technology
KCIA	Korean Central Intelligence Agency (Chungang Chŏngbobu)
KCP	Korean Communist Party (Chosŏn Kongsandang)

KDI	Korean Development Institute
KDP	Korean Democratic Party (Chosŏn Minjudang)
KEDI	Korean Educational Development Institute
KFLTU	Korean Federation of Teachers' Labor Unions
KIST	Korea Institute of Science and Technology
KNCW	Korean National Council of Women
KNP	Korean Nationalist Party (Han'guk Kungmindang)
KOTRA	Korea Trade Promotion Association
LCNS	Legislative Council for National Security (Kukka Powi Ippŏp Hoeŭi)
LP	Liberal Party (Chayudang)
MINCH'ŎNG	Chosŏn Minju Ch'ŏngnyŏn Tongmaeng (Alliance of Democratic Korean Youth)
MINCH'UWI	Minjujuŭi Ch'ujin Wiwŏnhoe (Committee for Promotion of Democracy)
MINT'ONGYON	Minjujuŭi T'ongil Yŏnmaeng (Joint Masses Movement for Democracy and Unification)
MP	Masses (People's) Party (Minjungdang)
MRC	Military Revolutionary Committee (Kunsa Hyŏngmyŏnghoe)
NCU	National Conference for Unification (T'ongil Kungmin Hoeŭi)

NCWO	National Council of Women's Organizations
NDP	New Democratic Party (Shinminjudang)
NDRP	New Democratic Republican Party (Shin Minju Konghwadang)
NDUP	New Democratic United Party (Shin-Minju Yŏnhaptang)
NIE	National Institute of Education
NIERT	National Institute of Educational Research and Training
NKDP	New Korea Democratic Party (Shin Han'guk Minjudang)
NKP	New Korea Party (Saehandang)
NNSC	Neutral Nations Supervisory Commission
NONGHYŎP	Nong'ŏp Hyŏptong Chohap (Association of Agricultural Cooperatives)
NPNPR	Party for New Political Reform (Shin-jŏngdang)
NTU	National Teachers' Union
PPD	Party for Peace and Democracy (P'yŏnghwa Minjudang)
RDP	Reunification Democratic Party (T'ongil Minju-dang)
SAM-MINT'UWI	Committee for the Three People's Struggles
SCNR	Supreme Council for National Reconstruction (Kukka Chaegŏn Ch'oego Hoeŭi)
SCNSM	Special Committee for National Security Measures (Kukka Powi Pisang Taech'aek Wiwŏnhoe)

SKIG	South Korean Interim Government (Nam Chosŏn Kwado Chŏngbu)
SKILA	South Korean Interim Legislative Assembly (Nam Chosŏn Kwado Ippŏp Ŭiwŏn)
SKWP	South Korean Workers' Party (Namchosŏn Nodongdang)
TAEHAN NOCH'ONG	Taehan Tongnip Ch'oksŏng Nodong Ch'ongdongmaeng (General Alliance of Laborers for Rapid Realization of Korean Independence)
TEAHAN NORYŎN	Taehan Nodong Chohap Ch'ongyŏnmaeng (General Federation of Korean Labor Unions)
TOKCH'OK	Tongnip Ch'oksŏng Kungmin Hyŏp'uihoe (National Council for Rapid Realization of Korean Independence)
UNCURK	United Nations Commission for Unification and Rehabilitation of Korea
UNKRA	United Nations Korean Reconstruction Agency
UNTCOK	United Nations Temporary Commission on Korea
UNP (UPP)	Unification National Party, also known as United People's Party (T'ongil Kungmindang)
USAFIK	United States Armed Forces in Korea
USAMGIK	United States Army Military Government in Korea
YUJŎNGHOE	Yushin Chŏng'uhoe (Political Fraternal Society for Revitalizing Reform)

HISTORICAL CHRONOLOGY

Dates prior to 1876 are those of the lunar calendar

ca. 30,000–2333 B.C.	**PREHISTORIC PERIOD**
ca. 30,000 B.C.	The appearance of the Paleolithic culture
ca. 6000 B.C.	The appearance of the Neolithic culture—pointed-bottom pottery, as well as flat-bottom pottery and the pottery with comb-marking.
ca. 2333–108 B.C.	**THE OLD CHOSŎN PERIOD**
ca. 2333 B.C.	Traditional data of the founding of the Kingdom of Chosŏn by Tan'gun.
ca. 1200 B.C.	The beginning of the Bronze Age; appearance of black pottery and agricultural tools.
ca. 1122 B.C.	The establishment of Kija Chosŏn.
ca. 300 B.C.	The beginning of the Iron Age.
ca. 194 B.C.	The rise of Wiman Chosŏn in the north and the three federations of the Han tribes in the south.
108 B.C.	Invasion of Korea by Emperor Wu of the Han dynasty of China.

57 B.C.–668 A.D.	**THE THREE KINGDOMS PERIOD**
57 B.C.	The founding of the state of Saro (later renamed Shilla).
37 B.C.	The emergence of the state of Koguryŏ in Manchuria.
13 B.C.	The emergence of the state of Paekche in central Korea.
313 A.D.	The end of the Lolang commandery of China in Korea.
372 A.D.	Official adoption of Buddhism and the establishment of a school for Confucian studies in Koguryŏ.
382 A.D.	Official adoption of Buddhism in Paekche.
427 A.D.	The relocation of the capital of Koguryŏ at Wanggŏmsŏng (now Pyongyang).
528 A.D.	Official adoption of Buddhism in Shilla.
612	Invasion of the Sui (Chinese) forces; a great military victory of the Koguryŏ forces.
644–655	Invasions of the T'ang (Chinese) forces.
663	The destruction of Paekche by the combined forces of Shilla and China.
668	The destruction of Koguryŏ by the combined forces of Shilla and China
668–918	**UNIFIED KOREA OF SHILLA**
ca. 670	Invention of the *idu* system of writing.
682	The establishment of a school for Confucian learning.

699	The emergence of the Kingdom of Parhae in Manchuria.
727	The return of Monk Hyecho from his pilgrimage to China and India.
ca. 750	The printing of Buddhist texts.
751	The reconstruction of the Pŏpryu Temple, built in 528, and renaming it the Pulguk Temple.
892	The founding of the Kingdom of Later Paekche.
901	The founding of the Kingdom of Later Koguryŏ.
918–1392	**THE KORYŎ PERIOD**
918	The overthrow of Kung'ye and the founding of the Kingdom of Koryŏ by Wang Kŏn.
935	The surrender of the last Shilla king to Koryŏ.
936	The overthrow of the Later Paekche: reunification of Korea.
993	Invasion of the Khitans.
998	Adoption of the Chinese civil service examination system.
1011	Publication of the *Tripitaka* with wooden blocks.
1018	Second invasion of the Khitans.
1104	Invasion of the Jurchens.
1135–1136	The Rebellion of Myoch'ŏng and other rebellions.

1145 The completion of Kim Pu-sik's *Samguk sagi.*

1170 Chŏng Chung-bu's rebellion.

1196 Ch'oe Ch'ung-hŏn's coup; the establishment of dictatorship of the Ch'oe clan.

1231 The first Mongol invasion.

1232 The flight of the Koryŏ court to Kanghwa Island; the second Mongol invasion.

1234 The casting of movable metal type.

1235 The third Mongol invasion.

1251 Production of new printing blocks; publication of the *Tripitaka Koreana.*

1258 The end of dictatorship of the Ch'oe clan.

1259 Establishment of the peace with the Mongols; and acceptance of Mongol domination.

1270 The returning of the Koryŏ court to Kaegyŏng; Korea's acceptance of vassalage to the Mongols; the Rebellion of the *Sambyŏlch'o.*

1273 The end of the Rebellion of the *Sambyŏlch'o.*

1274 The first Mongol-Korean expedition to Japan.

1281 The publication of Ilyŏn's *Samguk yusa;* the second Mongol-Korean expedition to Japan.

1313 April, first population census.

1388 Coup d'état of General Yi Sŏng-gye.

1392 The end of the Koryŏ kingdom.

1392–1910	**THE YI DYNASTY PERIOD**
1394	Hanyang (now Seoul) became the capital of Korea.
1403	The casting of new metal type.
1420	April, the founding of the Royal Academy of Scholars.
1432	Publication of *Geography of the Eight Provinces.*
1442	May, installation of the first rain gauge.
1446	October, promulgation of the new Korean script (*han'gŭl*).
1452	Publication of *History of Koryŏ.*
1454	Yi Ching-ok's rebellion.
1467	Yi Si-ae's rebellion.
1470	Publication of a new code.
1498	First purge of scholars.
1502	Second purge of scholars.
1519	Third purge of scholars.
1545	Fourth purge of scholars.
1562	Lim Kŏ-jŏng's rebellion.
1592	April, invasion of the Japanese; July, construction of ironclad war vessels (turtle boats); Admiral Yi Sun-sin's great naval victory.
1597	January, second Japanese invasion.

1598	October, withdrawal of Japanese troops from Korea.
ca. 1610	Introduction to Catholicism.
1624	Yi Kwal's rebellion.
1627	First Manchu invasion.
1628	The crew of a ship-wrecked Dutch vessel rescued off Cheju Island and taken to Seoul.
1636	December, second Manchu invasion.
ca. 1650	Beginning of the *Shirhak* movement.
1653	August, another Dutch ship, the *Sparrow Hawk,* wrecked off Cheju Island; its crew taken to Seoul.
1654	Korean rifle troops sent against the Russians in Manchuria in behalf of the Manchus.
1712	Establishment of the new Sino-Korean boundary line.
1728	Yi Rin-jwa's Rebellion.
1784	First Catholic church established in Seoul.
1785	The banning of Catholicism.
1790	Publication of An Chŏng-bok's *Outline of History of Korea.*
1801	First anti-Catholic persecution.
1812	The Rebellion of Hong Kyŏng-nae.
1831	Establishment of Korean Catholic diocese; arrival of French priests.

1839 Proclamation of anti-Catholic edicts.

1854 April, arrival of a Russian Admiral E.V. Putiatin.

1860 The founding of the *Tonghak* sect by Ch'oe Che-u.

1864 January 22, beginning of the reign of King Kojong and the regency of the Taewŏn'gun; execution of Ch'oe Che-u.

1866 February, beginning of a large-scale anti-Catholic persecution; August, the destruction of an American merchant ship, the *General Sherman;* September-October, invasion of French naval force.

1871 May-July, invasion of American troops; proclamation of policy of isolation.

1873 December, the end of the regency of the Taewŏn'gun.

1875 September, the *Unyō-kan* incident; landing of Japanese troops at Pusan.

1876 February, the arrival of six Japanese naval vessels; February 26, the signing of the Kanghwa Treaty with Japan; April-July, a Korean mission to Japan; August 26, the signing of a supplementary treaty and the trade regulation with Japan.

1879 The opening of Pusan to Japanese traders.

1880 May 1, opening of Wŏnsan to the Japanese; August-September, Kim Hong-jip's mission to Japan.

1881 January, establishment of the Office for the Management of State Affairs.

1882 March, beginning of modern military training; May 22, the signing of the Chemulp'o Treaty with the United States; June 9, beginning of the military insurrection and the abduction of the Taewŏn'gun to China by the Chinese; the signing of the Chemuplo'o Treaty with Japan; September 20, departure of a Korean mission headed by Pak Yŏng-hyo to Japan; December 26, establishment of the Foreign Office.

1883 January 1, renaming of Chemulp'o as Incho'ŏn; June, the opening of Inch'ŏn; September, the departure of the first Korean mission headed by Min Yŏng-ik to the United States; October 30, the publication of the first Korean newspaper, the *Hansŏng Sunbo;* November 26, the signing of Korean-British and Korean-German Treaties.

1884 June, the return of the Korean mission from the United States; June 21, the signing of the Korean-Italian Treaty; July 7, the signing of the Korean-Russian Treaty; September, arrival of first Protestant missionary, Dr. Horace N. Allen; December 4, the coup of the Progressives, Chinese military intervention, and the flight of the Progressives to Japan.

1885 January 9, the signing of the Korean-Japanese Agreement; April 15, the occupation of Kŏmun Island by British marines; April 18, the signing of the Tientsin Agreement between China and Japan; October 5, the return of the Taewŏn'gun from China to Korea.

1886 January, publication of the *Hansŏng Chubo;* establishment of the first school for girls named Ewha; June 4, the signing of the Korean-French Treaty.

1887 February 27, the evacuation of British troops from Kŏmun Island; October, the arrival of Pak Chŏng-yang in the United States as the first Korean minister.

1894 March, the beginning of the *Tonghak* uprising; July 25, the outbreak of the Sino-Japanese War; July 26, establishment of the Deliberative Council and the beginning of the *Kabo* Reform; August 26, the conclusion of mutual defense agreement between Korea and Japan.

1895 January 7, the taking of an oath by King Kojong before his ancestors' shrine, and the proclamation of a royal charter, *Hongbŏm sipsajo;* January 18, establishment of the cabinet system; April 17, the signing of the Treaty of Shimonoseki and the end of the Sino-Japanese War; October 8, assassination of Queen Min; December 30, proclamation of the Hair-Cutting Ordinance.

1896 January 1, adoption of the Gregorian calendar; arrival of Dr. Philip Jaisohn (Sŏ Chae-p'il) from the United States; February 11, the flight of the king and the crown prince to the Russian legation; April 7, the publication of *The Independent;* May 14, the conclusion of the Waeber-Komura Memorandum; June 9, the signing of the Lobanov-Yamagata Protocol; July 2, the conclusion of the Min-Lobanov Agreement; the establishment of the Independence Club; August, division of Korea into 13 provinces; November 21, construction of the Independence Gate.

1897 February 20, return of King Kojong from the Russian legation; October 12, the renaming of Korea to Empire of Tae-Han, and the adoption of imperial title by the king.

1898 February 22, the death of the Taewŏn'gun; May 20, opening of Sŏngjin, Kunsan, and Masan; November 4, the arrest of the leaders of the Independence Club and the abolition of the Independence Club.

1899 May 4, the opening of street-car operation in Seoul; partial operation of the Seoul-Inch'ŏn Railway.

1900 April 10, installation of street lights in Seoul; November 12, the opening of the entire Seoul-Inch'ŏn Railway line.

1901 March 23, the signing of the Korean-Belgian Treaty.

1902 July 23, the signing of the Korean-Austrian Treaty; July 15, the signing of the Korean-Danish Treaty.

1903 The founding of the YMCA in Seoul and Seoul Medical School.

1904 February 8, the outbreak of the Russo-Japanese War; February 23, the signing of the Korean-Japanese Protocol; August 22, the signing of the Korean-Japanese Agreement; the formation of the *Ilchinhoe.*

1905 March 21, official adoption of Western weights and measures system; May 25, the opening of the entire Seoul-Pusan Railway line; June, inauguration of a new monetary system; August 10, the publication of *The Korean Daily News;* September 5, the signing of the Portsmouth Treaty and the end of the Russo-Japanese War; November 17, the signing of the Japanese-Korean Agreement; November 29, the formation of the Corps for the Advancement of Individuals (Hŭngsadan).

1906 January 28, the renaming of the *Tonghak* sect as *Ch'ŏndogyo;* February 1, the opening of the Residency-General; arrival of Itō Hirobumi as the first Resident-General of Korea; April, the opening of the Seoul-Shinŭiju Railway line; August, promulgation of a new public school ordinance.

1907 May, formation of a new cabinet headed by Yi Wan-yong; June, adoption of a new cabinet system, and the arrival of Kojong's envoys at The Hague; July 20, the abdication of Kojong; July 24, the signing of a new Korean-Japanese Agreement; promulgation of a new press law and the Public Security Law; July 31, disbanding of the Korean Army, and the beginning of anti-Japanese guerrilla war of the Righteous Armies; August 27, coronation of Emperor Sunjong; November 18, proclamation of a six-article imperial charter.

1908 April, promulgation of the ordinance concerning the girls' schools; August, promulgation of an ordinance concerning private schools.

1909 February-April, promulgation of new tax laws; March 4, promulgation of the Family Registration Law; July 5, succession of Itō Hirobumi by Sone Arasuke as Resident-General; July 12, the assumption of judicial administration by the Japanese; July 31, abolition of the Ministry of Defense and the Korean military school; September 4, the signing of a treaty between China and Japan concerning Chien-tao (Kando), and the establishment of new boundaries between Korea and Manchuria; October 26, assassination of Itō Hirobumi; November 24, the opening of the Bank of Korea.

1910 August 22, the signing of the Treaty of Annexation, and the end of the Yi dynasty and Korean independence.

1910–1945 JAPANESE COLONIAL PERIOD

1910 Oct. 1, the establishment of the Government-General of Korea; beginning of land survey.

1911 December, the 105 Persons Incident.

1914 The Seoul-Wŏnsan railway line opened.

1918 Completion of the land survey.

1919 Jan. 22, ex-emperor Kojong died; February 8, Korean students in Tokyo issued the Declaration of Independence; March 1, beginning of the March First Independence Movement; April 11, establishment of the Korean Provisional Government in exile in Shanghai.

1920 March 5, publication of the *Chosŏn Ilbo;* April 1, publication of the *Tong-a Ilbo;* Oct. 21, a victory of the Korean insurgents at Ch'ŏngsan-ri.

1925 April 17, founding of the Korean Communist Party in Seoul.

1926 April 25, death of former emperor, Sunjong; June 10, independence demonstrations in Seoul.

1927 Feb. 15, Founding of the *Shin'ganhoe* and the *Kŭn'uhoe.*

1929 Oct. 30, the Kwangju student incident; November 3, beginning of the nationwide anti-Japanese student movement.

1931 July, the Manbosan (Wanpaoshan) incident in Manchuria; anti-Chinese activities in Korea.

1932 Jan. 8, Yi Pong-ch'an's attempt to assassinate the Japanese emperor at the Sakurada Gate in Tokyo; April 29, the bomb incident of Yun Pong-gil at the Hungk'uo Park in Shanghai.

1938 Feb. 26, enactment of the Special Army Volunteer Ordinance in Korea; Oct. 1, beginning of labor mobilization.

1940 Feb. 11, promulgation of the ordinance concerning the adoption of Japanese-style family and given names by the Koreans; Aug. 10, abolition of the *Tong-a Ilbo,* and *Chosŏn Ilbo,* and other Korean-language newspapers.

1942 May 8, mobilization of Korean youth into the Japanese imperial army; Sept. 1, the case of the Korean Linguistic Society and the arrest of its leaders.

1943 Oct. 20, mobilization of students into the Japanese army; Dec. 1, the Cairo Declaration of the Allies regarding Korea announced.

1944 Jan. 20, general mobilization of Korean

youth into the Japanese armed forces began.

1945 Aug. 8, declaration of war by the Soviet Union against Japan, invasion of Korea by Soviet troops; Aug. 15, 16, Japanese acceptance of the Potsdam ultimatum of the Allies, end of World War II, and liberation of Korea and the formation of the Committee for the Preparation of National Reconstruction.

1945–1948 THE ALLIED OCCUPATION PERIOD

1945 Sept. 1, formation of the Nationalist Party; Sept. 2, announcement of the Supreme Command of the Allied Powers in the Pacific regarding the division of Korea into two military operational zones of the U.S. and the Soviet Union along the 38th parallel line; Sept. 6, proclamation of the People's Republic of Korea; Sept. 7, landing of U.S. troops, Sept. 9, signing of the surrender document by the Japanese governor-general; Sept. 11, establishment of the United States Army Military Government in Korea (USAMGIK); Sept. 12, reestablishment of the Korean Communist Party in Seoul; Sept. 16, formation of the Korean (Han'guk) Democratic Party; Oct. 21, establishment of South Korean national police; Nov. 7, anticommunist uprising of the students in Shinŭiju in the north; Nov. 12, formation of the Korean People's Party; Dec. 28, announcement of the Moscow Agreement regarding Korea, eruption of antitrusteeship demonstration; Dec. 30, assassination of a right-wing Nationalist Song Chin-u of the Korean (Han'guk) Democratic Party.

1946 Jan. 3, nationwide antitrusteeship strikes and demonstrations; the fall of the Nationalists in the north and the flight of the Korean (Chosŏn) Democratic Party to the south; Jan. 19, formation of the Democratic People's Front; Feb. 14, establishment of the Representative Democratic Council; March 13, anti-communist student uprising in Hamhŭng in the north; March 30, Communist-inspired labor strikes in Taegu and elsewhere in the south; Oct., Communist-inspired labor uprising and railway workers' strike in Taegu; Oct. 7, formation of the Coalition Committee for Co-operation Between the Rightists and the Leftists; Nov. 12, formation of Socialist Workers' Party; Nov. 23, the Korean Communist Party renamed the South Korean Workers' Party (merged with the People's and the New People's Party); Dec. 12, establishment of the South Korean Interim Legislative Assembly.

1947 Feb. 18, establishment of the Supreme People's Assembly in the north, creation of the Central People's Committee as the central government of North Korea; May 24, formation of the Working People's Party in the south; June 3, establishment of the South Korean Interim Government in Seoul; July 19, assassination of a left-wing nationalist Yŏ Un-Hyŏng; Nov. 14, adoption of the Korean resolution by the U.N. General Assembly; creation of the U.N. Temporary Commission on Korea (UNTCOK); Dec. 2, assassination of right-wing leader, Chang Tŏk-su of the Korean (Han'guk) Democratic Party.

1948 Apr. 3, a rebellion on Cheju Island began;

Apr. 19–21, Kim Ku, Kim Kyu-shik and others made a journey to Pyongyang for a joint conference with the North Korean Communists; May 10, the U.N. sponsored general elections in South Korea; May 14, North Korea's suspension of electric power supply to the south; May 31, convening of the National (Constituent) Assembly of South Korea; July 12, adoption of a constitution, election of the president and the vice-president.

1948– **THE REPUBLIC OF KOREA**

Aug. 15, inauguration of President Rhee and the Republic of Korea; end of the U.S. occupation of South Korea; Sept. 22, promulgation of the Law Concerning Punishment of Those Who Committed Crimes Against the People (anti-traitor law); Oct. 2, a military insurrection on Cheju Island began; Oct. 19–22, the Yŏsu-Sunch'ŏn military insurrection; Nov. 2, a military revolt in Taegu; Nov. 13, promulgation of martial law; Nov. 30, passage of the National Security Law; Dec. 9, U.N. recognition of the Republic of Korea.

1949 Feb., renaming of the Korean (Han'guk) Democratic Party as the Democratic Nationalist Party; April 18, activation of the South Korean Marine Corps; May 20, arrest of ten National Assemblymen as North Korean spies; June 21, promulgation of the Land Reform Law; June 26, assassination of a right-wing nationalist and head of the Korean Independence Party, Kim Ku; June 29, completion of U.S. troop withdrawal; Oct. 12, establishment of South Korean Air Force; Oct. 29, outlawing of the

South Korean Workers' Party and its affiliated groups.

1950 May 30, National Assembly elections; June 25, North Korean invasion of the south; June 28, fall of Seoul, the flight of the South Korean government to Taejŏn first and then to Pusan; July formation of the U.N. Forces under the U.N. Command, Sept. 15, amphibious landing of U.N. troops at Inch'ŏn; Oct. 1–7, U.N. troops crossed the 38th parallel in pursuit of North Korean aggressors; Oct. 20, fall of Pyongyang; Oct. 15–25, arrival of the "Volunteers" of the Chinese People's Liberation Army; Nov., withdrawal of U.N. troops from North Korea.

1951 Jan. 4, fall of Seoul for the second time; Feb. 11, Koch'ang Incident; March 7, adoption of an educational system; Mar. 15, recovery of Seoul from the enemy; May 9, resignation of the vice-president (Yi Shi-yŏng); May 15, National Assembly elects a new vice-president (Kim Sŏng-su); July 10, truce negotiations began; Dec. 23, formation of the Liberal Party.

1952 Jan. 18, the declaration of the Rhee (Peace) Line; Apr. 17, constitutional revision proposed, resignation of premier; May 14, new constitutional revision proposed; May 25, martial law proclaimed in the Pusan area; May 29, resignation of the vice-president; July 4, passage of the first constitutional amendment; Aug. 5, reelection of President Rhee by popular vote.

1953 Feb. 15, a monetary reform, March 8 and May 10, passage of several labor laws; July 27, signing of the Korean armistice;

Aug. 15, return of the government to Seoul; Oct. 1, conclusion of U.S.-South Korea Mutual Defense Treaty.

1954 May 20, general elections for the National Assembly; April–June, Geneva Conference on Korea and Vietnam; Nov. 27, passage of the second constitutional amendment.

1955 Sept. 18, formation of the Democratic Party.

1956 Mar. 20, formation of the Republican Party; May 15, presidential election, reelection of Dr. Rhee, election of Chang Myŏn of the Democratic Party as vice-president; June 16, television broadcasting began; Sept. 28, assassination attempt on Chang Myŏn; Nov. 11, formation of the Progressive Party.

1957 July 2, headquarters of the U.N. Command moved to Seoul from Tokyo.

1958 Jan. 1., passage of the new election law; Jan. 13, Cho Pong-am and other leaders of the Progressive Party arrested as spies; Feb., promulgation of the new Civil Law; May 2, general elections for the National Assembly; Dec. 26, promulgation of the new National Security Law.

1959 Apr. 30, publication of the *Kyŏnghyang Daily News* suspended, July 31, Cho Pong-am executed; Oct. 14, Japan repatriated the first group of Koreans to North Korea; Oct. 26, the Federation of Labor Unions formed.

1960 March 15, presidential elections, reelection of Dr. Rhee and election of Yi Ki-bung as vice-president; demonstrations for nullification of election results began;

student demonstrations in Masan; April 19, student uprising in Seoul; April 24, resignation of Vice-president Chang; April 25, demonstration by college professors and others; April 27, resignation of President Rhee and his cabinet members; May 22, formation of the Teachers' Labor Union; May 29, Dr. Rhee exiled to Hawaii; June 15, passage and promulgation of constitutional amendments; July 29, general elections for the two houses of the National Assembly; Aug. 13, election of Yun Po-sŏn as the President; Aug. 15, emergence of the Second Republic; Aug. 28, formation of the Chang Myŏn cabinet; Nov. 23/28, adoption of the new constitution by both houses; Nov. 25, formation of the Federation of Korean Labor Unions.

1961 Jan., emergence of the Reform and the Unification Socialist Parties; Feb., formation of the New Democratic Party; Mar., student demonstrations against the Anti-Communism Law; May, student resolution to hold a conference of students of the north and the south at Panmunjom in May; May 16, the military revolution and the fall of the Second Republic; May 19, establishment of the Military Revolutionary Committee; May 20, the Military Revolutionary Committee renamed the Supreme Council for National Reconstruction; May 22, dissolution of all political parties and suspension of the National Assembly; June 6, promulgation of Law Concerning Extraordinary Measures for National Reconstruction; June 10, promulgation of the laws concerning the Supreme Council for National Reconstruction and the Central Intelligence Agency; July 3, promulgation of the

Anti-Communist Law; Oct. 10, formation of the General Federation of Labor Unions; Nov. 11–15, Gen. Park Chung-hee visited Japan and the United States.

1962 March 22, promulgation of the Political Activities Purification Law and resignation of President Yun; Gen. Park became acting president; June 10, second monetary reform; Oct., promulgation of the law concerning national referendum; Nov., publication of the revised constitution; Nov. 12, announcement concerning South Korea-Japan agreement (Kim-Ōhira Memorandum); Dec. 17, a national referendum on the new constitution; Dec. 26, promulgation of the new constitution and the Political Party Law and others.

1963 Jan. 1, lifting of the ban on political activities; Feb. 26, formation of the Democratic Republican Party (DRP); May 15, formation of the Civil Rule Party (CRP); July 18, emergence of the Democratic Party (DP); Aug. 1, formation of the Nationalist Party (NP); Sept. 3, establishment of the Liberal Democratic Party (LDP); Oct. 15, presidential election, election of Park Chung-hee as president; Nov. 26, general elections for the National Assembly (unicameral); Dec. 17, the emergence of the Third Republic.

1964 March-April, numerous demonstrations against the South Korea-Japan talks for the normalization of relations; June 2–3, violent student demonstrations in Seoul, promulgation of martial law in the Seoul area; Aug. 2, passage of the new press law; Oct. 5, the Democratic and the Nationalist parties merged as the Democratic Party; Oct. 31, signing of the South Korea-South Vietnam agreement on the dispatch of South Korean troops; Nov. 27, union of the Civil Rule and the Liberal Democratic parties as the Civil Rule Party.

1965 May 11, the Civil Rule and the Democratic parties merged and became the Masses (Minjung) Party (MP); May 16, President Park embarked on U.S. visit; June 22, the South Korea-Japan Normalization Treaty signed; Aug. 13, the National Assembly approved the dispatch of combat divisions to South Vietnam; Aug. 26, a garrision decree issued in the Seoul area.

1966 Feb., President Park embarked on state visits to Malaysia, Thailand, and Taiwan; South Korea-U.S. agreement on the dispatch of South Korean troops to South Vietnam signed; May 30, emergence of the New Korea Party (NKP); July 9, the U.S.-South Korea Status-of-Forces Agreement signed; Dec., emergence of the Democratic Socialist Party (DSP).

1967 Feb. 11, The NKP and the MP united into the New Democratic Party (NDP); Mar. 22, formation of the Populist (Taejung) Party; Apr. 7, establishment of the Unification Socialist Party; Apr. 27, emergence of the Liberal Democratic Party; May 3, presidential election, election of the incumbent President Park; May 6, birth of the Democratic Party; June 8, inauguration of President Park; July 8, the Korean CIA announced the East Berlin case.

1968 Jan. 21, North Korean commandoes attempted to storm the presidential mansion in Seoul and assassinate President Park; Jan. 23, U.S. intelligence ship, *Pueblo,* seized by North Korean naval ships; Apr. 1, formation of the Homeland Reserve Forces; Dec. 5, promulgation of the Charter for National Education.

1969 June-Aug., mass demonstrations against the revision of the constitution; Aug. 20, President Park embarked on U.S. visit; Sept. 14, passage of constitutional amendments; Oct. 17, a national referendum on the new constitution; Dec. 11, hijacking of a South Korean passenger plane to the north.

1970 Dec. 24, trade law amended to allow trade with non-hostile Communist countries.

1971 April 27, reelection of President Park; May 25, general elections for the National Assembly; Sept. 20, opening of talks between the Red Cross societies of the north and the south; Oct. 15, martial law proclaimed in the Seoul area; Dec. 6, promulgation of the state of national emergency; Dec. 26, passage of the Special Measures Law for National Security and Defense.

1972 April 11, the launching of the New Community Movement Plan; July 4, the statement concerning the opening of North-South political dialogue issued by the governments of both Koreas; Oct. 12, the first North-South Coordinating Committee meeting held; Oct. 17, national emergency decree proclaimed, the National Assembly dissolved, and the October *Yushin* reform began; Oct. 27, the revised constitution made public; Nov. 21, a national referendum on the *Yushin* Constitution; Dec. 15, the National Conference for Unification (NCU) established as an electoral college; Dec. 23, the NCU elected President Park; Dec. 27, President Park inaugurated, the *Yushin* Constitution promulgated, and the Fourth Republic emerged; Dec. 30, the new National Assembly Election Law and the new Political Party Law promulgated.

1973 Jan. 27, formation of the Democratic Unification Party (DUP); Feb. 27, general elections for the National Assembly; Mar. 10, formation of the Yujŏnghoe; Aug. 8, Kim Dae-jung kidnapped from Tokyo to Seoul; Oct. 2, anti-*Yushin* Constitution demonstrations began; Dec. 4, the movement to collect one million signatures for the revision of the constitution launched.

1974 Jan. 8, Presidential Emergency Decrees Numbers 1 and 2 issued; Jan. 14, Presidential Emergency Decree Number 3 issued; Apr. 3, Presidential Emergency Decree Number 4 issued; Aug. 15, assassination attempt against President Park by a pro-North Korean from Japan; Aug. 23, cancellation of Presidential Emergency Decrees Numbers 1 and 4.

1975 Feb. 12, a national referendum reaffirmed the 1972 *Yushin* Constitution; Apr. 8, proclamation of the Presidential Emergency Decree Number 7; May 13, proclamation of the Presidential Emergency Decree Number 9.

1976 Mar. 1, the Declaration of Democratic National Salvation issued by dissident leaders (the Myŏngdong incident); Mar. 9, U.S. President Carter announced his plan to withdraw the U.S. ground combat troops from South Korea; Aug. 18, two American army officers killed by North Korean troops at Panmunjon.

1977 Jan. 19, operation of the first atomic power plant began; Oct.–Dec., student demonstrations for constitutional reform intensified: association of dismissed professors formed and its Declaration of Democratic Education issued.

1978 Apr. 30, declaration of a twelve-mile limit to territorial waters; May 18, elections for members of the NCU; June 12–26, large student demonstrations in Seoul; July 6, reelection of President Park by the NCU; Sep. 13–14, violent student demonstrations in Seoul; Dec. 12, general elections for the National Assembly; Dec. 27, inauguration of Park as the ninth president.

1979 May 30, Kim Young-sam elected president of the NDP; Aug. 9, female workers of the Y.H. Trading Co. occupied the headquarters of the NDP; Sept. 8, large student demonstrations in Taegu; Sept. 9, Kim Young-sam's party presidency suspended by the government; Oct. 4, Kim Young-sam expelled from the National Assembly; Oct. 9, arrest of the leaders of the South Korean People's Liberation Front announced; Oct. 16, violent student demonstration in Pusan and Masan began; Oct. 20, proclamation of a garrison law in the Pusan and Masan region; Oct. 24, violent student demonstrations in Taegu; Oct. 26, assassination of President Park; Oct. 27, proclamation of a nationwide martial law; Premier Ch'oe Kyu-ha became acting president; Dec. 6, election of Ch'oe Kyu-ha as the president by the CNU; Dec. 12, Gen. Chun Doo-hwan's coup and arrest of the Martial Law Commander Gen. Chŏng Sŭng-hwa, formation of a new cabinet.

1980 April-May, mass student demonstrations in Seoul, Pusan, and other cities; April 21, coal miners' strike at the Sapuk Mine; May 17, proclamation of martial law and the Emergency Decree No. 10, all political activities, assemblies and rallies banned, key political leaders arrested; May 18–27, the Kwangju Uprising; May 31, formation of the Special Committee for National Security Measures (SCNSM); Aug. 16, resignation of President Ch'oe; Aug. 27, Gen. Chun elected as the president by the NCU; Sept. 1, President Chun inaugurated; Sept. 17, Kim Dae-jung given death sentence; Oct. 17, proclamation of martial law; Oct. 22, approval of the constitution of the Fifth Republic; the National Assembly dissolved and all political parties disbanded; Oct. 27, the Legislative Council for National Security (LCNS) established, replacing the National Assembly; Nov. 12, 835 former politicians were banned from politics for the next eight years; Nov. 10, new Political Party Law promulgated; Nov. 14, a drastic plan to reorganize mass media ("massacre of mass media") finalized; Nov. 15, partial lifting of martial law of 1980; Dec. 1, KBS-TV began color telecasting; Dec. 26, the LCNS adopted the new National Security Law; the Korean CIA renamed the Agency for National Security Planning (ANSP).

1981 Jan. 15, formation of the Democratic Justice

Party (DJP); Jan. 17, establishment of the Democratic Korea Party (DKP); Jan. 23, emergence of the Korean National Party (KNP); Jan. 23, Kim Dae-jung's death sentence commuted to life term; Jan. 28, President Chun embarked on U.S. visit; Feb. 11, elections for the new electoral college; Feb. 25, election of President Chun as the first president of the Fifth Republic; Mar. 3, inauguration of President Chun and the Fifth Republic; Mar. 25, general elections for the new National Assembly; June 25, President Chun embarked on a tour of the ASEAN member nations.

1982 Jan. 5, the 36-year-old midnight-to-4 a.m. curfew lifted; Apr. 28, May 21 and June 2 and 24, cabinet reshuffle; Oct. 16, a Chinese MIG landed; Dec. 23, Kim Dae-jung left Korea for U.S. for "medical treatment."

1983 Feb. 25, a North Korean MIG-19 landed and its pilot sought political asylum; May 5, a hijacked Chinese passenger plane landed; Aug. 7, a Chinese MIG-21 landed; Sept. 1, a Korean Air Lines passenger plane shot down by a Soviet fighter plane; Oct. 8, President Chun embarked on a tour to south Asian countries; Oct. 9, a remote-controlled bomb aimed at the assassination of President Chun exploded at the Martyr's Mausoleum in Rangoon, Burma, killing 18 South Korean ministers and advisers; Oct. 17, a new cabinet formed.

1984 May 3, Pope John Paul II visited South Korea and canonized 93 Korean and 10 French martyrs; May 25, the first subway line in Seoul opened; Sept. 6–8, President Chun's state visit to Japan;

Nov. 14, occupation of the headquarters of the DJP by students.

1985 Jan. 18, formation of the New Korea Democratic Party (NKDP); Feb. 8, Kim Dae-jung returned from U.S.; the largest student demonstration since 1980 in Seoul; Feb. 12, general elections for the National Assembly; Feb. 18, cabinet reshuffled; Feb. 23, Roh Tae-woo named chairman of the DJP; Mar. 6, the last group of political outcasts freed from the blacklist; Apr. 3, merger of the DJP into the NKDP; formation of the Council for Promotion of Democracy (CPD); Apr. 7, formation of a radical student organization named the Three People's Struggle Committee (Sammint'uwi); May 22, occupation of the U.S. Information Service building in Seoul by students; June 16, a partial cabinet reshuffle; July 18, arrests of the core members of the Three People's Struggle Committee and other radical student groups announced; Aug. 2, Kim Dae-jung and Kim Young-sam, co-chairman of the CPD, named advisers to the president of the NKDP; Dec. 31, formation of the New Conservative Club by lawmakers who defected from the NKDP.

1986 Jan. 6, President Chun disclosed that he had no intention of rewriting the Constitution during his tenure and said that the question of changing the presidential election system ought to be debated in 1989; Jan. 7, a cabinet reshuffle; Apr. 5, President Chun embarked on a four-nation European tour; May 29, rival political parties agreed to revise the Constitution, advocating a parliamentary form of government; Aug. 26, a cabinet reshuffle; Nov. 26, the government decided to construct a large dam near the 38th parallel in the eastern front in order to neutralize the "water assault" of North Korea.

1987 Jan. 11, the NKDP lawmakers began sit-in strike at the National Assembly; Feb. 19, 270 opposition politicians put under house arrest and headquarters of the NKDP closed; Mar. 11, Kim Dae-jung put under house arrest; Apr. 4, the government realigned 20 business firms; Apr. 8, Kim Dae-jung, Kim Young-sam and many NKDP lawmakers announced a plan to form a new party; Apr. 13, President Chun forbade debates on constitutional revision and stated that his successor will be chosen under the current constitution; wild antigovernment demonstrations began; Apr. 21, hunger strike of Catholic priests and nuns began; May 1, Kim Young-sam formed the Reunification Democratic Party (RDP) and became its president; May 26, a major cabinet reshuffle; June 1–26, nationwide antigovernment demonstrations; June 10, the DJP nominated Roh Tae-woo as its presidential candidate; June 24, President Chun agreed to reopen debates on constitutional revision; June 29, Roh Tae-woo announced his democratic reform plan; July 1, President Chun accepted Roh's demands; July 13, cabinet reshuffled; Aug. 5, Roh Tae-woo elected president of the DJP; Aug. 8, Kim Dae-jung joined the Reunification Democratic Party; Oct. 12, passage of a new constitution by the National Assembly; Oct. 28, the new constitution approved in a national referendum; Kim Jong-pil reconstituted the former DRP into the New Democratic Republican Party (NDRP); Nov. 12, Kim Dae-jung formed the Party for Peace and Democracy (PPD) and became its presidential candidate; Nov. 29, a Korean Air Lines passenger plane was destroyed over Burma by bombs planted by North Korean agents; Dec. 16, the first direct presidential election in 16 years held; Roh Tae-woo elected president.

1988 Feb. 8, Kim Young-sam resigned the party presidency of the RDP; Feb. 25, Roh Tae-woo took the oath of office as the president of the Sixth Republic; Mar. 8, the National Assembly passed the new National Assembly Election Law; Mar. 12, Kim Young-sam regained his party presidency; Mar. 17, Kim Dae-jung resigned his presidency of the PPD; Apr. 26, general elections for the National Assembly held; May 8, Kim Dae-jung regained his party presidency; July 10, radical students launched a movement to hold talks with North Korean students at Panmunjom for Korean unification; Sept. 17–Oct. 2, the 24th Olympiad held in Seoul; Oct. 27, the government lifted the ban on works of South Korean writers and artists who either emigrated or were abducted to North Korea; Nov. 23, former president Chun made formal apology for the misdeeds of his relatives and the Fifth Republic on a national television broadcasting and began a self-imposed internal exile with his wife at a Buddhist temple in a remote area; Dec. 5, a major cabinet reshuffle.

1989 Jan. 21, the National Coalition for a People's Democratic Movement (Chŏnguk Minjok Minju Undong Yŏnhap, or

Chŏnminyŏn) of some 200 dissident groups was formed; Jan. 31, 47 former high-ranking officials of the Fifth Republic were arrested on charges of irregularities and corruption; Feb. 1, South Korea made direct importation of North Korean coal for the first time; Feb. 13, 15,000 farmers staged a violent antigovernment rally in front of the National Assembly building, clashing with the riot police; Mar. 14, Minister of Government Administration resigned after issuing a warning against the growing leftism; Mar. 23, the Seoul subway workers' strike ended; Apr. 13, Rev. Moon Ik-hwan, who made a secret, unauthorized visit to North Korea in March was arrested upon his return to Seoul; May 3, six police officers perished in a fire set by rioting antigovernment students at Dongeui University in Pusan; the U.S. agreed to relocate its military base from Seoul to another location; May 6, two North Korean students, who defected from Poland, arrived in Seoul seeking political asylum; May 12–13, large peaceful antigovernment student demonstrations in Kwangju in commemoration of the May 1980 Kwangju Uprising; May 25, bills concerning the punishment of firebomb users and the restraining of teargas use were passed by the National Assembly's Internal Affairs Committee; May 28, a nationwide teachers union was formed in defiance of government ban; June 9, President Roh officially cancelled the midterm evaluation of his administration; radical student demonstrations followed, calling for the resignation of Roh and the withdrawal of U.S. troops from South Korea; June 14, the June 12–16 meeting of Kim Young-sam of the RDP of South Korea and Hŏ Dam, North

Korea's chairman of Peaceful Fatherland Unification Committee, in Moscow was announced; June 19, a cabinet reshuffle; six ministers and director of the ANSP were replaced; June 21, a coed, Lim Su-gyŏng, left Seoul on a secret mission to North Korea, representing National Council of Student Representatives (NCSR); June 27, the ANSP arrested Suh Kyŏng-wŏn, former lawmaker of the PPD, who made secret visits to North Korea in Aug. 1988 and met Kim Il-sung and received political funds; July 29, a Chinese delegate to the Korean Armistice Commission and his wife defected to South Korea across the DMZ; Aug. 2, Kim Dae-jung was questioned by the ANSP in connection with the case of Suh Kyŏng-wŏn; Aug. 13, some 5,500 students of 26 colleges held anti-U.S. demonstrations and some 300 students raided U.S. ambassador's residence; Aug. 15, coed Lim and a Roman Catholic priest Moon Gyu-hyŏn who visited North Korea from the U.S. to accompany coed Lim, were arrested upon arriving in South Korea across the DMZ line at Panmunjom; Aug. 25, Kim Dae-jung was indicted on charge of violation of the National Security Law and the Foreign Exchange Control Law (charges were dropped later); Sept. 11, President Roh proposed his new Korean reunification formula at the National Assembly; Sept. 26–30, the first athletic games of the overseas Koreans were held in Seoul; Oct. 4, the 44th International Eucharistic Congress opened in Seoul; Oct. 7, second Korea visit of Pope John II; Oct. 16, President Roh embarked on a U.S. tour; Oct. 22, a movement to form a new general federation of democratic labor unions was launched in Seoul; Nov. 13,

15,000 antigovernment students of 78 colleges clashed with riot police; Nov. 20, President Roh embarked on a state visit to three European countries and Hungary; Nov. 27; the movement to merge three political parties was accelerated; Dec. 27, the government separated the Ministry of Culture and Public Information into the Ministry of Culture and the Office of Public Information, and created a new Ministry of Environmental Control; Dec. 31, former president Chun testified at the National Assembly on the wrongdoings of the Fifth Republic; President Roh declared that the issues connected with the Fifth Republic were settled.

1990 Jan. 23, President Roh announced that his DJP would merge with RDP to form the Democratic Liberal Party (DLP); Feb. 9, the DLP was officially launched; Mar. 3, the 4th infiltration tunnel dug by North Korea was discovered; Mar. 17, a major cabinet reshuffle; Mar. 24, violent student movement and labor strikes at Korea Broadcasting System and Hyundai Heavy Industries began; June 4, President Roh met President Mikhail Gorbachev in San Francisco; June 6, formation of the Democratic Party; Sept. 19, a cabinet reshuffle; Sept. 30, establishment of diplomatic relations between South Korea and the Soviet Union; Dec. 13, President Roh embarked on a state visit to the Soviet Union; Dec. 27, a major cabinet reshuffle in which the premier, a vice-minister, and several ministers were replaced.

1991 Jan. 23, a 134-man military medical team left for Saudi Arabia to join Operation Desert Storm; Feb. 18, a cabinet reshuffle;

Mar. 26, the first elections for small cities, county, and ward councils held; Apr. 20–21, President Roh and President Gorbachev held a summit meeting on Cheju Island; May 22, resignation of Premier Ro Chaebong; May 24, a major cabinet reshuffle; June 20, elections for provincial and Special City assemblies held; Sept. 17, South Korea, along with North Korea, secured a full membership in the United Nations; Oct. 1, South Korean army units took over security in the DMZ and the joint security area in Panmunjom from U.S. military units; Oct. 23–24, the fourth talks of premiers of the North and the South held in Pyongyang; Nov. 8, President Roh called for a nuclear-free Korean peninsula in his 3-point Declaration; Dec. 13, Agreement on Reconciliation, Nonaggression and Exchanges and Cooperation between the South and the North signed; Dec. 31, Joint Declaration of the Non-Nuclearization of the Korean Peninsula was initialed by representatives of the North and the South.

1992 Jan. 10, formation of the Unification National Party; Jan. 15, formation of the New Korea Party; Feb. 7, merger of the Unification National Party and the New Korea Party as the Unification National Party; Mar. 24, the 14th National Assembly elections held; May 15–26, nomination of presidential candidates by three major parties; May 22, three North Korean soldiers who infiltrated into South Korea across the 38th parallel were killed by South Korean security forces.

MAPS OF KOREA

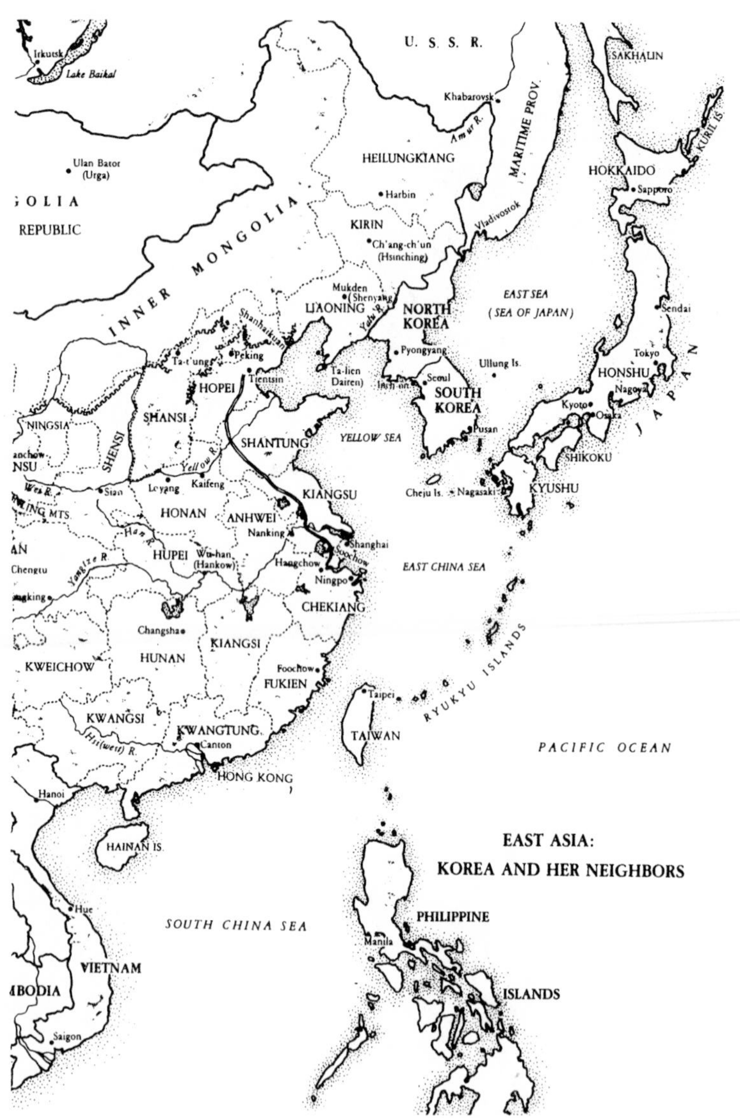

1. East Asia: Korea and Her Neighbors

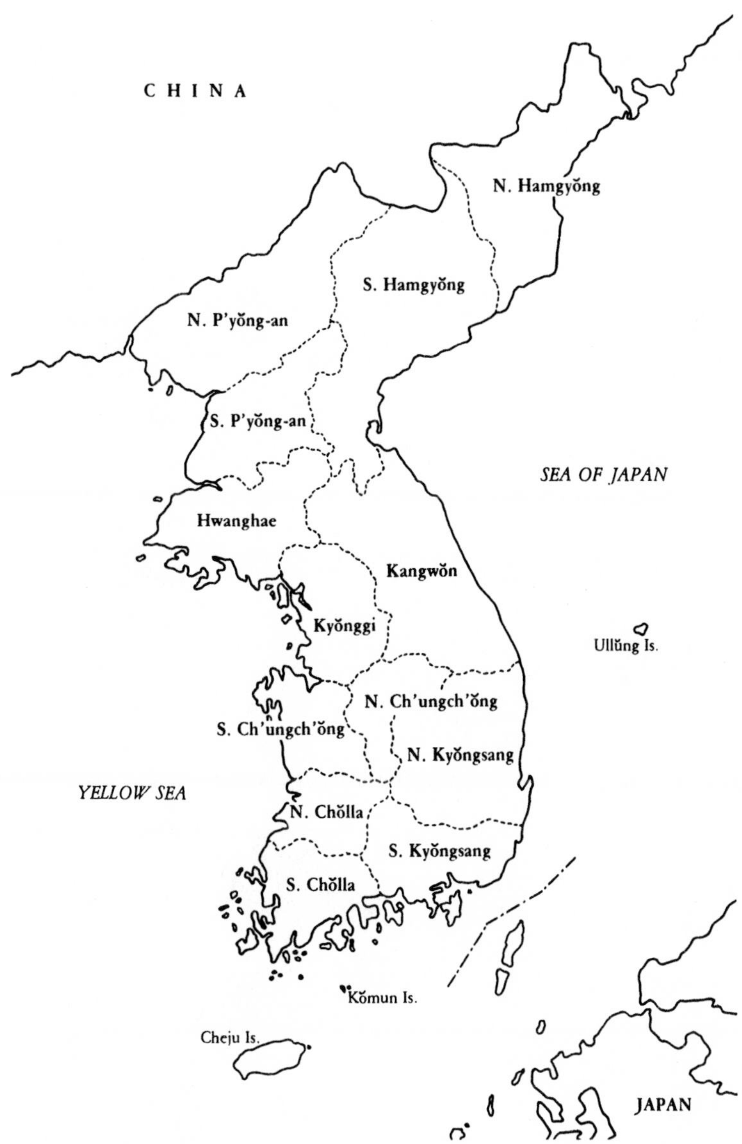

2. Korea Before Partition

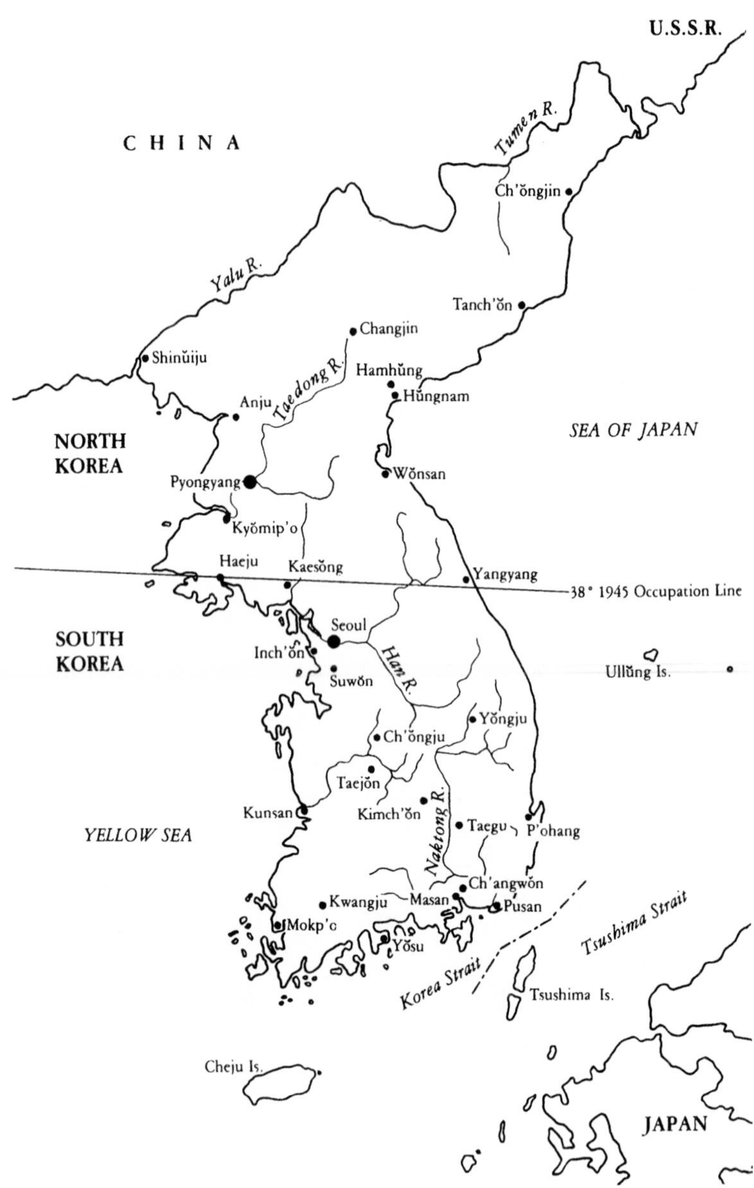

3. The Partitioned Korea, 1945

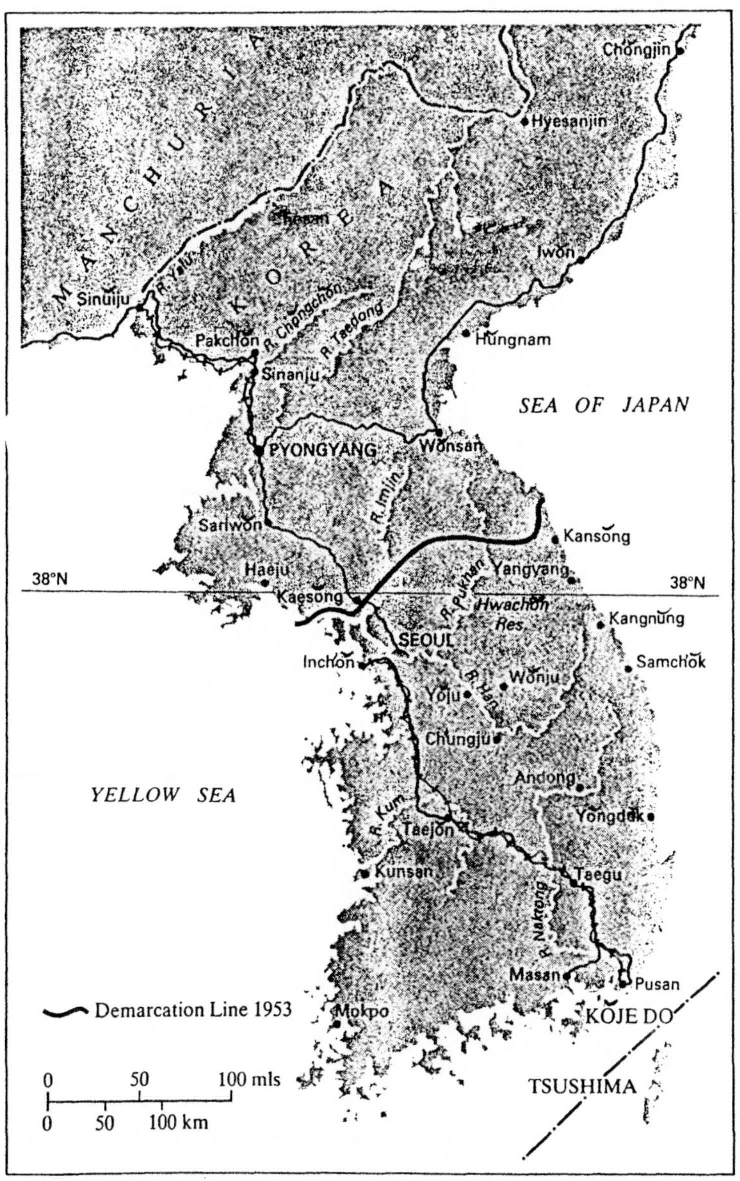

4. Military Demarcation Line and Demilitarized Zone

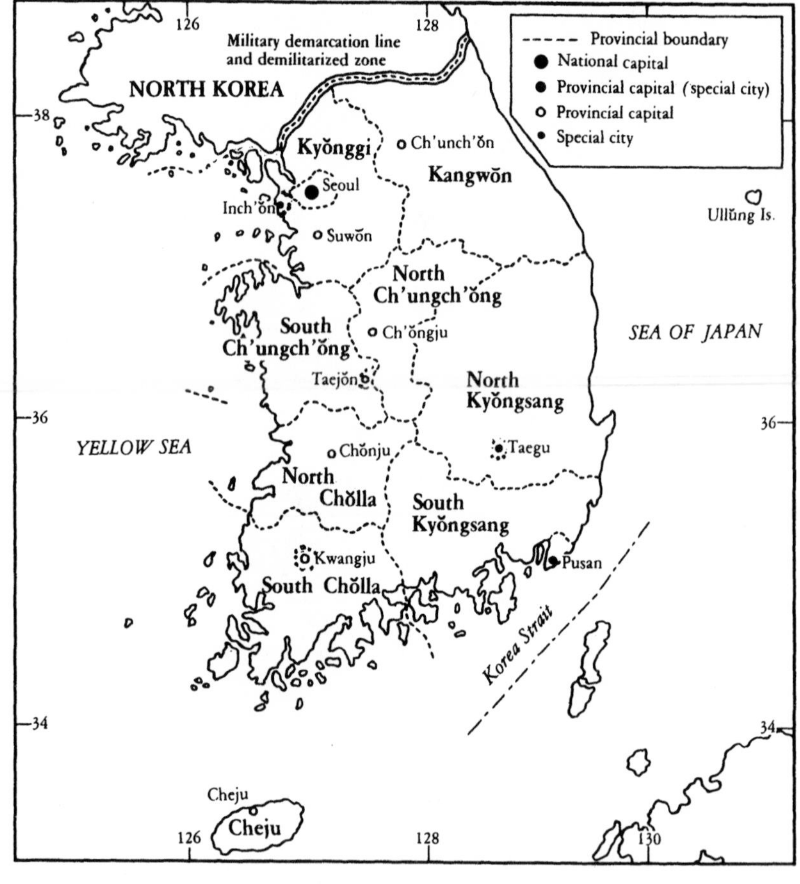

5. Republic of Korea, Administrative Districts (1953–)

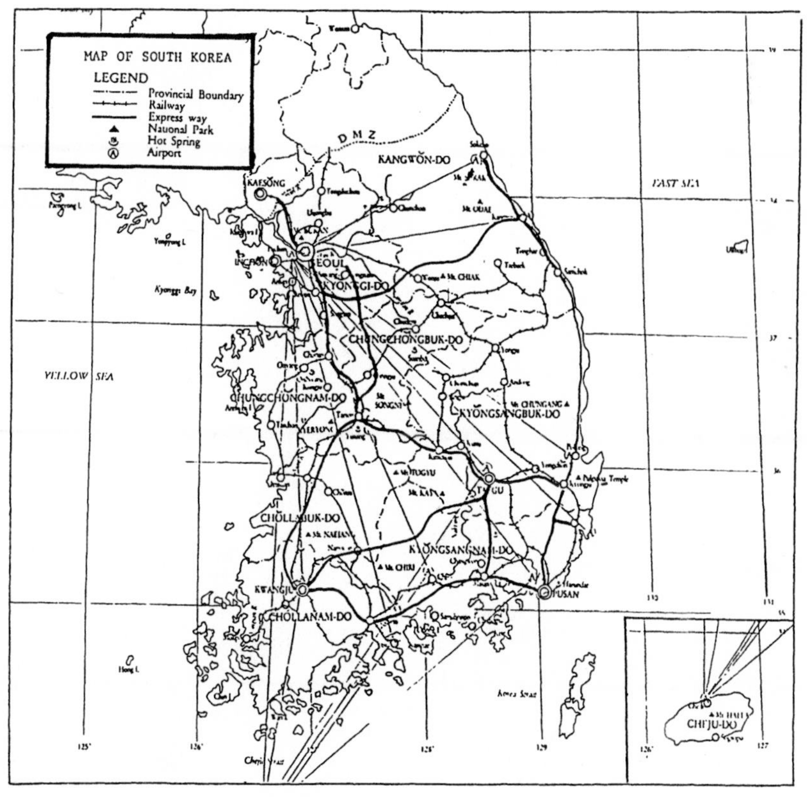

6. Map of South Korea

INTRODUCTION

The Korean Peninsula extends due south from Manchuria on the Asian mainland. Korea and all of its associated islands lie between longitudes 124° and 131° East, and between latitudes 33° and 43° North. The peninsular area of some 85,000 square miles is slightly larger than Minnesota. The peninsula is roughly 621 miles long and 134 miles wide at its narrowest point. It is separated from Manchuria by the Yalu and Tumen rivers, and it is surrounded by the Sea of Japan (East Sea), the Yellow Sea (West Sea), and the Korea Strait. A very short distance from its northeastern corner lies the Maritime Province of the Soviet Union.

Today, the peninsula is divided along the military demarcation (truce) line into two Korean states; the Democratic People's Republic of Korea (North Korea 46,768 sq. mi.) and the Republic of Korea (South Korea 38,131 sq. mi). The demilitarized zone (DMZ) which separates the two Korean states covers an area of some 477 square miles.

The name Korea is derived from the Koryŏ dynasty which ruled Korea from 936 to 1392 A.D. as a unified kingdom. The other name of Korea, Chosŏn, more popularly known in the West as "the Land of the Morning Calm," came from the kingdom which the Yi dynasty established in 1392 and ruled over until 1910.

PHYSICAL FEATURES

Korea is a mountainous country, but the west coast along the Yellow Sea and the southern coast both have low hills with some plains. In the north, the Changbaek Range and its branches cover an extensive area. The highest mountain in the Changbaek Range, which runs along both banks of the Yalu and Tumen rivers, is Mt. Paektu (9,000 feet), and in the Nangnin Range the Kaema and the Pujŏn plateaus constitute the "roof" of North Korea. The T'aebaek mountain chain, which is the backbone of the peninsula, runs almost the entire length of the peninsula and parallels the east coast from the eastern fringe of the Kaema Plateau. In this range are found such famous mountains as Mt. Kŭmgang, or Diamond Mountain (5,350 feet), Mt. Sŏrak (5,600 feet), and Mt. T'aebaek (5,100 feet). Running in a southwesterly direction is a branch of mountains called Sobaek, where the second highest peak in Korea, Mt. Chiri (6,250 feet), is located.

Whereas the east coast generally has smooth shorelines, the west and southern coasts have extremely irregular ones with numerous bays and inlets. Most of Korea's 3,400 islands are located near the west and southern coasts. Among the major islands are Kŏje and Wan off the south coast, the Chin Island off the southwestern corner of the peninsula, and the island of Kanghwa near Inch'ŏn on the west coast. Located some 100 miles off the southern coast is Cheju, the largest of the Korean islands, created by volcanic activities, which also boasts one of the highest and most majestic mountains, Mt. Halla (6,400 feet). Finally, in the Sea of Japan are the two Korean islands of Ullŭng and Tok.

All major rivers but two flow westward into the Yellow Sea. They are the Yalu, the Ch'ŏngch'ŏn, and the Teadong rivers in the north, the Imjin, the Han, and the Kŭm rivers in the south. The Tumen River flows into the Sea of Japan, and the Naktong River in the south flows southward into the Korea Strait. There are three major plains, one in the northwestern region, one in the west-central region, and one in the southwestern region of the peninsula.

Only about 22% of the land is cultivated, while the other 66% is mountainous or covered with forests. Most of the arable lands are located in the western and southern regions of South Korea, although a sizeable area of fertile farmlands is located in the western region of North Korea.

Climate

The climate of Korea is more continental than oceanic, and there are four distinct seasons. Spring generally begins in early March, accompanied by warm breezes from the south, and lasts until the end of June with light rainfall at regular intervals. Late June and the month of July are generally the heavy rainy season with July temperatures reaching 26-to-30 degrees centigrade in the south. The summer is hot and humid due to southern monsoon winds. Annual precipitation varies from about 24 inches in the northeast to more than 60 inches in the southern regions.

The autumn is a pleasant season, starting generally from late September and ending towards the end of November with the first frost. Autumn is a period of dry and sunny weather which the Koreans refer to as a time of "high, blue sky and fat horses." The winter begins around mid-December and lasts until February, being extremely cold in the north, where January temperatures fall to 8°F. Owing to the influence of the surrounding seas, the winter climate in the south is not as severe. The snowfall is generally light in the lowlands and the southern half of South Korea. The mean January temperature in Seoul is 23°F. The extreme southern area of South Korea has only very light snowfall or none at all.

THE PEOPLE

The Koreans are a homogeneous people, speaking the same language. In 30,000 B.C., homo sapiens inhabited the Korean Peninsula, leaving behind numerous Paleolithic culture sites. Later on, around 3,000 B.C., certain tribal units of the Tungusic people, such as the Han, the Kaema or Koma, the Maek, and the Puyŏ, migrated into the peninsula from the Altai Mountain region via Siberia, Mongolia and Manchuria, bringing with them the Neolithic culture—the Ural-Altaic language and Shamanism—and became the ancestors of the present-day Koreans. Ethnologically, the Koreans belong to the Altaic family of races, which includes the Turkic, Mongolian, and Tungusic peoples.

POPULATION

The total population of Korea was about 25 million when the country was liberated from Japan and partitioned into military operations zones of the Allies in 1945. The American zone had about 16 million and the Soviet zone a little over 9.5 million people. However, with the steady influx of two million refugees from the north and another two million Koreans who returned from overseas, the population of South Korea had grown to 20 million by 1948. Since then, the population has steadily increased: 24 million in 1965, 35 million in 1975, 42 million in 1985. In 1990, the total population of South Korea stood at 42.8 million, with a population density of 1,107 per square mile.

The average life expectancy was less than 45 years during the Japanese colonial period. As of 1945, only 12.5% of the total population was over the age of 50. Since liberation, the life expectancy has steadily increased, and in 1988 the life expectancy of men stood at 66.9 and that of women at 74.9 years.

The population grew at an annual average rate of 3% up until 1960. After that time, the growth rate fell gradually, declining to 0.93% by 1985. The average Korean woman had 2.4 children in 1988, compared to 2.5 in 1984, 2.8 in 1980, 4.2 in 1970, and 6.1 in 1960.

According to the 1985 census, the urban population stood at 26.5 million, representing 65.4% of the total population, and the rural population was 14 million, representing 34.6% of the total. This is in sharp contrast to the distribution as of 1948, when only 3.8 million were in the urban areas and 16.2 million in the rural areas. The urban population has grown at an annual average rate of 5% since 1955, while the population in the rural areas has shown a commensurate decrease. The population of Seoul grew from one million in 1948 to 10.7 million by 1990, representing 25% of the total population. The influx of rural population into Seoul Special City declined after 1970 as there was greater population migration into cities other than Seoul due to the rise of new commercial and industrial centers. Among the cities whose population has grown rapidly in recent years are the five other special cities of Pusan, Taegu, Inch'ŏn, Kwangju, and Taejŏn, in addition to such industrial centers as Ch'angwŏn, Masan, P'ohang, and Ulsan.

The most populated province in 1990 was Kyŏnggi, with a population of 5.6 million, followed by South Kyŏngsang with 3.6 million, North Kyŏngsang with 2.8 million, South Chŏlla with 2.5 million, and North Chŏlla with 2.1 million. South Ch'ungch'ŏng Province had 1.9 million, followed by Kangwen with 1.7 million and North Ch'ungch'ŏng with 1.3 million. The island-province of Cheju had the smallest population with 507,000 in 1990.

History

The long history of Korea may be divided into several distinct periods. The first of these is the period before the rise of the three kingdoms. The second covers the Three Kingdoms period (57 B.C.-936 A.D.), as well as the period during which the unified Korea was ruled by the Shilla dynasty. The third period is that of the Koryŏ dynasty (918–1392). The long fourth period (1392–1910) is that of the Yi dynasty, lasting until the dawn of the twentieth century. The relatively short fifth period (1910–1945) saw Korea under Japanese colonial rule, and the sixth even shorter period (1945–48) was that of the Allied occupation, at the end of which the two Korean states emerged.

1. History to 1945. Various groups of the Paleolithic people inhabited the Korean Peninsula from about 30,000 B.C., leaving behind many Paleolithic sites throughout the land. From about 3000 B.C., several groups of the Neolithic people began to migrate into the peninsula. They were the Tungusic tribes who arrived from central Asia via Siberia, Mongolia, Manchuria, and the northwestern Chinese coastal regions. It was this Tungusic people who brought to Korea their Ural-Altaic language, shamanistic religion, and a Neolithic culture. Many dolmens, menhirs, various types of pottery, and a variety of stone tools unearthed in Korea attest to this fact.

The new immigrants formed their tribal units and built walled towns and pit dwellings. In 2333 B.C., a mythological figure named Tan'gun (also known as Wanggŏm) is said to have formed a "nation," marking the beginning of the Old Chosŏn period. The territory of Old Chosŏn is said to have included the southern part of Manchuria and the northwestern part of the Korean peninsula along the Taedong River with its capital at Asadal. Many believe that Asadal was present-day Pyongyang, whose former name was

Wanggŏmsŏng. Although historical obscurity surrounds the findings of Old Chosŏn and its history, Old Chosŏn of Tan'gun was said to have been ruled by a new ruler named Kija and his successors from about 1120 B.C. until it was taken over by Wiman in 194 B.C., ushering in the Wiman Chosŏn period.

Wiman Chosŏn extended its domination into the northeastern part of the peninsula, establishing the Imdun district there, and into the central region of the peninsula, where it established the Chinbŏn district. As Wiman Chosŏn rose, a tribal state named Chin emerged in the southern region of Korea. The state of Chin founded by the refugees from Old Chosŏn, eventually gave way to the rise of the three federations of the Han people, namely Mahan in central Korea, Chinhan in the southeastern region, and Pyŏnhan in the southcentral coastal region.

In 190 B.C., Emperor Wu of the Han dynasty of China invaded Korea, and after overthrowing Wiman Chosŏn in 108 B.C. he established three Chinese commanderies of Lolang (Nangnang), Chenfan (Chinbŏn), and Lintu'un (Imdun) in Korea and a commandery named Hsungt'u (Hyŏnt'o) in southern Manchuria along the lower Yalu River region. However, the Chinese commandery of Lint'un was soon overthrown, and was replaced by two Korean states named Okchŏ and Eastern Ye in the northeastern region.

A new state of Koguryŏ of the Yemaek tribes which emerged in the central region of Manchuria in 37 B.C. conquered the state of Puyŏ which was located in the northwestern region of Manchuria, and extended its territory into the Korean Peninsula with its capital at Kungnaesŏng (T'ungkuo) on the middle region of the Yalu River, and after conquering both Okchŏ and Eastern Ye during the first century it became a bona fide kingdom in the third century. In 313, Koguryŏ overthrew the Chinese commandery of Lolang, as well as a new Chinese commandery of Taifang (Taebang), which was established around 204 A.D., soon thereafter. After this, Koguryŏ moved its capital from Kungnaesŏng to Wanggŏmsŏng (now Pyongyang) in 427, controlling most of the northern half of Korea and the southern part of Manchuria.

As political changes took place in the north, a political metamorphosis also occurred in the southern part of Korea as the state of Saro emerged in the Chinhan area in 57 B.C. and the state of Paekche in the Mahan area in 18 B.C. In the meantime, Pyŏnhan was split into several Kaya states. The state of Saro eventually absorbed other areas of Chinhan, establishing the Kingdom of Shilla in the third century, while the state of Paekche did likewise in the Mahan area, becoming a bona fide Kingdom of Paekche in the third century and extending its territory into the southwestern region of Korea. Six Kaya states which were located in the lower reaches of the Naktong River failed to become unified, and they were taken over one by one by Shilla in the sixth century. With the rise of Koguryŏ in the north, Shilla in the southeast, and Paekche in the central region of Korea, the Three Kingdoms period in Korean history began, ushering in a long period of warfare between them.

Koguryŏ was engaged in frequent warfare not only against Paekche and Shilla, but also against Chinese forces of the Sui and T'ang dynasties from the end of the sixth and in the early seventh centuries. Meanwhile, it was faced with serious internal disunity as well. Paekche also encountered numerous internal problems. On the other hand, Shilla increased its economic and military strength, thanks to the political and military leadership provided by able bureaucrats and military leaders known as *hwarang* ("flowery princes").

Shilla, in alliance with the T'ang forces of China, destroyed first Paekche in 663, and then Koguryŏ in 668, thus unification of Korea by Shilla was achieved as it ruled over approximately two-thirds of the Korean Peninsula. When Koguryŏ fell, its territory in western Manchuria was taken over by China, which established a puppet state named "Lesser Koguryŏ" in that area. Koguryŏ's eastern territory in both Manchuria and northeast Korea was invaded by the nomads named Khitans and Jurchens. However, a Koguryŏ general who fled after the fall of Koguryŏ to eastern Manchuria with a large number of followers established a new kingdom of Chin in 698 (renamed Parhae in 713) whose territory covered the former Koguryŏ territories in eastern Manchuria and northeastern Korea.

Shilla was able to prevent the reestablishment of Chinese control in Korea, but it encountered growing internal problems, and in 892 a rebel leader established the Later Paekche in the former Paekche territory in the southwestern region of the Korean Peninsula while another rebel established Later Koguryŏ in 898 in the central region of Korea. Thus, once again Korea entered into a brief period of division of the Later Three Kingdoms.

During the Three Kingdoms period, agricultural economy developed rapidly in the southern region as Chinese cultural influence grew in Korea as Buddhism, which was first introduced to Korea in the fourth century, flourished in Paekche and Shilla. As Chinese cultural influence increased the political system of the Korean kingdoms changed from a primitive democracy of the peasant society to a centralized bureaucratic rule with the establishment of monarchy. Such a political change also brought about social changes, establishing a new class structure dominated by the aristocracy. While Confucian learning grew, accompanying the rise of educational institutions and scholarship, Buddhism developed rapidly, bringing the rise of new art, architecture, crafts, music and dance, and scholarship. Thus, Korea became a cultural satellite of China.

In 918, Wang Kŏn, a general of the Kingdom of Later Koguryŏ, rebelled against his lord and, after overthrowing Later Koguryŏ, he established his own dynasty and a new kingdom named Koryŏ with its capital at Song'ak (now Kaesŏng). Soon after the last king of Shilla surrendered in Koryŏ in 935, Koryŏ conquered Later Paekche in 936, reunifying Korea, this time without the aid of a foreign power. Gradually, Koryŏ extended its territory up to the Yalu River region in the west and near Hamhŭng in the east, and after incorporating Cheju Island into the kingdom, Koryŏ ruled the entire Korean Peninsula except the northeastern region from the early 12th century.

The Koryŏ dynasty adopted the Chinese model of political structure, including the executive organ called Secretariat of State Affairs, which had six boards (ministries). It adopted the T'ang code of China as well as the civil examination system to select qualified civil and military officials into the centralized bureaucracy.

With the adoption of a new land system, farmlands were distributed to meritorious persons, and civil and military officials of high ranks were given stipend lands, creating a new pattern of absentee landlordism. Meanwhile, a new social structure emerged with the new landed-gentry class at the top, which was cushioned by a class of petty functionaries in the central and local bureaucracies. The commoner class included the artisans, the merchants, and the peasants (*paekchŏng*). At the bottom was the low-born class (*ch'ŏnmin*), which included mostly slaves and domestic servants.

While nurturing Confucian learning and scholarship with the

many new educational institutions it established, the Koryŏ dynasty made Buddhism the state religion and contributed toward the further development of Buddhist culture in Korea. However, it also encouraged a harmonious relationship between Buddhism and the native religion of Shamanism and its culture. A significant cultural and technical innovation was the production of better wooden printing blocks, printing many books, including the 81,137-page *Tripitaka Koreana (Koryŏ Taejanggyŏng)* in 1251. Among the many history books published were the *History of the Three Kingdoms (Samguk sagi)* by Kim Pu-sik and others in 1145, and that of Monk Ilyŏn entitled *Memorabilia of the Three Kingdoms (Samguk yusa)* in 1281.

Korea suffered invasions of the Khitans in 993 and 1018 and that of the Jurchens in 1104. Meanwhile a power struggle between the civil and military officials in the 12th century, which led to the rise of the military dictatorship of the Ch'oe clan in the late 12th century, coupled with numerous slave and peasant uprisings in the 12th century, weakened the nation and brought about the decline of the Koryŏ dynasty. The most serious threat to the Koryŏ dynasty came in the 13th century when the Mongols invaded Korea several times between 1231 and 1270, making Korea a vassal to the Mongol empire.

When the Koryŏ court surrendered to the Mongols, a rebellion of Korean military units called Three Elite Patrols (Sambyŏlch'o) erupted against both the Koryŏ court and the Mongols. The rebels fled from Kanghwa Island to the island of Chindo, off the southwest tip of the peninsula, but they were again forced to flee to Cheju Island, where they took their last stand in 1273.

The Mongol invasions not only destroyed the legitimacy of the Koryŏ dynasty, but countless cultural properties such as temples, pagodas, books and wooden printing blocks. A tremendous amount of property and farms were also destroyed, and in the two futile attempts of the Mongols to invade and conquer Japan in 1274 and 1281, Korea lost several thousand sailors, soldiers, and carpenters.

In 1388, a Koryŏ general, Yi Sŏng-gye, who subscribed to an anti-Mongol and pro-Ming (China) policy, carried out a coup, taking control of the government in disarray. When he met opposition to his reform measures, he overthrew the Koryŏ dynasty and established his own Yi dynasty (1392–1910) and a new kingdom which he named Chosŏn with Seoul as its capital.

Conquering the northeastern region of Korea, the Yi dynasty brought the entire Korean Peninsula under its control and strengthened its national defense. However, the Yi dynasty maintained Korea's vassalage to China of the Ming dynasty, which overthrew the Yuan dynasty of the Mongols in 1368, and the Ch'ing (Qing) dynasty of the Manchus, which overthrew the Ming dynasty in 1644.

The Yi dynasty established an elaborate bureaucracy completely patterned after that of Chinese model, legislated many new laws, adopted neo-Confucianism as a state creed and promoted educational development for Confucian learning, fully adopted the Chinese civil examination system, and reconstructed the social structure of Korea. The kingdom was divided into eight provinces governed by the central bureaucracy in Seoul through provincial governments. The central bureaucracy was headed by the Privy Council called Ŭijŏnbgu and the State Council, the executive branch of the central government which had six boards (ministries) of Personnel, Rites, Revenue, Punishment, Public Works, and Military. The Office of the Inspector-General and the Office of the Censors played important roles in controlling the behavior of the monarchy, the bureaucracy, and the bureaucrats. The top military organ was the Five Military Commands Headquarters.

The social structure of Korea of the Yi dynasty was similar to that of the Koryŏ period. However, the upper class was called *yangban,* which included high-ranking civil and military officials (scholar-gentry known as *sadeabu*) and their families. Petty functionaries in the central and local government were called the "middle people" (*chung'in*); the commoners were called *sangmin* or *sang'in*, the class which included the free peasants, the artisans, and the merchants in that social order; and at the bottom was the low born (*ch'ŏnmin*) people, which, as before, included slaves, domestic servants, and others who were engaged in unclean or undesirable professions (butchery, funeral business, public entertainment, etc.).

With the adoption of Neo-Confucianism as a state creed, the Yi dynasty rejected Buddhism, relegating it to be the religion of the rural masses. Shamanism, which was tolerated, was widely practiced by the people. Along with the creation of the Korean alphabet (*han'qŭl*) in the middle of the fifteenth century, the government of the Yi dynasty brought about a tremendous cultural development and the rise of scholarship and educational institutions for Chinese and Confucian studies from the primary to university levels. Meanwhile, folk culture flourished as a new form of poetry (*sijo*), genre painting, and popular literature developed rapidly.

However, the power struggle between the monarch and bureaucracy which was controlled by Confucian scholar-officials known as *sadaebu,* several purges of certain scholars carried out by the kings in the late fifteenth and early sixteenth centuries, and factional strifes of several politically ambitious groups of scholars brought about extremely serious political instability. In this situation, Korea suffered much from Japanese invasions ("seven-years war") of the 1592–98 period and Manchu invasions in 1627 and 1636. Numerous rebellions and uprisings which erupted in the seventeenth century created serious economic and social problems from which the Korean government was unable to recover.

Two reform-minded monarchs, Yŏngjo (1724–76) and Chŏngjo (1776–1800) adopted several reform measures, including tax reform, but they were unable to restore national strength after the disastrous Japanese and Manchu wars, and they could not reestablish political morality and social stability. Then came the popular uprisings in 1811–12 in the northwest and in 1862 in the southern region.

The various reform measures proposed by a new breed of Confucianists known as *Shirhak* ("Practical learning") scholars in the eighteenth and early nineteenth centuries fell upon the deaf ears of conservative Neo-Confucian scholars and policy makers.

Korea was in a hopeless state of affairs when a young boy was put on the throne in 1864 as Kojong, succeeding his uncle who died without an heir. The boy-king's father was selected to be his regent with the title of Taewŏn'gun. The regent was not only ambitious to strengthen his son's monarchical power, but also to recover the prestige and glory of the Yi dynasty. Therefore, he launched various reform measures and made plans to reconstruct palace buildings which were destroyed by the Japanese during the "seven-years war" of 1592–98. However, his reform measures antagonized reactionary Confucian scholars and conservative officials, and his new taxes and coinage antagonized the commoners. In the end, he was forced to relinquish the regency in 1873, leaving his inept son under the shadow of his wife, Queen Min, and other ladies and their relatives in the court.

From the 1850s onward, Korea, the "hermit kingdom," was

under pressure from the Western Powers to open her doors for trade. But it was Japan which brought about a direct military threat to Korea, forcing her to establish a new relationship by signing a diplomatic and commercial treaty in 1876. The signing of this treaty was followed by the conclusion of diplomatic and commercial treaties between Korea and the United States in 1882 and with other Western powers thereafter.

The opening of Korea to the West brought forth a group of nationalist reform advocates who were collectively called Kaehwa-dang, or the "party of the Progressives." The king, who became fond of the Americans, was willing to adopt a new policy and modernize his kingdom. Thus, a new era of national reconstruction began after 1881. However, the growing power struggle between the conservative and progressive officials, together with the increasing international rivalries among the powers in Korea, brought about serious political disturbances and social problems. Some of the most serious domestic events were the military insurrection of 1882, the coup d'état carried out by the Progressives in 1884, and the Tonghak Uprising of a religiously rebellious group and the poverty-stricken and socially mistreated people, including the peasants, in 1893–94.

The first serious international conflict which developed in Korea was that between China and Japan. Whereas China refused to disclaim her suzerainty over Korea and recognize her as a completely sovereign and independent nation, the Japanese challenged both Chinese political claims and her economic position in Korea, which eventually led to the Sino-Japanese War of 1894–95. After removing Chinese domination over Korea, the Japanese in turn increased their encroachment in that country, leading the Korean government to seek Russian aid.

Korea's growing ties with Russia increased Japan's apprehension for their national security in the face of growing Russian expansionism in Manchuria and Korea. At this juncture, the Independence Club and other reform advocates emerged, preaching self-oriented national regeneration, cultural modernization, and the strengthening of national independence. However, the Korean government was both unwilling and unable to adopt policies which these reform groups advocated. Meanwhile Russo-Japanese friction increased, culminating in the Russo-Japanese War of 1904–05.

During the war, Korea became the victim of Japanese aggression and domination, and in 1905 when the Japanese won the war over Russia, they made Korea a protectorate, superimposing the Japanese Residency-General (Tōkanfu) over the Korean government. In 1910, Japan actually annexed Korea, ending the rule of the Yi dynasty as well as any aspirations for Korean independence.

During the Japanese colonial period (1910–45), Korea was ruled by a colonial government named the Government-General of Korea (Chōsen Sōtokufu), which was a military bureaucracy headed by a Japanese army general on active duty. Contrary to the Imperial Rescript on Annexation of the Meiji Emperor, which promised the extension of "benevolent rule" of the Japanese emperor to Korea, the Japanese imposed military rule there, referring to Korea as *gaichi* ("outer land"), and treated it as a colony rather than an integral part of the empire. The Koreans were given no constitutional protection, having no voting rights or voice in politics. The Japanese referred to the Koreans as *senjin,* a derogatory Japanese noun for "the people of Chosŏn." Social integration between the Koreans and the Japanese was nonexistent and intermarriage between them was rare.

In the beginning of their colonial rule, the Japanese made vigorous efforts to suppress and stamp out Korean nationalism. To achieve this end, they closed down all Korean newspaper presses and magazine companies, shut down hundreds of private schools which were allegedly engaged in anti-Japanese activity, outlawed the teaching of Korean history and confiscated all Korean history books, and forbade the publication of nationalistic books and magazines. After this, they proceeded to appropriate farms and forest lands, forcing hundreds of thousands of Korean farmers into tenancy.

After suffering a humiliating Japanese colonial rule for ten years, the Koreans launched independence movements at home and abroad in 1918. Shortly after the Korean students in Japan wrote the Korean Declaration of Independence and took the action for independence in February 1919, the leaders in Korea wrote the Declaration of Independence, signed by thirty-three leaders, and led the Koreans of all walks of life, sex, and age to demonstrate their desire for independence in a peaceful manner. The culmination was the March First Movement in 1919 for national independence in which over two million Koreans were reported to have participated throughout the country.

The March First Movement was crushed and its leaders, along with thousands of those who participated in the demonstrations, were imprisoned, several hundreds of them were killed, and hundreds of nationalists were forced to flee from their native land. In April 1919, those Korean nationalists who were in Shanghai, China, established the Provisional Government of Korea with Dr. Syngman Rhee, who was in the United States, as premier (later president). After that, in cooperation with other nationalists in Korea and elsewhere, they continued to sustain Korea's national liberation movement.

The efforts made by the Korean nationalists at home, including students, were fruitless, but the relentless resistance which the Japanese continued to encounter convinced them that Korea could not be ruled by force and intimidation alone. Thus, in 1937, the Japanese Government-General in Korea adopted various programs and policies to Japanize the Koreans in order to make them "loyal imperial subjects." To do so, it launched what is called the *Kōminka undō* ("Movement for the Conversion of the Koreans to be Imperial Subjects"), and under a law the Koreans were forced to adopt Japanese-style family and given names, memorize and recite the "Pledge of the Imperial Subjects," and speak only the Japanese language in public. The teaching of the Korean language was first discouraged, but in 1938 Korean language instruction was abolished altogether. Even the ministers of churches were ordered to deliver their sermons only in Japanese. The Koreans were also forced to abandon their traditional white clothes and be converted to the Shintoism of Japan. In essence, this movement was to wipe out Korean ethnic identity and nationalist consciousness.

During the colonial period, the Koreans made both voluntary and involuntary efforts to modernize their economy, culture, and society, and various Japanese policies and plans brought about the modern transformation of Korea. First of all, the Japanese replaced old laws and administrative and judicial systems with new ones. They also developed the Korean economy so as to strengthen the power of their empire, and modern financial and commercial institutions, along with industrial establishments arose. Although inadequate, education was modernized as both public and private schools grew in number and communication and transportation systems were modernized by the installation of telegraph and telephone systems, construction of more railways and highways, and improvement of harbor facilities.

However, Korea paid a high price for those changes. Their natural and human resources were exploited ruthlessly by Japanese capitalist (*zaibatsu*) firms. Rich farmlands and forests were taken over by the Japanese, and increasing rice production only helped the Japanese rather than the Koreans as an increasing amount of rice was shipped to Japan. Workers' wages for the Koreans were always low, working hours were long, and working conditions were poor. If Korea was "thriving," as the Japanese said, it was "thriving" only to enrich Japan. Korean youth lagged far behind the Japanese in regard to educational opportunity, as it was the policy of the Japanese not to educate too many Koreans or train Korean scientists and technicians. Indeed, the lack of educational opportunity kept the rate of illiteracy as high as 75% even at the end of the Japanese colonial period.

Without giving any political rights and social equality to the Koreans, the Japanese mobilized more than two million workers after 1937 and shipped about half of them to factories and mines in Japan. Tens of thousands of the Korean youth as well as college students in Korea and Japan were drafted into the Japanese army and navy during World War II, and several thousand Korean women were forced to go to the war fronts in China and elsewhere to provide sexual service to Japanese troops. Little wonder then why most Koreans remained anti-Japanese to the bitter end as the savage war between the Allies and Japan was being waged in the Pacific area.

2. Liberation, Partition, the Allied Occupation, and the Birth of the Republic of Korea. In November 1943, the three Allies (the U.S., Britain and China) held a conference in Cairo, Egypt, and in their communique released on December 1, 1943 stated that "mindful of the enslavement of the people of Korea" under Japanese colonial rule, the three Allies have resolved that "in due course Korea shall become free and independent." The Soviet Union accepted the Cairo Agreement of the three Allies.

As agreed at Yalta with the U.S. and Great Britain in February 1945, the Soviet Union declared war on Japan on August 8, Soviet troops poured into Korea, and within a short period of time they put most of the northern half of Korea under their occupation. At this juncture, the American government proposed the partition of Korea into two military operational zones along the 38th parallel line—the area south of the line as the U.S. zone and the northern area as the Soviet zone—in order to prevent the Soviet occupation of the entire Korean Peninsula. The Soviet Union accepted this arrangement.

Realizing in early August 1945 that the emperor was ready to capitulate to the Allies, the Japanese Governor-General in Korea became concerned about the safety of the Japanese in Korea. As a result, he made an attempt to establish a transitional government in Korea in the hands of a group of prominent Korean leaders, hoping this would prevent possible anti-Japanese retaliation and allow time to make arrangements for safe repatriation of Japanese subjects. After failing to secure the cooperation of a right-wing nationalist leader, the Japanese turned to Yŏ Un-hyŏng, a well-known left-wing nationalist leader, who had formed a secret Alliance for Korean Independence in 1944. When approached by the Japanese, Yŏ laid down five conditions for his consideration of the Japanese offer, requesting the transfer of major governmental functions to his organization in order to preserve law and order, to prevent political chaos, and to establish a Korean government according to the wishes of the people. Specifically, the five conditions were: (1) immediate release of all political prisoners; (2) noninterference by the Japanese in his activities for national reconstruction; (3) freedom to organize the student and youth corps; (4) freedom to organize labor unions; and (5) guarantee of a three-month supply of food.

Yŏ's conditions were met on August 15, the day Japan surrendered to the Allies, accepting the unconditional surrender terms included in the Potsdam Declaration of July 1945. On August 16, with acceptance of his conditions by the Japanese, Yŏ organized the Committee for the Preparation of National Reconstruction (CPNR), and it began to function as a government with its own public security units. Provincial, district, and local committees of the CPNR were organized and maintained law and order.

Learning on September 2 that the Allies' plan was to partition Korea into two military operational zones, the CPNR called a "National Assembly" of some 1,000 delegates, and on September 6 it established the Korean People's Republic and its cabinet. Dr. Syngman Rhee, who was yet to return to Korea from his exile in the United States, was appointed chairman, and Yŏ Un-hyŏng was appointed vice-chairman of the Republic. Hŏ Hŏn, a prominent leftist, was named premier, and most cabinet ministers appointed were well-known right-wing nationalists.

Whereas the Soviets who occupied the north recognized the legitimacy of the People's Republic, the American occupation authorities, who landed in Korea the day after the formation of the People's Republic, did not. After accepting the surrender from the Japanese Governor-General, General John R. Hodge, commander of U.S. occupation forces in Korea, outlawed the People's Republic, and established the United States Army Military Government in Korea (USAMGIK) in September. Meanwhile, exiled political leaders returned to Korea from China and the United States. A contingent of Korean Communist troops under Kim Il-sung had already entered the north with the Soviet forces, followed by Korean Communist troops from the Yenan (Yan'an) area in China in late December.

Freedom of assembly, speech, religion and the press granted by the American military government in the south resulted in the proliferation of political parties of various political and economic orientations, and many social and labor organizations of various ideological persuasions, as well as newspaper presses and magazine publishers in the fall of 1945. Among the major political parties which emerged in the south were the Korean (Han'guk) Democratic Party, the Korean (Han'guk) Independence Party, and the National Council for Rapid Realization of Korean Independence, or Tokch'ok, all of which represented the conservative nationalist camp, and the Korean (Chosŏn) Communist Party and the People's Party, which represented the leftist camp. In the north, a similar event occurred, bringing the rise of the branch of the Korean Communist Party as well as the Korean (Chosŏn) Democratic Party of the right-wing nationalists and Ch'ŏng'udang, which was a political/social organization of a religious group (Ch'ŏndogyo, formally Tonghak). However, in early 1946, these right-wing organizations in the north were broken up by the Soviets and Korean Communists.

While the right-wing groups were more concerned with political matters, the Communists were quick to take advantage of a favorable situation for the promotion of socialist and labor movements, and they established subordinate groups of the Korean Communist Party such as the General Council of Labor Unions (Chŏnp'yŏng) in November 1945, the General Federation of Farmers' Unions (Chŏn'nong) in December 1945, the General Alliance of Korean Women (Chosŏn Punyŏ Tonghaeng) and the Alliance of Korean Youth (Chosŏn Minju Ch'ŏngnyŏn Tongmaeng, or Minch'ŏng) in the spring of 1946. All of these leftist organizations in the south were broken up in 1947 when the American military government cracked down on them for their illegal activities. The right-wing organizations in the south belatedly formed their labor unions in late 1945 and in March they formed the General Alliance of the Laborers for Rapid Realization of Korean Independence.

From December 16 to 26, 1945, the foreign ministers of the three Allies (the U.S., Great Britain and the Soviet Union) met in Moscow and adopted the Moscow Agreement, providing for the formation of a U.S.-U.S.S.R. Joint Commission, consisting of the occupation authorities of the two powers, for the purpose of establishing in consultation with the Korean leaders an independent nation of Korea and its government. They also agreed to put the newly established Korean government under a five-year trusteeship of the four Allies (the U.S., Great Britain, China and the Soviet Union).

When the news of the Moscow Agreement reached Korea on December 29, all Koreans, including the Communists, opposed the trusteeship plan of the Allies, and violent antitrusteeship demonstrations swept the country. Then, suddenly, the Communists in both zones changed their stand in favor of the plan, polarizing the Korean people, and bloody clashes between the Rightists and the Leftists ensued in both zones.

In March 1946, in the midst of a chaotic political situation, the U.S.-U.S.S.R. Joint Commission was formed to carry out the mandate of the Moscow Agreement. The first session of the Joint Commission was held in Seoul in March-May 1946, but it was unable to achieve its primary objective when the Soviets refused to talk with the right-wing leaders, condemning them as "undemocratic" because of their opposition to the trusteeship plan. It became clear to the U.S. that the Soviet intended to establish a national Korean government dominated by the leftists, if not completely in their hands. Witnessing the difficulties which the Joint Commission had faced, in October 1946 Kim Kyu-shik, a moderate nationalist, and Yŏ Un-hyŏng, a moderate leftist, organized the Coalition Committee for Cooperation between the Rightists and the Leftists in order to unite the strength of the middle groups and establish "a democratic transitional government" in accordance with the Moscow Agreement. In May 1947, the second session of the Joint Commission met in Pyongyang after a lengthy recess, but it similarly failed to achieve any agreement, and in June the Commission's business was suspended indefinitely.

Realizing that the establishment of Korean unity and a national government by the Joint Commission was a remote possibility, the American occupation authorities adopted new plans for "Koreanization" of the American military government. After establishing the South Korean Interim Legislative Assembly (SKILA) in December 1946, replacing an advisory Democratic Council of the Koreans which had been set up in February 1946 by Gen. Hodge, in June 1947 the South Korean Interim Government (SKIG) was established to assist the American military administration. Meanwhile, the Soviets in the north, after arresting the nationalist leaders, proceeded to establish its puppet regime under Kim Il-sung, and implemented several economic measures to socialize North Korea.

In September 1947, discarding the Moscow Plan unilaterally, the United States placed the Korean question before the United Nations. The U.N. General Assembly adopted the Korean resolution in November 1947, and formed the U.N. Temporary Commission on Korea (UNTCOK), authorizing it to conduct a national election in Korea to create a national government for the whole country so as to end the occupation of the country by the Allies.

The U.N. decision on Korea was welcomed by the United States and by most people in Korea, but the Soviets did not accept it and they did not allow the UNTCOK to visit North Korea. It soon became apparent that the U.N. plan would not work in the whole of Korea, and the UNTCOK adopted an alternative plan to hold elections in those areas where it was possible, namely in South Korea only. It was assumed by the UNTCOK that U.N.-sponsored and supervised elections would be held in the north in the near future, that a national assembly created by two-thirds of the Korean people in the first democratic elections in Korea should have the legitimacy to represent the entire country, that the government would be that of all Korea, and that the people in the north would elect their representatives to the national assembly later.

Whereas the right-wing nationalists in Dr. Rhee's camp welcomed such an alternative plan, the moderate and progressive nationalists, such as Kim Kyu-shik, as well as extreme right-wing nationalists, such as Kim Ku, vehemently opposed it, fearing that it would turn the temporary division of Korea into a permanent political partition. Thus, they visited North Korea in April 1948 and talked with the Communist leaders there, but they failed to achieve their objective, which was to solve the Korean question by the Koreans themselves, primarily because of Kim Il-sung's betrayal and deception.

The Soviet authorities in the north had already begun to transfer power to the Koreans and to Sovietize North Korea. Thus, the North Korean Provisional People's Committee was established in February 1946 as the central authority in the north and the People's Assembly was established in February, 1947 as North Korea's "legislative" body. Unlike their counterparts in the south, these administrative and legislative organs in the north exercised greater authority. In 1948, the People's Army was formed in the north.

On May 10, 1948, a month after a Communist-inspired rebellion broke out on Cheju Island, the U.N.-sponsored elections were held in the south, electing members of a Constituent Assembly. About 7.5 million people, or 75% of the eligible voters cast their ballots in the first democratic elections (although bloodshed accompanied the process) and elected 198 of 200 representatives to the National Assembly for the south, while 100 seats were left vacant to be occupied in the future by the representatives elected in the north.

The Constituent Assembly drew up a democratic constitution for the Republic of Korea, and it elected Dr. Rhee to be the first president and Yi Si-yŏng as vice-president of the Republic for a four-year term of office. On August 15, 1948 the Republic and its government were inaugurated as Dr. Rhee took the oath of office as president, and the U.S. occupation of South Korea came to an end.

Meanwhile, in the latter part of August, the Communists in the north held an election and established a new Supreme People's Assembly, which adopted a constitution, named the north as the Democratic People's Republic of Korea, and elected Kim Il-sung premier of North Korea. The Communist Republic and its government were inaugurated on September 9, ending the Soviet occupation of the north.

The rival regimes in the divided Korea made conflicting claims for political legitimacy, declaring that the entire Korean Peninsula was its national territory. South Korea claimed its legitimacy by declaring that the Republic of Korea was established by a majority of the Korean people under the U.N. resolution and its supervision, and that the United Nations General Assembly recognized it in November as "the only and lawful government in Korea." Meanwhile, North Korea claimed that the Democratic People's Republic of Korea was established by "all the Korean people," saying that while elections were held in the north, underground elections were also held in the south, electing 360 delegates to the 572-member Supreme People's Assembly by 77.8% of the eligible voters in the south. Needless to say, no such elections were held in the south.

Thus, the inability of the Allies to carry out their previous agreements, due to growing distrust and antagonism between the United States and the Soviet Union, bringing the Cold War between the East and the West, led to the establishment of two separate states in Korea with conflicting ideologies and systems, opening a tragic chapter in the history of the Korean people.

3. History of the Republic of Korea. The history of South Korea began in a turbulent domestic and international environment, and the many tragic events that took place in the Korean Peninsula shaped the particular character of Korean society as it is today. The original aim of building a democratic country was soon overwhelmed due to many unfortunate circumstances among which the major ones were the traditional bureaucratism which the government exercised, the Korean War, and the lack of experience in self-rule.

The history of South Korea which spans a half century consists of seven periods: 1948–60, 1960–61, 1961–63, 1963–72, 1972–79, 1979–81, and 1981–88, followed by the eighth period which began in 1988. Although the South Korean people's desire for democracy is yet to be fully fulfilled, various efforts made by the government and the people after 1948, particularly after 1963, brought about a remarkable progress in cultural, economic and social development, dramatically modernizing Korean society.

(A) The First Republic, August 1948–April 1960. The foundation of the Republic had hardly settled when a Communist-inspired military rebellion broke out on October 19, 1948 in the Yŏsu and Sunch'ŏn areas in South Chŏlla Province, followed by that in Taegu, North Kyŏngsang Province, on November 2. These rebellions were crushed but they demoralized the nation and increased the suppressive character of the government. Democratic aspirations suffered as the government became increasingly autocratic with the passage of the National Security Law in November 1948.

Despite the growing fear of further Communist uprisings and possible North Korean invasion, withdrawal of U.S. troops from South Korea was completed in June 1949, leaving behind the infant South Korean defense forces of some 50,000 men. Although a group of 500 American military advisers remained in South Korea to help train South Korean troops, these troops were inadequately equipped, having neither fighter planes or bombers, nor tanks, nor naval craft. They had been given only training aircraft and naval ships, and they were equipped with light arms, mostly those which had been surrendered by Japanese troops. The newly established Officers Candidate School was yet to function fully, and the complete annihilation of Communist guerrillas in the mountainous south central regions was yet to be achieved. As the new nation faced such a situation, tension mounted. The assassination of the Rightist leader, Kim Ku, by an army officer, and the arrest in October of some sixteen National Assemblymen under the recently passed National Security Law for their collaboration with Communists made the situation only worse.

Although it was not made public, military clashes between troops of North and South Korea had been taking place in the western frontiers as North Korean leaders prepared for an invasion to "liberate the southern half [South Korea] from American imperialists." Then, the new nation was struck by a calamity when, on June 25, 1950, North Korea launched a surprise attack. Some 80,000 well-trained North Korean troops, supported by Soviet-built tanks, crossed the 38th parallel and invaded South Korea to annex what North Koreans called "the southern half of the republic." Three days later, the aggressors captured the capital city of Seoul and pushed southward. U.S. troops, which were sent back to Korea from Japan, were unable to check the advance of the aggressors.

Responding to the appeal made by the United States, the U.N. Security Council, after condemning North Korea as an aggressor, organized the U.N. force, consisting of troops contributed by fifteen U.N. member nations, and dispatched it to South Korea. Meanwhile, North Korean troops occupied most of South Korea, leaving the southeastern corner of the country—the Pusan perimeter—unoccupied. After the arrival of U.N. troops and the formation of the U.N. Command under Gen. Douglas MacArthur, the U.N. forces launched a counterattack, beginning with the seaborne landing by U.N. forces at Inch'ŏn in September 1950. Seoul was recovered on September 28, the invaders were pushed back beyond the 38th parallel, and U.N. troops advanced into North Korea in pursuit of the fleeing enemy in early October under the authorization of the U.N., capturing the North Korean capital of Pyongyang on October 19. On November 21, the advance units of the U.N. forces reached the Chinese border on the Yalu River.

At this juncture, the People's Republic of China sent in its troops to the Korean Peninsula to save North Korea, and some 250,000 "volunteers" of the Chinese People's Liberation Army crossed the Yalu River, forcing the evacuation of South Korean and U.N. troops from the north. Over a million Chinese troops participated in the Korean War as Soviet pilots joined in air battles against the U.N. forces. The U.N. forces regrouped and mounted a counterattack, retaking Seoul on March 12. After this, stalemate was reached roughly along the 38th parallel.

The Soviet government called for truce negotiations, but peace talks that began at Kaesŏng in July 1951 failed to end the fighting. Hostilities continued until an armistice agreement was finally signed at Panmunjom on July 27, 1953 between the U.N. Command and the North Koreans and the Chinese. However, the South Korean government refused to sign the armistice. Be that as it may, the 1953 cease-fire (military demarcation) line, became a new boundary between North and South Korea, with a narrow demilitarized zone (DMZ) separating the two countries. The war caused more than a million casualties in South Korea, as well as enormous property damage, and political and social conditions became chaotic as economic hardships multiplied. On August 15, 1953, the South

Korean government returned to the war-devastated capital city of Seoul.

During the Korean War, President Rhee and his Liberal Party (LP, formed in 1951) acted high-handedly toward their opponents in the National Assembly who refused to approve a series of constitutional amendments proposed by the government in January 1952, creating a political crisis known as the "Pusan political disturbance" of May. After proclaiming martial law in the Pusan area on May 25, President Rhee and his party forced the National Assembly in July 1952 to pass a constitutional amendment bill, instituting a direct, popular election of the president and the vice-president.

Under the amended constitution, Dr. Rhee was reelected by popular vote in 1952, but the vice-presidential candidate nominated by the LP was defeated by an aged, independence candidate, who was helped by the police under a secret instruction given by Rhee himself. In November 1954, the National Assembly dominated by the LP adopted another series of constitutional amendments by dubious means, providing exemption to the incumbent president from the two-term limitation in office, and abolishing the office of prime minister.

In the 1956 presidential election, a new opposition Democratic Party (DP, founded in 1955) nominated candidates for the offices of president and vice-president. The sudden death of its presidential candidate (Shin Ik-hui) assured victory for Dr. Rhee, but the DP candidate (Chang Myŏn) for the vice-presidency defeated the LP candidate. Encouraged by such an event, Cho Pong-am, a Socialist and former minister of agriculture, formed the Progressive Party in November.

As corruption among government officials and members of the Liberal Party became rampant and repression by the police increased, a widespread desire for change grew, particularly among the urban voters. In the general elections for the National Assembly in 1958, the DP increased its number of seats substantially and, aware of the danger of losing its absolute control, the Liberal Party-dominated National Assembly repealed local autonomy law and passed a new National Security Law, promulgated on December 26, so as to strengthen the government's control.

In the fourth presidential election, held in March 1960, Dr. Rhee and Yi Ki-bung ran as the presidential and vice-presidential candidates of the LP, respectively. Three weeks before the election, the DP presidential candidate (Cho Pyŏng-ok) died while receiving medical treatment in the United States, once again assuring the election of Dr. Rhee. However, the election of Yi was uncertain. As a result, the ruling party resorted to corrupt and fraudulent means to elect Yi, who defeated Chang Myŏn, the vice-presidential candidate of the DP, by a large margin.

Popular reaction against the autocracy of President Rhee and the corrupt and fraudulent practices of the administration and the LP exploded immediately after the March election of 1960. Fierce student riots erupted throughout the country, particularly in the Pusan-Masan area, producing casualties among students and leading up to the Student Uprising of April 19, 1960 in Seoul. These incidents combined with mounting pressure from the United States forced President Rhee and his cabinet to resign *en masse* on April 26.

(B) The Second Republic, August 1960–May 1961. A caretaker government was set up under Foreign Minister Hŏ Chŏng, and in mid-June the National Assembly adopted constitutional amendments. In July, general elections for the new upper House of Councillors, and the House of Representatives were held, and in August, both houses of the National Assembly elected Yun Po-sŏn as president and Chang Myŏn as prime minister, and the Second Republic emerged.

The Second Republic was handicapped from the start. It had no mandate from the people and both President Yun and Prime Minister Chang lacked fortitude and political skills. The Chang administration was indecisive in dealing with former leaders of the Rhee regime and seemed too tolerant toward left-wing radicals. It was unable to cope effectively with the ideological and social cleavage between political and social groups, and failed to gain the confidence of the people.

The ruling DP itself was badly split and it had no suitable solutions to economic and social problems. Meanwhile, new student demonstrations erupted as the influence of the Communists among the students grew. Agitation by students for direct negotiations with North Korean students, aimed at reunification of the country, created anxiety and turmoil. The danger to national security increased as shortages of food and jobs became more acute.

Such a state of the nation set the stage for the military revolution which would usher in another important period in Korean history.

(C) The Military Rule, May 1961–Dec. 1963. On May 16, 1961 a military revolution, led by a small group of young, disgruntled army officers headed by Major General Park Chung-hee overthrew the Second Republic. The revolutionaries proclaimed that their aims were to protect the country from Communist threats and reconstruct its political, economic, and social systems, establishing a clean government and social justice.

The Military Revolutionary Committee (MRC), which emerged on May 16 and took over the government, declared martial law, dissolved the National Assembly, forbade all political activity, banned student demonstrations, and imposed press censorship. President Yun was persuaded to remain in office as the Second Republic fell on May 18. Thereupon, the MRC, headed by Lt. Gen. Chang To-yŏng, Army Chief of Staff, who did not participate in planning of the revolution, but became its chairman, issued its six pledges, and on the following day, acting as a legislative body, it adopted the Law Concerning Extraordinary Measures for National Reconstruction. In late May, the MRC was renamed the Supreme Council for National Reconstruction (SCNR), making the SCNR the supreme organ of the nation, and a new executive branch (cabinet) of the government headed by the chairman of the SCNR, and the new judicial branch in the hands of the revolutionaries were established. Meanwhile, the Korean Central Intelligence Agency (KCIA) was established as stern measures for political and social purification were carried out. In November 1961 the General Alliance of the Laborers for Rapid Realization of Independence and the National Council of Labor Unions, which had been organized in October 1960, were united into General Federation of Korean Labor Unions (Han'guk Noryŏn).

In July 1961, Gen. Park became chairman of the SCNR, and in August he announced that political activity would be permitted in early 1963 to pave the way for the restoration of a civilian government. Meanwhile, the activities of the Political Purification Committee, which was established under the Political Purification Law of March 16, 1962, created much controversy. In a bitter political controversy over the law, President Yun resigned, and Gen. Park became acting president. The constitution, which was amended by the SCNR was presented to the people, and in late

December 1962 it was approved in a national referendum. Meanwhile, the Political Party Law was promulgated on December 30, reviving political activities of those who were not purged.

In January 1963, as the ban against political activity was removed, the revolutionaries quickly formed the Democratic Republic Party (DRP), and nominated Gen. Park as its presidential candidate. When, in mid-March, the discovery of an alleged plot to overthrow the military junta was announced, the acting president disclosed that a plebiscite would be held on a four-year extension of military rule. However, when a strong negative reaction against his plan developed, the acting president withdrew the plan, and the restoration of civilian rule was once again promised. In August, Gen. Park retired from the army and ran for the four-year-term presidency.

The opposition forces were split into four political parties, and in the presidential election held in October 1963, Gen. Park defeated by a narrow margin former President Yun, who ran as the presidential candidate of the Civil Rule Party. The Democratic Republican Party, of which Gen. Park was president, also won a majority in the National Assembly elections held in November, giving former military junta members control over the new civilian government. With the inauguration of President Park on December 17, the Third Republic emerged.

(D) The Third Republic, December 1963–December 1972. Although a civilian government was restored, all important positions were occupied by ex-military men and the National Assembly was completely dominated by the DRP.

Considerable economic progress was achieved under the two consecutive Five-Year Economic Development Plans (1962–66 and 1967–71), and social stability was restored, but the Third Republic failed to promote democracy. In March and April 1964, large student demonstrations broke out in Seoul, protesting against the negotiations with Japan to establish normal relations between the two countries. The government declared an emergency decree in the Seoul area in June, and despite violent opposition, the government signed the treaty with Japan on June 22, 1965 establishing new diplomatic and commercial relations. To make matters worse, the National Assembly, without the participation of the opposition lawmakers, passed the bill authorizing the government to dispatch South Korean troops to South Vietnam under the U.S.-South Korean agreement signed on October 1964. Violent demonstrations against these government actions broke out, forcing the government to declare martial law in the Seoul area again in August 1965.

In order to promote a parliamentary democracy, if not to weaken the power monopoly of the ruling DRP, the opposition leaders formed a new party named the New Korea Party (NKP) in May 1966. However, formation of the Democratic Socialist Party, and another party in the fall of 1966 by two prominent dissident groups allowed the ruling party to maintain its control. In February 1967, the NKP and the Masses Party (MP) were united into the New Democratic Party (NDP), and Yun Po-sŏn was nominated as its presidential candidate. But in the May 1967 presidential election, the incumbent president defeated Yun again, this time by a large margin, and the ruling party won a substantial majority of seats in the National Assembly elections of July.

While the announcement in July regarding the arrest of a pro-North Korean espionage team consisting of over 100 members, whose main operational base was located in East Berlin, shocked and dismayed the people, the attempt made by a North Korean commando team in January 1968 to assassinate President Park, the abduction of a U.S. intelligence ship, *Pueblo,* by the North Korean naval vessels soon after that, and the arrest of an underground espionage group of the phantom "Unification Revolutionary Party" in August increased tension and a sense of insecurity in South Korea, providing the government with ample excuses to tighten its control over the country. In April 1968, the 2.5 million-man Homeland Reserve Forces were formed and the government proceeded to give military training to college students in September. Despite strong opposition, the ruling party amended the Constitution in mid-September 1969 allowing the incumbent president to run for the third term of office while the members of the opposition party were boycotting the National Assembly sessions, and a national referendum held in October approved the amended constitution.

A calmer political atmosphere prevailed in 1970. In September, seven months after former president Yun Po-sŏn departed from the NDP, Kim Dae-jung was nominated as its presidential candidate. In December, the National Assembly revised the foreign trade law, allowing trade with "non-hostile Socialist countries."

In the presidential election held in April 1971, President Park defeated the nominee of the NDP, by a narrow margin. However, in the National Assembly elections held in May, the ruling DRP won a larger majority. Shortly after President Park took the oath of office on July 1 for the third term, the government adopted the New Community Movement Plan.

Antigovernment student demonstrations continued to be rampant, and observing carefully the development of the talks between the Red Cross societies of North and South Korea (the talks began in September 1971), the government declared a state of national emergency on December 6, 1971, ostensibly to help the nation better meet the rapidly changing domestic and international situations. Meanwhile, the withdrawal of South Korean troops from South Vietnam began in early December. On December 26, the National Assembly adopted the Special Measures Law on National Defence, giving an extraordinary power to the president.

The secret negotiations conducted between Seoul and Pyongyang some time in early 1972 resulted in the issuance of an identical statement by the two Korean governments on July 4, 1972, regarding their agreement on the Korean reunification formula. The momentous statement issued simultaneously by Seoul and Pyongyang on that day announced the opening of a dialogue between the two governments to achieve national unification by peaceful means without outside intervention.

The two successive Five-Year Economic Development Plans (1962–71) had laid a good foundation for economic development, and the future of the nation seemed brighter both politically and economically. However, the sudden changes in the international situation, due to the Sino-U.S. détente, the new development in North-South relations, and certain changes in U.S. Asian policy provided the ruling party with a convenient pretext to perpetuate President Park's rule. As a result, the government proclaimed a national emergency decree on October 17, 1972, dissolved the National Assembly, and suspended the constitution, bringing the October *Yushin.* New (seventh) constitutional revisions proposed by the government on October 17 were approved in a national referendum held on November 21.

Martial law was lifted in mid-December, the new electoral college known as the National Conference for Unification (NCU), whose 2,350 members were elected by popular vote on December 15, was established, and the NCU elected President Park as the eighth president of the Republic.

(E) The Fourth Republic, December 1972–October 1979. With the inauguration of President Park on December 27, 1972 the Fourth Republic emerged, and the new constitution, known as the *Yushin* ("Revitalizing Reform") Constitution was officially proclaimed on December 30, followed by the promulgation of the new National Assembly Election Law and the Political Party Law.

The elections for the National Assembly held in February 1973 under the new election law gave the ruling DRP a majority. Meanwhile, a new political society named Political Fraternal Society for Revitalizing Reform (Yushin Chŏng'uhoe, or Yujŏnghoe) was set up as a companion political body of the ruling party, and 73 of its members were elected by the NCU, on the president's recommendation, to serve a three-year term in the National Assembly under the new constitution.

The Fourth Republic encountered an increasing number of domestic and foreign problems. Unrest increased among dissident groups following the kidnapping of Kim Dae-jung in August 1973 from Tokyo to Seoul by agents of the Korean CIA. Antigovernment agitation and demands for the abolition of the 1972 *Yushin* Constitution grew, increasing political instability in 1974 and after. Meanwhile, the government faced rising diplomatic problems with Japan and the United States in connection with the kidnapping of Kim Dae-jung and increasingly repressive measures against civil liberties.

To cope with the situation, under the Presidential Emergency Decrees Nos. 1-4 of January–April 1974, the government banned all antigovernment activities and agitation for constitutional reform, making the political situation only more unstable. In this tense situation, President Park's wife (Yuk Yŏng-su) was killed on August 15 by pistol shots fired by a pro-North Korean from Japan whose aim was to assassinate President Park as he was addressing the audience at the National Theater commemorating the liberation of Korea and the establishment of the Republic.

In late August, the Emergency Decrees Nos. 1-4 were lifted, but the NDP and other groups relentlessly pressed for constitutional reform and the release of political prisoners. While college students of some 18 universities were engaged in violent antigovernment and anti-Japanese demonstrations in September and October, reporters of the *Tong-A Daily* and a group of 101 writers each issued their "Declaration for the Realization of Freedom of Speech and the Press," and in late November some 71 dissident leaders, including former President Yun, formed the National Conference for Restoration of Democracy.

Despite the national referendum held in February 1975, which reaffirmed the *Yushin* Constitution by some 73% of the voters, and the release of those who had violated the presidential decrees soon after that, antigovernment demonstrations and the movement for the revision of the constitution continued.

Facing such a situation, the Presidential Emergency Measures No. 7 of April and No. 9 of May, 1975 imposed further restrictions on the opponents of the 1972 constitution, banned student demonstrations, and outlawed public defamation of the government. However, political turbulence persisted as many dissidents were imprisoned. In March 1976, the three major dissident political leaders issued a joint statement entitled the "Democratic National Salvation Declaration," bringing what is known as the "Case of Myŏngdong Cathedral" of March 1. It demanded the abolition of the 1972 constitution and the restoration of complete human and civil rights. This was followed by a series of student demonstrations.

An embarrassment to the Korean government was the disclosure by *The Washington Post* in October 1976 of illegal lobbying activity of a Korean businessman named Pak Tong-sŏn in Washington, D.C., followed by the investigation of Pak and other Koreans, including a former ambassador to the United States, by the House of Representatives of U.S. Congress in the spring of 1977. Meanwhile, the reelection of President Park by the new members of the NCU in December 1978 only made the situation worse as the student unrest, supported by the opposition party, caused greater political turmoil.

After the National Assembly elections held on December 12, 1978, President Park took the oath of office as the ninth president on December 27, and released some 1,000 political prisoners, including Kim Dae-jung. However, the voice of the dissidents grew louder in March and May 1979 as Kim Young-sam, who became president of the opposition NDP in May, initiated a new movement for constitutional revision. His antigovernment speeches and press interviews led the government to suspend his party presidency and his expulsion from the National Assembly.

The student protests led to a series of uprisings in the Pusan and Masan areas in mid-October, bringing about the issuance of a garrison decree in that region. The situation became more critical toward the end of October as college students in Seoul prepared for a large-scale uprising, similar to that of April 1960. On October 26, in the midst of the crisis, came the shocking news that Kim Chae-gyu, director of the Korean CIA, shot and killed President Park. As the country faced an unprecedented national crisis, Prime Minister Ch'oe Kyu-ha was named acting president as martial law was proclaimed. Kim and his accomplices were executed in late May 1980.

(F) The Interim Period, October 1979–March 1981. The NCU elected Ch'oe Kyu-ha as the new president on December 6, but Lt. Gen. Chun Doo-hwan, commander of the Defense Security Command, who carried out a coup on December 12, arresting the Martial Law Commander Gen. Chŏng Sŭng-hwa, overshadowed both the president and the government.

The government restored the civil rights of former President Yun, Kim Dae-jung and others in February 1980, and formed the Constitution Revision Deliberation Committee in March, but both the opposition NDP and students became impatient with the slow progress in political reform. Conditions deteriorated further when Gen. Chun was appointed as acting director of the Korean CIA in April without leaving his army post. Many campus rallies followed, demanding the immediate end of martial law, the adoption of a new constitution without delay, and the resignation of Gen. Chun as acting director of the Korean CIA. Tens of thousands of students marched into the streets in Seoul and elsewhere in mid-May, clashing with riot police. Troops were mobilized, and on May 17 the government proclaimed nationwide martial law, followed by the issuance of the Martial Law Decree No. 10. With this, some 30 political leaders, including Kim Jong-pil, head of the DRP, Kim Young-sam, head of the NDP, and Kim Dae-jung were put under house arrest, and the National Assembly was closed as were colleges. All political activities, assemblage and public demonstrations were banned. In spite of these restrictions, the rebellious students and dissidents in the city of Kwangju and its vicinity rose up, bringing the bloody Kwangju Uprising of May 18–27, 1980.

On May 20 all cabinet members tendered their resignation, and a new cabinet emerged in an extremely unstable situation. The newly arrived troops stormed the city of Kwangju and recaptured it from the rebels after bloody fighting as other nearby towns were occupied by troops. A Special Committee for National Security Measures (SCNSM) was formed on May 31 to cope with the crisis with President Ch'oe as its chairman and Gen. Chun as chairman of its Standing Committee. Gen. Chun resigned as acting director of the Korean CIA in June, but he and 15 other generals in the SCNSM exercised absolute power, instituting many changes, including a drastic educational reform in July.

President Ch'oe suddenly stepped down on August 16, succeeded by Gen. Chun. When Gen. Chun was elected by the NCU as the president and took the oath of office on September 1, he said that he would do his best to make the forthcoming government an "honest and efficient one, which can win the confidence of the nation," and he pledged that he would eradicate past ills and restore public faith in honest rule.

However, President Chun soon displayed his dictatorial tendencies: in late September the police rounded up 13 NDP members on suspicion of playing a key role in the political melee in the 1976 NDP national convention, and Kim Dae-jung, who was charged with instigating the Kwangju Uprising, was given the death sentence in September by the military court. On October 22, the new (eighth) constitutional revisions proposed by the SCNSM were approved in a national referendum, replacing the *Yushin* Constitution and paving the way for the Fifth Republic. Meanwhile, the National Assembly was dissolved, replaced by the 81-member Legislative Council for National Security (LCNS), whose members were appointed by President Chun himself. In late October, all political parties were dissolved, and on November 12, the government announced that a total of 835 persons were to be banned from political life for the next eight years. Meanwhile, the government brought about the dismissal of 937 journalists (editors and reporters) and forced consolidation of radio-TV broadcasting systems and newspaper presses, causing what is known as "the massacre of the mass media" of October-November 1980. In essence, a new military revolution took place under the dictatorial leadership of Gen. Chun. In December, the Korean CIA was renamed the Agency for National Security Planning (ANSP) without losing any of its former power.

With the partial lifting of the Martial Law Decree No. 10 on November 15, 1980 political activity was renewed, and in January 1981 the Democratic Justice Party (DJP) of President Chun, the Democratic Korean Party (DKP) of Yu Ch'i-song, and the Korean National Party (KNP) of Kim Chong-ch'ŏl emerged. On February 25, 1981, the 5,278-member Presidential Electoral College, which was popularly elected on November 11 and replaced the NCU, elected the incumbent president as the first president of the Fifth Republic for a nonrenewable seven-year term of office under the new constitution.

(G) The Fifth Republic, March 1981–February 1988. With the taking of the oath of office for a single seven-year term by President Chun on March 3, the Fifth Republic emerged, followed by the general elections for a new National Assembly in late March. The 11th National Assembly was inaugurated on April 11, replacing the short-lived LCNS, with the DJP as the majority party.

Although the Fifth Republic of President Chun sustained the momentum of economic modernization and development that began in the 1970s, his government displayed little indication of promoting democracy as it failed to win the confidence of the people. Not only that, it misused power only to strengthen government control and benefit the ruling party and those individuals and business firms which supported it. As a matter of fact, the Chun administration was regarded by the people as "the hotbed of illegality and irrationality," and the dubious financial dealings of President Chun's wife, his brother and other relatives were rampant. Consequently, the democratic aspirations of the people suffered, and frequent student riots and labor unrest, accompanied by violence, erupted as the demand for democratic reform increased.

President Chun made state visits to five nations of the Association of Southeast Asian Nations (ASEAN) in June 1981, to Japan in September 1984, to the United States in February 1981 and April 1985, and to five European nations in April 1986, improving South Korea's diplomatic and commercial ties with them. However, his plan to visit six Southeast Asian nations in October 1983 was cut short by the bomb incident in Rangoon, Burma on October 9, aimed at the assassination of President Chun by North Korean agents, in which many of his top advisers and cabinet ministers were killed.

To be sure, President Chun granted amnesty to some 1,061 political prisoners who had been imprisoned in connection with the Kwangju Uprising in June 1981, reduced the death sentence given to Kim Dae-jung to life imprisonment and allowed him to travel to the United States for "medical treatment" in December 1982, and gradually removed (in February 1983 and February and November 1984) some 835 former political leaders from the political blacklist, restoring their political and civil rights. However, he and his government utterly failed to promote democracy, as President Chun refused to revise the constitution before 1989.

Following the founding of an underground radical student organization named the Committee for Promotion of Democracy (Minch'uwi) in October 1984, a group of radical students occupied the headquarters of the ruling DJP, demanding further democratic reform. But President Chun made no concession, except the removal of 84 names out of 103 persons who were still on the political blacklist as of November 1984. The final group of 19 former political leaders (Kim Jong-pil, Kim Dae-jung and Kim Young-sam and others) did not regain their political and civil rights until March 1985.

Those who regained their political and civil rights in November brought about the establishment of a new political party named the New Korea Democratic party (NKDP) in January 1985, and agitated for an immediate revision of the constitution. At this juncture, Kim Dae-jung returned to Seoul from the United States in early February, ending his self-imposed exile since December 1982.

In the general elections for the National Assembly, held in mid-February, the opposition NKDP won the majority of urban votes, but the ruling DJP managed to maintain its overall majority. Shortly after that, President Chun named Roh Tae-woo as new chairman of the DJP in order to strengthen the party. Meanwhile, the opposition party leaders formed the Council for the Promotion of Democracy (CPD), calling for the merger of all opposition parties, naming Kim Dae-jung and Kim Young-sam co-chairmen of the CPD, and increasing its pressure on the government for constitutional revision. In mid-April, the radical students who formed the Committee for the Three People's Struggle (Sammint'u) with the representatives of 23 universities brought about much student unrest. Students belonging to this and other radical groups occupied the U.S. Information Center in Seoul in late May, as well as the training institute of the ruling DJP.

When, in March, Kim Young-sam officially joined the NKDP, becoming adviser to party president, the NKDP launched a more determined movement for the revision of the constitution to institute the direct election of the president and to restore the prime ministership responsible to the National Assembly.

In the turbulent political climate of the spring of 1986, the police placed 270 opposition politicians under house arrest as it blocked a mass rally planned by the NKDP. Nonetheless, large mass rallies were held in Seoul, Inch'ŏn, Kwangju, Taegu and Pusan in support of the constitutional revision drive. It was the first time since 1981 that such large outdoor mass political rallies had been held in South Korea and openly criticized the current regime and its policy. While demonstrators even demanded the immediate resignation of President Chun, several groups of university professors issued joint statements calling for the immediate revision of the constitution, and a group of some 325 women leaders issued a statement calling for the promotion of social democracy and women's rights under a new constitution.

Political peace was restored temporarily when, following the meeting between the president and the opposition leaders, the president agreed to form a Constitution Study Committee to prepare for the constitutional revision. However, President Chun refused to revise the constitution before 1989 in order to enable his successor to be chosen by the Electoral College under the current constitution. Thereupon, the opposition groups such as the NKDP, the CPD, and Catholic and Protestant societies increased their demand for the constitutional revision in 1986 so that the presidential election would be held in 1987 under a revised constitution.

The rise of radical groups and increasing demonstrations caused considerable problems for the government. In late October 1986, a group of young revolutionaries whose aim was to form a Marxist-Leninist party was arrested. It was followed in early November by a mass demonstration at Kŏnguk University in Seoul of some 1,270 radical students from various universities. Meanwhile, the police cracked down on the dissidents who organized the Joint Masses Movement for Democracy and Unification (Mint'ongyŏn) in mid-November, and the police also arrested the leaders of a pro-North Korean Anti-Imperialist League.

The political situation rapidly deteriorated as antagonism between the DJP and the opposition NKDP grew following the adoption by the ruling DJP in October 1986 of a resolution to permit the police arrest of opposition Assemblymen. The passage of the 1987 national budget bill by the ruling DJP lawmakers in early December without participation of the opposition lawmakers only worsened the situation. The death by police torture of a university student in December further radicalized antigovernment students, forcing the president to replace the home minister and the director of the National Police in January 1987.

President Chun's April 13, 1987 ban on any further talks for constitutional reform until after the 1988 Seoul Olympics precipitated violent reaction against the government and its party. Hundreds of Protestant ministers and Catholic priests and nuns carried out hunger strikes, demanding Chun's resignation, as professors of many universities and many lawyers issued political statements, criticizing the policy of the president and his party. Meanwhile, hundreds of thousands of students and others staged antigovernment demonstrations throughout the spring and in early summer, clashing with the "combat" police. The city of Seoul became a battleground as the odor of teargas filled the air over the city and traffic stoppage occurred day after day.

In this turbulent political situation, some 71 lawmakers who defected from the NKDP formed a new Reunification Democratic Party (RDP) on May 1, with Kim Young-sam as its president and Kim Dae-jung as his mentor, declaring their determination to carry out their struggle for democratization.

The nomination on June 10 of Roh Tae-woo, chairman of the ruling DJP who was hand picked by President Chun to be his successor, as presidential candidate of the DJP, precipitated more violent reaction as the opposition RDP demanded (1) an immediate revision of the constitution, (2) restoration of full freedom of the press, (3) release of all political prisoners, and (4) restoration of full civil rights for Kim Dae-jung. In the wake of this, some 500 persons, including vice-president of the RDP, were arrested on June 10, as violent clashes between the "combat" police and protesters continued day after day. A total breakdown of law seemed imminent.

On June 24, President Chun met with Kim Young-sam to seek solutions, but the two leaders failed to reach an accord as President Chun made no major concessions. Thereupon the opposition RDP mobilized the masses and carried out a "Grand Peace March" on June 26, on which day hundreds of thousands of people took to the streets, clashing with the riot police. Kim and others were seized by the police, and Kim Dae-jung, who was freed the previous day from 78 days of detention in his home, was again placed under house arrest. An extremely serious national crisis similar to that of April 1960 developed.

Realizing that inevitability, Roh Tae-woo, backed by his loyal supporters of the party, presented his "Democratization Declaration" on June 29 to the people, and demanded that President Chun accept his proposals, indicating that he would resign his chairmanship of the party and candidacy for presidency if his demands were not met. The nation was stunned by his unexpected public announcement, but welcomed it with cautious optimism. Roh met with President Chun and convinced the latter that the only peaceful way to defuse the crisis was to implement his reform policy. Persuaded by Roh, President Chun announced to the nation on July 1 that he had accepted Roh's proposals, thus paving the way for a peaceful settlement of the most troublesome political issues that the nation had faced for some time.

In a conciliatory mood, the government granted amnesty on July 10 to some 2,335 political prisoners, including Kim Dae-jung, and their civil rights were restored. President Chun relinquished the presidency of the DJP to Roh in early August as the two major political parties agreed on the basic outline of a new constitution.

As the winds of democracy rose, labor unrest increased while radical students continued their antigovernment demonstrations. More than 500 industrial disputes erupted mainly in the motor, mining and shipbuilding industries as striking workers demanded higher wages, better treatment, and better working conditions. Most of these were settled quickly, but violent clashes between striking workers and riot police took place at the Hyundai Motors in Ulsan. By mid-October, however, nearly all labor strikes ended with the government's concession on the swift revision of labor laws, guaranteeing workers's right to form a union to bargain collectively, and raising minimum wages.

On the political front, negotiations carried out between Kim Young-sam and Kim Dae-jung failed to result in selection of a single presidential candidate of the RDP. Kim Young-sam declared his candidacy for president in mid-October, and on November 12 Kim Dae-jung, taking 27 of the RDP's lawmakers with him, formed his own party named Party for Peace and Democracy (PPD), and became its head as well as its presidential candidate. With this, the two major opposition parties—the NKP and the NKDP—were virtually dissolved. Meanwhile, Kim Jong-pil revived the DRP which had been defunct since early 1980, and renamed it the New Democratic Republican Party (NDRP), and became its head as well as its presidential candidate. For the first time in the history of South Korea, a woman, Hong Sook-ja of the Socialist Democratic Party, ran for the presidency, although she later withdrew her candidacy.

The democratization process moved ahead when on October 12 the National Assembly passed the ninth constitutional amendment providing for direct presidential election, and the new constitution was put to a national referendum on October 27, to take effect on February 25, 1988. Some 20 million of the country's 25.6 million eligible voters cast their ballots, approving the constitution by 93.3% "yes" votes. Thus the stage was set for the establishment of the Sixth Republic.

The first direct, popular presidential election in 16 years was conducted on December 16, 1987. Some 23 million, or 89.2% of the eligible voters, cast their ballots, electing Roh Tae-woo of the DJP as president for a nonrenewable five-year-term of office with 36.6% votes. Kim Dae-jung received 28.1% of the votes and Kim Young-sam received 27.1% of the votes. It was clear that the failure to present a single candidate by the two major opposition parties which received 55.5% of the votes "gave" the presidency to Mr. Roh. Kim Jong-pil of the NDRP received 8.1% of the votes, while the fifth candidate received only 0.2% of the votes.

(H) The Sixth Republic, February 1988–. On February 25, 1988 President Roh took the oath of office for a single five-year term, and was inaugurated, bringing a peaceful transfer of power after the expiration of the term of office of former President Chun.

With this, the Sixth Republic emerged. In his inaugural address, President Roh proclaimed that the era of "ordinary people" had arrived, and the "day when freedom and human rights could be relegated in the name of economic growth and national security has ended."

Looking toward the National Assembly elections under the new National Assembly Election Law of March 8, 1988, which restored the single-member constituency for the first time in 17 years and increased the number of seats in the legislature from 276 to 299, Kim Young-sam resigned the presidency of the DRP, hoping to bring about the merger of the two major opposition parties. However, Kim Dae-jung refused to do likewise until criticism against him grew to such an extent that in mid-March he was forced to step down from the presidency of his party. However, the two opposition parties failed to merge, and both Kims returned to the presidency of their respective parties.

In the general elections for the National Assembly held on April 26, for the first time, the ruling DJP failed to win the majority as only 87 of its candidates were elected. The PPD of Kim Dae-jung won 54 district seats, thus becoming the first opposition party. The RDP of Kim Young-sam won 46 district seats and the NDRP of Kim Jong-pil won 27 district seats. A minor party won one, and nine seats were taken by the Independents. The 75 at-large (national) seats were distributed to each party according to the percentage of votes each received. Thus, the DJP received 38, the PPD 17, and RDP 13, and the NDRP 8 seats.

Political Development The nature of politics remained undemocratic, the uncooperative relationship between the ruling and opposition parties continued, the behavior of politicians and government officials remained dishonest and bureaucratic, and the unrest of students, farmers, and workers did not subside. Despite these unfavorable factors, the government of the Sixth Republic took several significant steps to promote democracy and restore harmony between the government and the people. First of all, in April 1988, the government redefined the May 1980 civil disturbances in Kwangju as "part of the efforts by students and citizens . . . for democratization of the nation," and offered an apology to the people in Kwangju, making a promise to take compensatory measures for the victims. Secondly, in July it removed a long-standing ban on the published works of some 120 writers who had defected to North Korea after 1945, and in October it lifted another longstanding ban on the pre-Korean War songs and art works of some 100 musicians and artists who had either defected, or were abducted to North Korea, provided their material included no North Korean propaganda. Meanwhile, the government liberalized the press law, permitting the establishment of new newspaper presses and radio-television broadcasting corporations. It also allowed the sale of some books published in North Korea and elsewhere on Communism, as well as studies on Marxism at colleges.

In May 1988, the Roh administration established the Administrative Reform Commission to study "future-oriented government systems" to help the country move forward with democratic development, including a plan to implement local autonomy in 1991 (to be discussed ahead.). Meanwhile, President Roh made efforts to promote cooperative relationships between the ruling DJP and the opposition parties in solving domestic and foreign problems, especially those issues related to the Fifth Republic, as it made other efforts to quiet down students and workers.

These and other measures taken by the government brought about a temporary truce among conflicting groups for the primary purpose of hosting the 24th Summer Olympics in Seoul as scheduled. As a result, Seoul was able to witness the opening on September 17 and closing on October 2 of the largest and the most peaceful Olympics in history. Following this, the Roh administration was able to persuade former President Chun to make a nationwide television appearance, making apologies for wrongdoings of his administration and its officials. After making the TV appearance on November 23, Chun and his wife left Seoul for a self-imposed internal exile at a Buddhist temple in a remote mountainous region where they stayed until December 1990. Three days later, on November 26, President Roh appealed for leniency for his predecessor, and in a five-point formula which he presented to the nation he promised to launch a broad reform plan to ensure democratic rule and to end abuse of power by the government. His plan also included reorganization of the government and the ruling party to realize "a spirit of a new era," institutionalization of the impartial method for raising and allocating political funds, and promotion of "liberal democracy."

In order to calm several months of political storm that engulfed his administration over the matters related to the Fifth Republic, as well as to improve public confidence in his administration's commitment to democratization, on December 5, President Roh carried out a major cabinet reshuffle, appointing Dr. Kang Young-hoon as prime minister and replacing 20 of the 25 cabinet ministers and the mayor of Seoul. This was followed by the granting on December 21 of amnesty for more than 2,000 "politically motivated offenders" and release of 281 political prisoners, including those students who were serving 20-year sentences for fire-bombing the U.S. Cultural Center in Pusan in 1982.

While the issues related to former President Chun and the Fifth Republic, as well as the alleged involvement of President Roh as former commander of a military unit in the Kwangju "massacre" incident continued to trouble the Roh administration, the announcement made by President Roh on March 20, 1989, regarding the postponement (cancellation?) of a national referendum on his administration, which he had promised in 1987 during his presidential campaign, brought about more antigovernment demonstrations of students, workers, and farmers.

The two most significant political developments in South Korea in the early 1990s were the emergence of the "super" ruling Democratic Liberal Party (DLP) and the restoration of partial local autonomy. The first was achieved when the interests of the ruling DJP, which had no majority in the National Assembly, and two opposition parties, the RDP and the NDRP, both of which badly needed to strengthen their positions, converged in January 1990. Following secret negotiations carried out among the presidents of these three parties during the month of January, in February 1990 the DJP, the RDP, and the NDRP merged, forming the Democratic Liberal Party as the "super" ruling party with 216 seats in the 299-seat National Assembly, making the lone opposition PPD with 70 seats in the National Assembly altogether powerless. Meanwhile, those former members of the RDP who refused to join the newly established DLP formed their own parties, such as the New Democratic United Party and the Democratic Party. Eventually these two parties merged with PPD, forming the new viable opposition New Democratic Party in 1991.

Shortly after the launching of the new ruling DLP, and facing a variety of economic problems in mid-March, President Roh carried out a major cabinet reshuffle, replacing all but one minister concerned with the economy, including the Deputy Premier and the Economic Planning Minister. Premier Kang was retained at that time. However, in December 1990, Dr. Ro Jae-bong replaced Kang when President Roh carried out another major cabinet reshuffle. Be that as it may, the disclosure of involvement of the government and party officials in financial scandals, including the one that was related to an illicit allotment of a large tract of land in Seoul's Susŏ district to a developer, the death of a college student beaten by riot police, and other political and labor problems led President Roh to carry out the third major cabinet reshuffle in February 1991 when he replaced Premier Ro with Chŏng Wŏn-skik, former college professor who had served as Minister of Education from 1988.

The most constructive political development during the period of the Sixth Republic was the partial restoration of local autonomy. It was achieved in 1991 in two stages under a new local autonomy law adopted by the National Assembly in December 1990. In the first stage, on March 25, 1991, members of small district councils were elected. The small districts included small cities, counties, and wards of large municipalities. In these elections, only 55.9% of the 24 million eligible voters cast their ballots, displaying the disinterest of local electorates. All small district councils were opened on April 15.

In the second stage for the restoration of local autonomy, on June 20 members of the large district councils were elected. The large districts were Seoul and five other special municipalities and nine provinces. In the large district council elections, only 58.9% of the 28 million eligible voters cast their ballots. The elections for provincial governors and mayors of the special municipalities were to be held during the first half of 1992, but they were postponed until 1995.

Looking toward the National Assembly elections to be held in 1992, and in order to cope more effectively with the superior position of the ruling DLP, in September 1991 the Democratic Party of Yi Ki-t'aek and the New Democratic Party of Kim Dae-jung and Yi Wu-jŏng merged to form the Democratic Party, strengthening the position of the opposition party in the National Assembly. Shortly before the elections for the National Assembly (14th) were held in March 1992, in January Chŏng Chu-yŏng, founder and honorary chairman of the Hyundai Group who had no political experience, organized the Unification National Party (UNP) while Dr. Kim Tong-gil, professor of history at Yonsei University, organized his Asia-Pacific-Era Committee into the New Korea Party (Saehandang) in mid-January. At this juncture, Pak Ch'an-jong formed the Party for New Political Reform. Be that as it may, on February 7, the Unification National Party and the New Korea Party were united into the Unification National Party (UNP), otherwise called the United Peoples' Party (UPP), with Chŏng as its president and Kim as its executive chairman.

In the general elections for the National Assembly held on March 24, 1992, the ruling DLP, the DP, and the UNP and three other splinter parties competed for seats. Despite its size, the ruling DLP won only 38.5% of the votes, winning 116 district seats, while the major opposition DP won 29.2% of the votes (75 Assembly seats), and the newly formed UNP won 17.3% of the votes (24 Assembly seats). The Independents won some 11.5% of the votes (21 Assembly seats). Even with 33 at-large Assembly seats allocated to the ruling DLP, it failed to have a majority in the National Assembly. Only when seven Independents joined the DLP, and one Assemblyman-elect from the UNP and another from the DP defected to the DLP did the ruling DLP gain a majority (159 seats) in the National Assembly. Meanwhile, the remaining Independents formed their own Fraternal Society of the Independents while three major parties were in a quandary. In the 1992 general elections for the National Assembly, only 71.9% (20.8 million) of the 29 million eligible voters cast their ballots, displaying the declining interest of the voters in politics. It was the lowest turnout of voters in the history of National Assembly elections.

As the term of office of President Roh was due to expire in February 1993, in the middle of May 1992 the major parties selected their presidential candidates. Thus the ruling DLP nominated Kim Young-sam, the DP nominated Kim Dae-jung, the UNP nominated Chŏng Chu-yŏng, and the PPR nominated Pak Ch'an-jong as presidential candidates of their respective parties. The DP selected its presidential candidate in a democratic manner when it selected one from two candidates, while the PNPR and the UNP nominated their presidential candidates without any contenders. The way in which the ruling DLP selected its presidential candidate aroused not only a bitter intraparty conflict, but also criticism by the voters. One of the two candidates of the ruling DLP who sought his party's nomination not only launched his bitter attack on the president and executive chairman of the party, but also failed to show up at the party convention after refusing to compete with another candidate without officially withdrawing his own candidacy.

In the spring of 1992, the South Korean people looked forward to a new politics for the promotion of democracy after restoring partial local autonomy, electing the new National Assembly, and witnessing the nomination of presidential candidates by major parties.

Economic Development. Despite various problems caused by labor disputes and appreciation of the won currency, South Korea achieved 12.2% GNP growth in 1988, raising the GNP to $169.2 billion from $128.4 billion in 1987. Per capita GNP jumped from $3,098 in 1987 to $4,040 in 1988 when the inflation rate of consumer goods was 7.5%. More than 500,000 new jobs were created in 1988 as the percentage of unemployment remained at 2.5%. South Korea's exports grew by 28.3% to $60.7 billion ($47.3 billion in 1987), while its imports rose by 26.3% to $51.8 billion ($41 billion in 1987), making South Korea one of the world's ten largest trading nations. With the increase in exports, in 1988 South Korea reduced its foreign debts from $35.6 billion in 1987 to $31.2 billion at the end of 1988.

South Korea's economic growth slowed down after 1988 due to many factors. Among them was rising labor wages. It was reported that the average annual rate of wage increase between 1988 and 1991 was 20%, following the adoption of a minimum wage system and several labor strikes at such places as Hyundai Motors, Daewoo Heavy Industries (shipbuilding), and Lucky-Goldstar Electronics in 1988 and 1989. The increasing wages of urban workers brought about the shift in income of the urban and farm households. For instance, in 1988 the annual average income of urban workers' households was $11,938.48 while that of farm households was $12,507.79, but in 1990 the annual average income of urban workers' households grew to $16,170.00 and in 1991 it increased to $18,537.37 while the annual average income of farm households grew to $15,751.37 in 1990 and $17,473.32 in 1991. The exchange rate between U.S. dollar and Korean won was 1 to 680 in 1988, 1 to 700 in 1990, and 1 to 750 in 1991. The inflation rate of consumer goods in 1989 was 5.2%, but it jumped to 9.4% in 1990 and 9.5% in 1991.

Due to rising wages and overimportation of foreign goods, plus other factors, South Korea's GNP growth was slowed down as its balance of trade shifted from plus to minus. For example, in 1989 South Korea's GNP growth rate was 6.5% raising the GNP to $204 billion with the per capita GNP of $4,830. The downward trends in economic development continued in 1990 and 1991 as South Korea's overseas markets shrank due to growing competition from other "Mini Dragons," as well as China. Despite this, South Korea's GNP growth rate in 1991 rose to 8.7% with the total GNP of $272.2 billion and per capita GNP of $6,498. South Korea's exports grew by 10.5% in 1991 reaching the $71.8 billion mark, but its imports jumped by 16.8% to $81.5 billion, producing a trade deficit of $9.7 billion which was twice as large as that of the 1990 trade deficit of $4.8 billion. Of this, $759 million was with the United States and $8.8 billion with Japan.

South Korea's two-way trade with China, the Soviet Union and former socialist countries grew substantially from $3.7 billion in 1988 to $8.1 billion in 1991 with an annual rise of 40%. Exports jumped from $2 billion to $3.7 billion. However, the annual growth rate of imports from them was 49.8%, exceeding the annual growth rate of exports that was 30%. As a result, the trade balance shifted from $329 million in favor of South Korea in 1988 to a deficit of $299 million in 1989, $159 million in 1990, and the $591 million in 1991. While trade balance vis-à-vis the Soviet Union and Eastern European and other socialist countries was in favor of South Korea by $499 million in 1991, South Korea's trade balance with China created a deficit of $2.43 billion in 1991 ($1 billion in exports and $3.4 billion in imports), due primarily to a large amount of agricultural products and medicinal herbs imported from China. Meanwhile, South Korea's market-share in the United States shrank from 4.6% in 1988 to 3.5% in 1991 due to the growing market-share of Chinese goods from 1.9% to 4.8% during the corresponding period.

The growth of the GNP was sustained due primarily to the population increase from 41.9 million in 1988 to 43.9 million in 1991, increasing domestic demands for goods and services, especially housing and transportation. However, in view of the declining rate of the GNP growth, coupled with the growing trade deficit, the

South Korean government reduced the share of military spending in the national budget from 33% in 1987 to 30% (4.37% of the GNP) in 1988. It was further reduced to 27.6% (3.77% of the GNP) in 1991, and 25.3% (3.71% of the GNP) in 1992. The government announced in May 1992 that the military spending would be further reduced to 24.4% of the national budget, or 3.69% of the projected GNP, by 1997.

Despite many economic problems, including the shortage of workers in the industrial sector, in November 1991, the South Korean government made public the finalized seventh socioeconomic development plan for 1992–1997. Its targets were to achieve an average annual GNP growth rate of 7.5% and to raise the GNP to $492.6 billion and per capita GNP to $10,908 by 1996.

Foreign Policy and Diplomacy. President Roh made various efforts to improve South Korea's ties with its allies and expand its diplomatic arena, seeking relations with those countries which had no ties with South Korea but had already established relations with North Korea. Another key foreign policy goal of his administration was South Korea's entry into the United Nations Organization as a full member. In order to achieve these objectives, President Roh himself took an active role.

President Roh made several overseas trips, making state visits as well as attending the U.N. General Assembly to improve South Korea's standing in the world. In October 1988, he traveled to the United States, delivering an address before the U.N. General Assembly on October 18, proposing the creation of a six-nation consultative conference, which would include the United States, the Soviet Union, China and Japan plus North and South Korea, to discuss a "broad range of issues concerning peace, stability, progress and prosperity" within Northeast Asia. Then on October 20, he and President Ronald Reagan held a summit meeting at the White House, agreeing to combine the efforts of the two nations "to ensure peace in the Korean Peninsula."

President Roh welcomed President George Bush to Seoul on the latter's return trip from Beijing in February 1989, and Roh and Bush had a cordial meeting, discussing various issues and trade in particular. In September, when Vice President Dan Quayle of the U.S. paid a visit to South Korea, Roh and Quayle had a talk, stressing the needs for mutual cooperation to solve problems between the two countries. In September 1991, President Roh met

President Bush in New York and agreed to make cooperative efforts to solve problems existing between the two nations, particularly those issues related to trade. After making a speech before the U.N. General Assembly on September 24 as president of a new member state of the United Nations, he made a state visit to Mexico, agreeing on economic cooperation with that nation.

South Korea and the United States arrived at various agreements during the Sixth Republic period. These included: the reduction of the size of U.S. forces in South Korea; the withdrawal of nuclear weapons of the United States from South Korea; the relocation of the U.S. military base in Seoul to Taejon and elsewhere; the increase of South Korea's share in U.S. military expenses in South Korea; the revision of the U.S.-South Korean Status of Forces Agreement; the abolition of the twelve-year-old Combined Field Army; the appointment of a Korean general as head of the Ground Component Command of the U.S.-South Korea Combined Forces Command; and South Korea's increase of imports of U.S. goods, including tobacco and other agricultural commodities.

The South Korean government also made special efforts to improve ties with Japan and induce it to revise its laws in dealing with the status of Koreans residing in Japan. The trade imbalance of South Korea vis-à-vis Japan was also a subject of intense discussion.

Japanese Premier Takeshita Noboru had already met President Roh on the day Roh was inaugurated in February 1988, and both had pledged to cooperate in many areas. However, it was President Roh's state visit to Japan in May 1990 that brought about better relations between Seoul and Tokyo. Roh delivered an address before the Japanese Diet and met with Emperor Akihito who expressed his "deepest regrets" for the Koreans who had suffered under Japanese colonial rule. In January, when Japanese Premier Kaifu Toshiki visited Seoul, Roh and Kaifu conferred on the matters related to Japan-North Korea negotiations for the normalization of relations. Efforts made by the Seoul government led to the abolition of the offensive practice of fingerprinting the Koreans residing in Japan as well as the extention of privileges to them. After many endeavors, the South Korean government persuaded the Japanese Ministry of Education to revise its secondary school history books, frankly admitting Japanese aggression and harsh rule in Korea. However, such issues as those which were related to Koreans who were forced to serve in the Japanese military as soldiers, those conscripted Korean workers who died in Japan, and those Korean women who were taken to the battlefields as "comfort women," or *teishintai,* as well as the trade imbalance with South Korea's huge deficit, still needed to be addressed further.

President Roh also made state visits to other allies and friends of South Korea in order to strengthen the ties with them. In November 1988, he made state visits to Australia, Brunei, Indonesia, and Malaysia, and in November 1989, he held cordial talks with heads of the states of France, Great Britain, Switzerland, and West Germany, as well as Hungary which had established diplomatic relations with South Korea in February.

The two most significant achievements in South Korea's foreign affairs were the establishment of diplomatic and commercial relations with former socialist countries as well as an expanding relationship with China, and the securing of a full membership in the United Nations Organization. Less than a week after taking the office, on March 1, 1988, President Roh indicated that his government would actively seek establishment of diplomatic relations with China, the Soviet Union and other socialist countries. Accordingly, on July 7, he announced the adoption of the foreign policy known as *Nordpolitik,* or "Northern Diplomacy." The new policy that President Roh adopted had been advocated by the late President Park who, in June 1973, disclosed a new foreign policy of the Fourth Republic, expressing South Korea's willingness to establish diplomatic and commercial relations with any country irrespective of differences in ideology or political systems so long as they harbored no hostile intentions against South Korea. At the same time, the late President Park called for the taking of reciprocal action by those countries which had no ties with South Korea.

The *Nordpolitik* which President Roh adopted was similar to West Germany's *Ostopolitik* launched by former Chancellor Willy Brandt to improve relations with the Soviet Union and Eastern European countries. In his July 7 declaration, President Roh also indicated that his government would promote various inter-Korean exchanges for the establishment of amicable relations between North and South Korea.

Taking advantage of the 1988 Summer Olympics scheduled to be held in Seoul, the South Korean government initiated cultural and economic diplomacy vis-à-vis socialist countries, inviting their cultural groups and trade missions. Following the exchange of trade missions with Hungary in March and Yugoslavia in June, in September the Bolshoi Ballet of the Soviet Union made its South Korean debut. Meanwhile, many Soviet and Chinese academicians participated in international conferences in Seoul in August while many Russian musicians and writers with Korean ancestry visited their ancestral land and gave musical recitals or academic talks. In August, La Scala from Italy performed in Seoul for the first time as the 52nd International PEN Congress in which many from socialist countries participated was held in Seoul.

After hosting the 1988 Summer Olympics in Seoul from September 17 through October 2, the South Korean government continued its efforts to promote its relations with socialist nations, implementing the *Nordpolitik.*

Aspiring the enhancement of national security and hoping to pressure North Korea to come to the conference table to reduce tension in the Korean Peninsula, the Roh administration made particular efforts to establish relations with the socialist countries in general, and particularly with the Soviet Union and China, the two members of the U.N. Security Council and close allies of North Korea.

The efforts made by the Roh administration brought about highly satisfactory results. After Hungary exchanged trade offices with South Korea in June, 1988, Bulgaria, Poland and Yugoslavia exchanged trade offices with South Korea in 1988, and in 1989 Czechoslovakia and the Soviet Union did likewise. Trade relations between South Korea and those countries led to the establishment of diplomatic relations with them. After South Korea and Hungary established diplomatic relations in February 1989, Poland did likewise in November followed by Yugoslavia in December, and in March 1990, South Korea expanded its diplomatic arena, exchanging ambassadors with Bulgaria, Czechoslovakia, Romania, and Mongolia. Meanwhile, in January 1990, South Korea and Algeria established normal relations, followed by the conclusion of a diplomatic treaty between South Korea and the socialist state of South Yemen in May. In June, South Korea restored its diplomatic relations with the Congo, which had been severed in 1965 when the Congo recognized North Korea and concluded a diplomatic treaty with it.

The establishment of full diplomatic relations with the Soviet Union was the high point in foreign affairs of the Sixth Republic and its *Nordpolitik.* South Korea had long been attempting to establish some kind of relations with China and the Soviet Union, the two powerful allies of North Korea which provided an enormous amount of economic and military assistance to their client state of Kim Il-sung. It was highly desirable for the Seoul government to weaken the ties between them and North Korea by whatever means possible and establish amicable relations with China and Russia in order to enhance South Korea's national security, as well as its chance to secure a full U.N. membership. The Seoul government had made various gestures on several occasions to Peking and Moscow, but they showed no interest in responding favorably to Seoul until the adoption of the policy of *glasnost* and *perestroika* by President Mikhail Gorbachev of the Soviet Union.

Taking advantage of Russia's new domestic and foreign policy, and after the Soviet Union indicated its decision to participate in the Summer Olympics in Seoul (South Korea had boycotted the 1981 Summer Olympics in Moscow), and receiving various signals from Moscow, President Roh took positive steps to achieve his foreign policy objectives in the rapidly thawing Cold War situation. In August 1988, President Roh made an overture to Moscow when he sent his aid to Moscow with a letter to President Mikhail Gorbachev, and received Gorbachev's reply through a Korean-Russian academician who visited Seoul in December. In September 1988, Gorbachev had clearly indicated the possibility of opening the way to forming economic relations with South Korea. Thus official contacts were established between Seoul and Moscow.

Nongovernmental Koreans also created new contracts with the Soviet Union. Among them were Chŏng Chu-yŏng and Kim Young-sam. In January 1989 Chŏng Chu-yŏng, founder and chairman of the Hyundai Group, visited Moscow and concluded agreements with the Soviet Union's Chamber of Commerce and Industry to set up South Korea-Soviet Union joint ventures in the timber, fishery, and shipbuilding industries. Chŏng visited the Soviet Union again in August, taking a 31-man study team with him to explore the possibilities for other joint ventures. At the same time, in June 1989, Kim Young-sam, president of the opposition Reunification Democratic Party, visited Moscow and talked with the director of the Institute of World Economics and International Relations of the Soviet Union on various matters, including the conclusion of a diplomatic treaty between South Korea and the

Soviet Union. Following this, two key members of the Soviet government visited South Korea in September, and in October the new director of the Institute of World Economics and International Relations, Vladlen A. Martynov, himself visited Seoul, bringing a 12-man delegation with him. Results of these contacts led to the establishment of consular offices of South Korea and the Soviet Union in each other's capital in December 1989, as well as the beginning of South Korean-Russian joint ventures in April 1990.

In 1990, South Korea-Soviet Union relations took a dramatic turn following the Moscow visit of Kim Young-sam, now executive chairman of the newly formed Democratic Liberal Party. In March he took a delegation composed of high-level party and government officials to Moscow, and negotiated with the Soviet leaders as President Roh's personal envoy. After this, in May, Anatoly Dobrynin, former ambassador to the United States, flew to Seoul and had a meeting with President Roh, making arrangements for a possible meeting between Roh and Gorbachev while the latter was on his state visit to the United States. Meanwhile, direct air services between Seoul and Moscow were officially opened in April.

The meeting between Roh and Gorbachev in San Francisco on June 4–5, 1990 clearly marked the crucial turning point in South Korea-Soviet Union relations. Although no official statements were issued regarding the establishment of diplomatic relations between the two nations, it became unmistakably clear that the establishment of full diplomatic and commercial relations between the two was only a matter of time. In September 1990, Soviet Foreign Minister Eduard Shevardnadze visited Pyongyang and informed the North Korean government regarding the intention of the Soviet Union to establish diplomatic relations with South Korea.

Various efforts the South Korean government made bore fruit, and on September 30, in New York, Soviet Foreign Minister Shevardnadze and South Korean Foreign Minister Ch'oe Ho-jung announced the establishment of full diplomatic relations between the two nations. Following this, in November, Gorbachev sent a Soviet delegation to Seoul with a letter of invitation to President Roh to visit the Soviet Union. In mid-December 1990, President Roh made a state visit to the Soviet Union, consolidating the ties with that nation. While in Russia, President Roh also met with Boris

Yeltsin in Leningrad, and after that he delivered a speech at Moscow University.

After President Roh's Soviet visit, in January 1991, Deputy Foreign Minister of the Soviet Union, Igor Rogachez, visited Seoul, and shortly after that Yuri Maslyukov, Deputy Prime Minister for Economic Affairs, took a 20-man mission to Seoul and obtained South Korea's agreement to provide $3 billion in aid over the next three years. A "tied" loan of $1.5 billion that included a $1 billion bank loan and $472 million in export credits had already been provided to Moscow before the collapse of the Soviet Union. In April 1991, President Gorbachev himself visited South Korea, holding a summit meeting with President Roh on the Korean island of Cheju, opening up a new chapter in South Korea's diplomatic history. After the fall of the Soviet Union, South Korea recognized and nurtured cordial relations with the Russian Republic.

China was reluctant to establish direct relations with South Korea lest it might antagonize North Korea. However, following its new economic policy the Chinese government opened its markets to South Korean companies. Thus in 1987 the Daewoo Electronics company established a joint venture in China, investing $3 million, followed by its $10 million investment in 1988 in the manufacturing of refrigerators and refrigerator equipment.

The participation of China in the 1988 Summer Olympics, despite North Korea's boycott, led to the development of new relations between Seoul and Beijing. After the Seoul Olympics, the Lucky-Goldstar Electronics company made a $5 million investment in China in 1989 to produce color television sets in a joint venture. After this, several other South Korean firms, including the Samick Music and the Samyang Food companies, made direct investments in China. By June 1989, total South Korean investment reached the $30 million mark.

The steadily developing relations between South Korea and China were interrupted by the Tiananmen Square Incident of June 1989. The momentum of growing economic ties between the two countries was dampened, but in view of the importance of China's friendly and cooperative attitudes toward South Korea, the Seoul government renewed its efforts to expand the bilateral relations in a variety of fields. Thus, in early 1990, Seoul welcomed a Chinese delegation headed by Deng Xiaoping's son, Deng Pugang. In June,

Lu Peijian, Director General for Audit Administration of China visited Seoul, increasing ties with Seoul.

Taking advantage of the Asian Games held in Beijing, September 22 to October 7, 1990, South Korea not only sent its team to the Asiad, but it also provided technical and financial assistance to China. Such a cooperative step taken by the Seoul government led to the publication of an announcement on October 20 that South Korea and China would exchange trade offices before the end of the year.

After exchanging trade offices which were authorized to handle consular business such as issuance of visas, sea transportation between Inch'ŏn and Weihai and Inch'ŏn and Tianjin were established. Direct air flight between South Korea and China was yet to be brought about, but charter flights of South Korean planes were authorized to land in China. Diplomatic relations between South Korea and China were yet to be established. However, in view of China's unwillingness to exercise its veto in the U.N. Security Council when South Korea was recommended to be admitted into the U.N., and rapidly increasing economic and cultural ties between the two countries, the conclusion of a diplomatic treaty became a matter of time.

South Korea's securing of a full membership in the United Nations was another significant accomplishment in its diplomacy. This had been South Korea's long cherished national aspiration ever since the Republic of Korea was established in 1948 under U.N. sponsorship and supervision. However, its desire had been frustrated by both China and the Soviet Union. Be that as it may, when South Korea established cultural and economic ties with China and diplomatic relations with the Soviet Union its chances of admission were enhanced.

After obtaining the Soviet Union's assurance of its positive support for a U.N. membership and after receiving the assurance from Beijing that it would not exercise its veto in the Security Council of the U.N., the South Korean government submitted its application on August 5, 1991. Three days later, the U.N. Security Council voted, China abstaining, to recommend that the General Assembly admit South Korea into the U.N. On September 17, South Korea secured its coveted U.N. membership as its 161st member nation. North Korea had also been admitted as the 160th member.

One of the latest developments in the foreign affairs of South Korea was its conclusion in April 1992 of an agreement with Vietnam to exchange liaison offices as a preliminary step for normal diplomatic relations between the two nations. The other significant achievement was the conclusion of a diplomatic treaty with Tanzania in May, bringing the number of countries which established diplomatic relations with South Korea to 165. After the collapse of the Soviet Union, South Korea recognized most of the newly formed commonwealth and independent states, as well as those of the Baltic states.

DICTIONARY

ACHESON'S STATEMENT ON KOREA. On January 12, 1950, Dean Acheson, then Secretary of State of the United States, spoke on Asian policy at the Press Club in Washington DC. Speaking "off the cuff" from notes, he said that the U.S. defense perimeter in the Pacific ran along the Aleutians to Japan, to the Ryukus, and to the Philippine Islands, which must and will be held by the United States. In his statement, the Republic of Korea and the Republic of China on Formosa were conspicuously absent from the line of the U.S. defense perimeter. *See also:* KOREAN WAR.

AGENCY FOR NATIONAL SECURITY PLANNING. *See:* CENTRAL INTELLIGENCE AGENCY (KCIA).

AGREEMENT ON RECONCILIATION, NONAGGRESSION AND EXCHANGES AND COOPERATION BETWEEN THE SOUTH AND THE NORTH. This Agreement was concluded at the fifth round of talks of the premiers of North Korea and South Korea in Seoul in December 1991. The first three premiers' talks were held in September, October, and December 1990, and the fourth in October 1991. The Agreement was dated December 13, 1991. The preamble of the Agreement said: "Whereas in keeping with the yearning of the entire people for the peaceful unification of the divided land, the South and the North reaffirm the unification principles enunciated in the July 4 (1972) South-North Joint Communique; Whereas both parties are determined to resolve political and military confrontation and achieve national reconciliation; Whereas both desire to promote multi-faceted exchanges and cooperation to advance common national interests and prosperity; Whereas both recognize that their relations constitute a special provisional relationship geared to unification; and Whereas both pledge to exert joint efforts to achieve peaceful and unification; Therefore, the parties hereto agree as follows:"

South-North Reconciliation

Article 1: The South and the North shall respect each other's political and social system. *Article 2:* Both parties shall not interfere in each other's internal affairs. *Article 3:* Both parties shall not slander and vilify each other. *Article 4:* Both parties shall not attempt in any manner to sabotage and subvert the other. *Article 5:* Both parties shall endeavor to transform the present armistice into a firm state of peace between the South and the North and shall abide by the present Military Armistice Agreement (of July 27, 1953) until such time as such a state of peace has taken hold. *Article 6:* Both parties shall cease confrontation on the international stage and shall cooperate and endeavor together to promote national interests and esteem. *Article 7:* To ensure close consultation and liaison between both parties, a South-North liaison office shall be established at Panmunjom within three months of the effective date of this Agreement. *Article 8:* A South-North Political Subcommittee shall be established within the framework of the Inter-Korean High Level Talks within one month of the effective date of this Agreement with a view to discussing concrete measures to ensure the implementation and observance of the accords on South-North reconciliation.

South-North Nonaggression

Article 9: Both parties shall not use armed force against each other and shall not make armed aggression against each other. *Article 10:* Differences of opinion and disputes arising between the two parties shall be peacefully resolved through dialogue and negotiations. *Article 11:* The South-North demarcation line for nonaggression shall be identical with the Military Demarcation Line specified in the Military Armistice Agreement of July 27, 1953, and the areas that have been under the jurisdiction of each party respectively thereunder until the present. *Article 12:* To abide by and guarantee nonaggression, the two parties shall create a South-North Joint Military Committee within three months of the effective date of this Agreement. The said Committee shall discuss and carry out steps to build military confidence and realize arms reductions, including the mutual notification and control of major movements of military units and major military exercises, the peaceful utilization of the Demilitarized Zone (DMZ), exchanges of military personnel and information, phased reductions in armaments including the elimination of weapons of mass destruction and surprise attack capabilities, and verifications thereof. *Article 13:* A telephone hotline shall be installed between the military authorities of both sides to prevent accidental armed clashes and other military emergencies and avoid their escalation. *Article 14:* A South-North Military Subcommittee shall be established within the framework of the Inter-Korean High-Level Talks within one month of the effective date of this Agreement in order to discuss concrete measures to ensure the implementation and observance of accords on nonaggression and to resolve military confrontation.

South-North Exchanges and Cooperation

Article 15: To promote an integrated and balanced development of the national economy and the welfare of the entire people, both parties shall conduct economic exchanges and cooperation, including joint development of resources, trade in goods as a kind of domestic commerce and joint investment in industrial projects. *Article 16:* Both parties shall carry out exchanges and cooperation in diverse fields, including science, technology, education, literature, the arts, health, sports, the environment and publishing and journalism, including newspapers, radio, television and publications in general. *Article 17:* Both parties shall guarantee residents of their respective areas free inter-Korean travel and contacts. *Article 18:* Both parties shall permit free correspondence, reunions and visits between family members and other relatives dispersed South and North, shall promote the reconstitution of divided families on their own and shall take measures to resolve other humanitarian issues. *Article 19:* Both sides shall reconnect railroads and roads that have been cut off and shall open South-North land, sea and air transport routes. *Article 20:* Both parties shall establish and link facilities needed for South-North postal and telecommunications services and shall guarantee the confidentiality of inter-Korean mail and telecommunications. *Article 21:* Both parties shall co-operate on the international stage in the economic, cultural and various other fields and carry out joint business undertakings abroad. *Article 22:* To implement accords on exchanges and cooperation in the economic, cultural and various other fields, both parties shall establish joint committees for specific sectors, including a South-North Economic Exchanges and Cooperation Committee, within three months of the effective date of this Agreement. *Article 23:* A South-North Exchanges and Cooperation Sub-committee shall be established within the framework of the Inter-Korean High-Level Talks within one month of the effective date of this Agreement with a view to discussing concrete measures to ensure the implementation and observance of the accords on South-North exchanges and cooperation.

Amendments and Effectuation

Article 24: This Agreement may be amended or supplemented by concurrence between both parties. *Article 25:* This Agreement shall enter into force as of the day both parties exchange instruments of ratification following the completion of their respective procedures for bringing it into effect.

Note: The document above is an official translation of the Agreement by the South Korean government. This Agreement was approved by President Roh Tae-woo of South Korea on January 17, 1992, and by President Kim Il-sung of North Korea on January 18, 1992. The approved document was exchanged at the sixth round of the high-level (premiers) talks held in Pyongyang, February 18–21, 1992, making the Agreement effective.

AGRICULTURAL COOPERATIVES. Some 3,744 agricultural cooperatives of various categories were organized throughout the country in February 1958 as mutual aid associations, while some 2,200 others were being formed. The number of these cooperatives grew to about 20,000 by 1960. In July 1961, a new Agricultural Cooperatives Law was promulgated by the Supreme Council for National Reconstruction, establishing a semigovernment agency named Association of Farmers Cooperative (Nong'ŏp Hyŏptong Chohap) in August 1961.

Under the law of 1961, newly combined agricultural cooperatives were organized, one in each district (*myŏn*), throughout the country to promote the welfare of the farmers, increase production, and advance cooperative spirit and efforts. By 1977, some 1,500 combined agricultural cooperatives were formed, each unit claiming an average of 1,300 members. *See also:* THE NEW COMMUNITY MOVEMENT.

AN CHAE-HONG (1891–1965). A progressive nationalist, An graduated from Waseda University in Tokyo in 1914, and in 1919 he was sentenced to three years of imprisonment for his activity in the March First Movement. (See the Introduction, pages 13–14.) In 1923, along with others, he founded a Korean-language newspaper, *Shidae Ilbo,* and served on its editorial board. Later, he became president and editor in chief of another Korean newspaper, *Chosŏn Ilbo,* a position he held for ten years, but was imprisoned again in 1925, 1936 and 1942 for his nationalistic remarks.

Upon Korea's liberation, he became a founding member of the Committee for the Preparation of National Reconstruction, and established his Nationalist Party. When the South Korean Interim Government was established in 1947 by the American military authorities, An became Civil Administrator.

During the Korean War, he was abducted by the Communists to North Korea where he died in 1965. *See also:* COMMITTEE FOR THE PREPARATION OF NATIONAL RECONSTRUCTION; KOREAN NATIONALIST PARTY (KUNGMINDANG); SOUTH KOREAN INTERIM GOVERNMENT.

AN HO-SANG (1902–). Educated at Jena University, Germany, An taught at Korea University and Seoul National University between 1933 and 1945, and 1945 and 1948, respectively. Dr. An served as the minister of education from 1948 to 1950. He was the author of South Korea's Education Law of 1949, which reflected his conservative philosophy. *See also:* EDUCATION LAW.

ANTI-COMMUNISM LAW. Promulgated on July 3, 1961 by the Supreme Council for National Reconstruction, the purpose of the law was to strengthen the anticommunist posture of the nation, to block the activities of Communist organizations, and to secure the safety of the nation and freedom of the people. It consisted of 11 articles, barring the affiliation and solicitation of affiliation with antistate organizations, praising, encouraging, or cooperating with antistate organizations, or escape to or secret entry from regions under control of antistate organizations, offering assistance to persons who had committed offences in violation of this law or the National Security Law. Those who violated the law or failed to report to the authorities any criminal offenders under it would be punished. In December 1980, the Anti-Communism Law was consolidated with the National Security Law. *See also:* NATIONAL SECURITY LAWS; EAST BERLIN, CASE OF.

APRIL STUDENT UPRISING. This refers to antigovernment demonstrations of the people, led by students, which forced President Rhee and his cabinet to resign in April 1960, ending the problem-ridden First Republic. It is also known as the April Student Righteous Uprising or student "revolution."

It began immediately after the March 15, 1960 presidential and vice-presidential elections when the opposition Democratic Party and students protested the "rigging" of elections by the Liberal Party in collusion with the police. The protesters clashed with the police, and several persons were killed and many were wounded by the shots fired by the police. The discovery in Masan on April 11 of the body of a student who had been shot and killed by the police provoked even more violent antigovernment demonstrations. Police stations, the Liberal Party headquarters, and some public buildings in Masan were wrecked.

Students in Seoul and other cities and towns began their demonstrations, demanding the nullification of the March 15 election results, as well as resignation of President Rhee and his cabinet members. On April 18, some three thousand students of Korea University in Seoul staged a mass rally and marched to downtown Seoul. On their way back to the campus following their rally in downtown Seoul, they were attacked by hundreds of thugs presumably hired by the Liberal Party. A new wave of student demonstrations, joined by professors and thousands of citizens, erupted on April 19, resulting in clashes with the police. The demonstrators marched toward the presidential mansion, while police fired upon the demonstrators. Further provoked, students burned down police stations, sacked the building of the government organ, *Seoul Shinmun,* and broke into the headquarters of the Liberal Party in Seoul.

Greatly outnumbered and facing such a dangerous situation, many police officers fled, but others continued to fire at the demonstrators, killing 125 persons and wounding some 1,000. President Rhee declared martial law in the afternoon of April 19, and mobilized army troops accompanied by tanks, but the troops refused to act against the demonstrators. In an attempt to save the president, all cabinet members submitted their resignations *en masse.*

Under pressure from Washington, and facing impossible odds, President Rhee himself resigned on April 26. *See also:* STUDENT MOVEMENT.

ASSASSINATION AND ASSASSINATION ATTEMPTS. The history of assassination of prominent political leaders began on December 28, 1945, when Song Chin-u, a major leader of the Korean (Han'guk) Democratic Party, was assassinated by a leftist in the midst of antitrusteeship protest. The killing of Song was followed by the assassination on July 19, 1947 by a refugee from North Korea of Yŏ Un-hyŏng, a prominent moderate left-wing nationalist who was the head of the Working People's Party. On December 2, 1947, Chang Tŏk-su, another key leader of the Korean (Han'guk) Democratic Party was assassinated by a leftist.

On June 26, 1949, Kim Ku, an ultra-rightist leader and the head of the Korean Independence Party, was assassinated by an army lieutenant of South Korea, who charged him with being an obstacle to the Republic and to the promotion of democratic government in South Korea.

On September 28, 1956, a would-be assassin shot and wounded Vice-President-elect Chang Myŏn at the Citizen's Hall in Seoul. On early January 21, 1968, a 31-man team of North Korean commandoes infiltrated into the northern part of Seoul in order to gain access to the Blue House (presidential mansion) and assassinate President Park. All but one of the commandoes were killed by the police.

On August 15, 1974, a Korean resident from Japan made an attempt to assassinate President Park Chung-hee at the National Theater in Seoul. President Park escaped the assassin's bullets, but his wife, Madame Yuk Yŏng-su, who was sitting on the platform, was shot and died shortly thereafter at a hospital.

In the evening of October 26, 1979, President Park was fatally wounded by pistol shots fired by the director of the Korean CIA, Kim Chae-gyu, and he died early the next morning. The assassin allegedly said that he killed the president to promote democracy in South Korea. On that occasion, President Park's security service chief was also killed.

On October 9, 1983, North Korean agents attempted to assassinate President Chun Doo-hwan at the Martyr's Mausoleum in Rangoon, Burma, by detonating remote-controlled bombs which they had planted at the structure in advance. President Chun, who was on a state visit tour in Southeast Asia, was on the way to the Martyr's Mausoleum, but was behind schedule because of traffic congestion, thus escaping certain death. However, Chun's top advisors and several cabinet ministers were killed.

-B-

BUDDHISM. Arriving in 372 A.D. from China, Buddhism (Mahayana sect) became the religion of the masses, including the upper class. Although it was introduced to Koguryŏ first, it did not flourish there. However, it became the state religion of Paekche in the 4th century and that of Shilla in the 6th century, contributing greatly toward the development of art, architecture, crafts, music, scholarship, and sculpture, as well as metallurgical technology. Several sects, including *Sŏn* (*Zen* in Japanese), rose in Shilla.

During the Koryŏ period, like the latter half of the Shilla period, Buddhism reached its golden age in Korean history as many books, such as massive *Tripitaka Koreana,* were printed in the 13th century. During the Yi period, Buddhism was rejected by the government and the ruling class. However, it survived as a religion of the rural population.

Buddhism gained strength during the Japanese colonial period, and it became the religion of the majority. The growth of Buddhism continued after the liberation of Korea from Japan. Among several sects of today, the most prominent one is the Chogye Sect which combines *Sŏn* practices with evangelistic drive. Two other important sects are the T'aego and the Wŏn sects. In 1985, there were eight million Buddhists, representing some 20% of the population. *See also:* RELIGIONS.

-C-

CAIRO AGREEMENT. In November 1943, a summit conference of the United States, Great Britain and China was held in Cairo, Egypt, to adopt an Allied plan to deal with Japan during and after the Second World War. Regarding Korea, the communique issued on December 1, 1943 by the Allies, stated that "the . . . great powers, mindful of the enslavement of the people of Korea, are determined that in due course Korea shall become free and independent." This decision was made in accordance with their resolution that Japan be stripped of all the islands in the Pacific which she had seized or occupied since 1914, that all the territories which Japan had "stolen" from China be returned to her, and that Japan be expelled from all other territories which she had taken by violence and greed.

CENTRAL ELECTION COMMITTEE. Under the amended Constitution of 1960, this committee was established "for the purpose of conducting fair elections." It included three members elected by the justices of the Supreme Court and six members recommended by the political parties. All disputes over the results of elections were decided upon by this committee.

CENTRAL INTELLIGENCE AGENCY (KCIA). The Korean Central Intelligence Agency (KCIA) was established in June 1961 under the Central Intelligence Agency Law of June 10, 1960 "for the purpose of countering indirect aggression of the Communist forces and to remove obstacles to the execution of the revolutionary tasks." It was to "coordinate and supervise activities of government ministries, including armed forces, concerning information and investigation of matters at home and abroad related to the ensuring of national security and the investigation of criminal activities."

It not only dealt with external threats, but was also involved in domestic affairs, providing valuable services to the administration in exercising its autocratic power. In December 1980, it was renamed the Agency for National Security Planning (Kukka Anjŏn Kihoekpu) without losing any of its power.

CHANG MYŎN (1899–1966). Educated in the United States, Chang taught at a secondary commercial school in Pyongyang during the Japanese colonial period. Following the liberation of Korea, he served as a member of the Representative Democratic Council and a member of the South Korean Interim Legislative Assembly. He was elected to the Constituent Assembly in May 1948 as a moderate nationalist. He was sent to the United States by President Rhee as ambassador in 1949, and in 1950 he served as head of the South Korean observer mission to the United Nations.

After serving as prime minister in 1951, he resigned from the post and became a prominent opposition leader, forming the Democratic Party in 1955 in cooperation with Shin Ik-hŭi. Elected in 1956 as vice-president of the Republic, he was shot and slightly wounded by a would-be assassin in September. He was nominated by the Democratic Party as vice-presidential candidate for the March 1960 presidential elections, but was defeated.

In the heat of the Student Uprising of April 1960, he resigned the vice-presidency although his term of office did not expire until May. When the First Republic fell and a new constitution was adopted by the National Assembly, in August 1960 he was chosen as prime minister by the National Assembly. The May Military Revolution of 1961 forced him to resign on May 18, 1961. Being purged by the military junta, he retired from politics.

CHANG T'AEK-SANG (1893–1969). Educated at Edinburgh University, he was appointed as chief of Metropolitan Police in Seoul in 1945 by the American military government. He became a legislator in 1950, and then was appointed as prime minister in 1952. Reelected to the National Assembly in 1954 and 1958, he served as chairman of the Anti-Communist Struggle Committee. Reelected in 1960 to the National Assembly, he was purged in 1961 by the military junta. In 1963 he reconstituted the Liberal Party, but he and the new party played no significant role. *See also:* LIBERAL PARTY.

CHANG TO-YŎNG (DO-YOUNG, 1923–). Born into a Christian family in a village near Shinŭiju, North P'yŏngan Province, he enrolled at Tōyō University in Tokyo, but his education was interrupted by student mobilization which the Japanese government carried out in January 1944. Drafted into the Japanese Imperial Army, he served as an instructor of the Officers Candidate Training School in Nanjing, China, toward the end of World War II. When the war ended, he returned to his hometown and became a high school teacher.

When an anticommunist uprising of his students broke out in November 1945, he fled to South Korea.

Graduating in 1946 from the Military English School, which was established by the American military government to train Korean officers in the Constabulary, he was commissioned as lieutenant, and remained in the military after the Korean armed forces were established in 1948. During the Korean War, he commanded combat divisions and an army corps.

Chang received further military training at the Command and General Staff College in the United States in 1953, and rising in rank rapidly Gen. Chang became Army Chief of Staff in February 1961.

When in May the military revolution came he, as Army Chief of Staff, acquiesced to it in view of the circumstances. Hoping to avoid large-scale bloodshed, believing that many commanders of army divisions were behind the revolution, mindful of the persistent military threats from North Korea, and with the idea of "guiding" the revolutionaries, he accepted the chairmanship of the Military Revolutionary Committee (MRC).

In late May, the MRC was renamed the Supreme Council for National Reconstruction (SCNR), and as chairman of the SCNR, he served as head (prime minister) of the cabinet until July when he was charged with an alleged antirevolutionary plot. He was tried and was given a death sentence by the lower military court. This was reduced to a life term by a higher military court. The case then went to the highest military court, but, while his case was being reviewed, he received a pardon from Gen. Park who had become chairman of the SCNR and dismissed the case in May 1962. Shortly after that Chang was allowed to leave Korea and go into exile in the United States.

CHANG TŎK-SU (1894–1947). A prominent right-wing nationalist who was educated at Waseda University in Tokyo and received a Ph.D. from Columbia University. He served as chief editor of *Tong-a Daily News* from 1920, and championed the Korean cause. He was a key founding member of the Korean (Han'guk) Democratic Party and chairman of its Political Committee. He was assassinated by a policeman on December 2, 1947 because of his support for the Moscow Agreement despite his party's opposition to it.

CHARTER FOR NATIONAL EDUCATION. On December 5, 1963, the government promulgated this charter to set the goal and standard of Korean education. It called for the promotion of a "posture of self-reliance . . . by revitalizing the illustrious spirit of our forefathers" with a keen sense that "we have been born into the land, charged with the historic mission of rejuvenating the nation." *See also:* EDUCATIONAL DEVELOPMENT.

CHEJU REBELLION. On April 3, 1948 some 3,000 Communist guerrilla bands in opposition to the May 10th general elections brought about this rebellion in collusion with Communist elements in the Korean Constabulary units of Cheju Island. Their main targets were the police force and right-wing youth groups on the island. The rebellion started in the northern part of the island, and spread into other parts as other islanders joined the rebels.

After reinforcements of police and constabulary arrived from the mainland the counterinsurgent campaign began, causing a large number of casualties on the part of the rebels. The rebellion lasted until May 1949, although some guerrilla activities continued well into 1953.

During the rebellion some 15,000 persons were reported to have been killed by the Communists, and 300 to 400 villages were ravaged, 20,000 houses were burned down, 34 schools and 15 town halls were destroyed, and 65,000 islanders were displaced and made homeless. Between 20 and 30,000 rebels were reported to have been killed. Of some 2,000 captured insurgents, 250 were executed and the remainder were given prison terms ranging from seven years to life.

On May 10, 1949, one year after the general elections were held on the mainland, elections were held on Cheju Island to elect the two Cheju representatives to the Constituent Assembly.

CHI CH'ŎNG-CH'ŎN (1888–1959). Born with the name of Chi Tae-hyŏng, he graduated from an army cadet school in Tokyo in 1913. In 1919, he fled from Korea after taking part in the March First Movement, and joined an anti-Japanese military group of Koreans in Manchuria. When the Korean Independence Party was organized in China in 1930, Chi became chairman of its military committee, establishing the Korean National Restoration Army. In 1940 he became its commander.

Chi returned to Korea after her liberation and organized the Taedong Youth Corps, an extreme rightist organization. He later became minister without portfolio, one of the founders of the Korean Nationalist Party, and in 1950 a member of the National Assembly loyal to President Rhee.

CHO PONG-AM (1898–1959). After serving a one-year prison term in 1919 for his participation in the March First demonstrations (see the Introduction, pages 13–14), he went to Tokyo to study, joining a radical leftist group there. In 1919 he went to Shanghai, and then went to Moscow to study at the Communist University of Toilers of the East. Upon returning to Korea, in 1925 he became a founding member of the Korean Communist Party, and he collaborated with other Socialists in forming the General Federation of Farmers and Laborers, playing an active role in promoting social revolution, as a result of which he served several prison terms. After his release from prison in August 1945, he played an active part in the labor movement and, in September 1945, in cooperation with other Communists, he reestablished the Korean Communist Party. However, in 1946, he left the Korean Communist Party following a disagreement with head of the party Pak Hŏn-yŏng.

Elected in 1948 to the Constituent Assembly, he became the first minister of agriculture, forestry and fisheries of the Rhee administration, and advocated radical land reform and a progressive economic policy which led to his dismissal by President Rhee. He was reelected to the National Assembly in 1950, and ran for the presidency in the 1952 election. In 1956, he formed the Progressive Party and in the same year ran for the presidency.

In January 1958, he was arrested and sentenced to a five-year prison term for illegal possession of firearms and a minor violation of the National Security Law. He was found guilty of "treason against the state in collaboration with the Communists," and was executed on July 30, 1959. *See also:* PROGRESSIVE PARTY.

CHO PYŎNG-OK (1894–1960). Born to a Christian family, Cho was educated at Christian schools in Korea and then studied at Columbia University where he was strongly indoctrinated by liberal and democratic ideas. After earning a Ph.D. in 1925, he returned to Korea, becoming a professor of economics at Yŏnhŭi College (now Yŏnsei University). He joined a pan-national society of men named Shinganhoe, and in 1929 he was imprisoned for three years for his involvement in the Kwangju student incident. After his release from prison, he became a staff member at a vernacular daily paper, *Chosŏn Ilbo.* In 1940, he was again imprisoned for his nationalistic activity.

In September 1945, he with others founded the Korean (Han'guk) Democratic Party, serving briefly as director of the Department of Public Security of the U.S. Army Military Government in Korea. When the Republic was inaugurated he served as minister of home affairs. In 1952 he visited the United States and other democratic countries as a presidential envoy, campaigning for membership of the Republic in the United Nations. From 1951, he, as secretary-general of a small Democratic Nationalist Party, struggled to promote democracy.

He was elected to the National Assembly in 1954 and again in 1958, and in 1955 he became a cofounder of the Democratic Party. In 1959, he was nominated by the Democratic Party as its presidential candidate, but he died on February 15, 1960 while receiving medical treatment in the United States.

CH'OE KYU-HA (1919–). Born to a family of a Confucian scholar in Wŏnju, Kangwŏn Province, he graduated from Tokyo High Normal School in 1941, taught at National Taitung Institute in Manchukuo from 1943 to 1945, and Seoul National University from 1945 to 1950. After serving as director of the Bureau of Trade of the Ministry of Agriculture, Forestry and Fisheries, he became a member of the Korean mission to Japan (1952–1957), becoming counsellor and minister of the Korean Mission to Japan (1957–1959). Other posts held include vice-minister of foreign affairs (1959–60), advisor to the chairman of the Supreme Council for National Reconstruction (1961–63), ambassador to Malaysia (1964), minister of foreign affairs (1967–71), special assistant to the president in foreign affairs (1971), acting prime minister (1975), chairman of the National Conference for Unification (1979), and prime minister (1976–79). Following the death of President Park, he became acting president (October–December 1979), and he was elected by the NCU in December 1979 as president, resigning the position in August 1980.

CH'OE NAM-SŎN (1890–1957). Ch'oe was a poet and one of the early leaders of the new culture movement in Korea. He was publisher of magazines for Korean youth, such as *Sonyŏn* (*Children,* 1908) and *Ch'ŏngch'un* (*Youth,* 1914). With his poem, "From the Sea to Children," he established a new form of Korean poetry. He authored the Declaration of Independence of 1919, and after serving a prison term in connection with his activity in the March First Movement, in 1924 he and others organized a vernacular newspaper named *Shidae Ilbo.*

In 1949, he was imprisioned as a traitor for his collaboration with the Japanese. Released from prison in 1950, he published many historical works, including *Korean People's History, Korea's Culture,* and *Korea's Mountains and Rivers.* He edited the *Korean Historical Dictionary* in 1955.

CH'ŎNDOGYO. A new native religion named Tonghak ("Eastern Learning") was founded by Ch'oe Che-u in 1860, and it became the religion of the oppressed. Combining superstitious religious beliefs in a better future with the concept of the unity of god and man, as well as the equality of man, it became an antiestablishment and antiforeign (particularly anti-Christian) force in the late 19th century, bringing the Tonghak Uprising in 1893–94.

In 1906, its leaders changed the name of their religion to Ch'ŏndogyo, or the Teaching of the Heavenly Way, which asserted that through self-discipline and cultivation of mind one could obtain the divine virtue of being able to influence everything without conscious effort of volition. The leaders of Ch'ŏndogyo played an important part in the March First Movement in 1919 (see the Introduction, pages 13–14) and of other Korean independence movements. A minor religion today, it had some 53,000 followers in 1985. *See also:* RELIGIONS.

CHŎNG IL-GŎWN (1917–). A graduate of the Japanese military academy in Manchukuo in 1940, he joined the Japanese army there. After the liberation of Korea, he returned to Korea, joining the newly established Korean army, and rose in rank during the Korean War. After serving as head of Command and Staff College (1954–56), he became chairman of Joint Chiefs of Staff.

Retiring from the army as Lt. General in 1975, he served as ambassador to Turkey (1957), France (1959), and U.S.A. (1960–63), and in 1963 he became minister of foreign affairs. Appointed to the premiership in 1964, he served the Third Republic until 1970. He was elected to the National Assembly in 1971 and 1979, and served as acting chairman of the Democratic Republican Party (1972–79). With the fall of the Fourth Republic in 1979, his political fortune declined, but he remained active as a member of the advisory council of state affairs to President Chun.

CHŎNMINYŎN. *See:* NATIONAL COALITION FOR A PEOPLE'S DEMOCRATIC MOVEMENT.

CHRISTIANITY. Both Catholicism and Protestantism had flourished since their introduction to Korea. Catholicism was first introduced to Korea in the seventeenth century from China, and it grew in the eighteenth century despite many difficulties and several anti-Catholic persecutions. It was called *Sŏhak* ("Western Learning") before 1900. In the anti-Catholic persecution of 1866, some 7,000 faithful, including several French priests, were beheaded. Catholicism continued to grow after 1900, and as of 1985 there were some two million Catholics in South Korea. In May 1984, Pope John Paul II visited Korea and canonized 93 Korean and ten French martyrs as he celebrated the bicentennial of the founding of the first Catholic church in Korea. He made the second Korea visit in October 1989.

Protestantism was introduced to Korea in the late nineteenth century, first by Scottish missionaries in Manchuria and then American and other missionaries who arrived after the conclusion of the U.S.-Korean Treaty in 1882 and other treaties with the Western nations. Protestantism played an important role not only in promoting a new religion in Korea, but also modern education. Protestantism was identified by the Koreans as a modernizing influence.

Since the liberation, members of Protestant churches have become political and social leaders of South Korea as the membership of Protestant churches increased rapidly. As of 1985, there were some nine million Protestant church members in ten sects. *See also:* RELIGIONS.

CHUN DOO-HWAN (1931–). Born in a small village in South Kyŏngsang Province, in 1950 he enrolled at the Taegu Technical Middle School, but in 1951, he enrolled at the Korean Military Academy, graduating in 1955 as the "Class of '55," and served in various posts in the army.

After serving as a member of the Civil Affairs Section of the Supreme Council for National Reconstruction in 1961 and Personnel Section chief of the Korean CIA (1963–67), he became battalion commander of the Capital Garrison Command in 1967. Between 1969 and 1970, he served as senior aid to the Army Chief of Staff, and in 1970 he went to South Vietnam as commander of the 29th Regiment of the Korean Army. Returning home in 1971, he became commander of the First Paratrooper Special Force.

After serving as assistant deputy chief of the Blue House security force from January 1973, Chun rose to the rank of major general in February 1978, commanding the First Army Division, and in March 1979 he became commander of the Defense Security Command, an army intelligence unit.

On December 12, 1979, he carried out a coup, gaining power over the South Korean armed forces, and in 1980 he became acting director of the Korean CIA and chairman of the Standing Committee of the Special Committee for National Security Measures.

When President Ch'oe resigned in August 1980, Chun was elected by the NCU as president, and in February 1981 he was reelected to be the president of the Fifth Republic by the newly created electoral college. As the Democratic Justice Party was formed by his supporters, many of whom were the members of the "Class of '55," he was made its president, the post he held until June 1987.

His term of office expired on February 25, 1988, and after making a nationwide television appeal, admitting many wrongdoings of his administration, he and his wife retired to a Buddhist temple in a remote mountain region in Kangwŏn Province, staying there until December 1991. *See also:* DECEMBER 12, 1979 COUP; DEMOCRATIC JUSTICE PARTY; SPECIAL COMMITTEE FOR NATIONAL SECURITY MEASURES.

CIVIL DEFENSE CORPS. It was established in September 1975 to protect lives and property in times of enemy attack or national disasters, as well as to provide support to rescue and rehabilitation activities and to augment military operation. All male citizens between the ages of 17 and 50, except members of constitutionally-established government agencies, police, firefighters, military and civilian personnel serving in the armed forces, members of the Homeland Defense Forces, and members of the Students National Defense Corps, were obligated to serve in the corps.

The government designated the 15th day of each month as a civil defense day, having mock antiwar raid drills and other exercises under the direction of the Civil Defense Headquarters. In June 1988, the government revised the minimum age from 17 to 20, benefitting some 300,000 youths in that age group.

CIVIL DEFENSE FORCE SCANDAL. The Civil Defense Force was a paramilitary force organized to augment regular armed forces against the Communist aggressors in the heat of the Korean War. Those able-bodied Korean males between the ages of 18 and 40 who were not in regular military services were obligated to join the force and fight in the war. This case involved embezzlement of a large amount of funds and misappropriation of supplies allocated for the force by Gen. Kim Yun-gŭn, commander of the force, and his coterie.

The investigations conducted by the National Assembly found the commander and other officers in the force guilty, and they were executed in August 1951. The Civil Defense Force was abolished at the end of the Korean War.

CIVIL RELIEF IN KOREA. A program of the United Nations which began during the Korean War to provide aid for civilian relief programs. Under the resolution of the Security Council of the U.N. on July 31, 1950, the U.N. Command determined the requirements for civil relief, and a military unit known as the U.N. Civil Assistance Command (later reorganized as the Korean Civil Assistance Command) was delegated to make necessary requests for civil relief in Korea.

CIVIL RULE PARTY. In May 1963, this political party known in Korean as Minjŏngdang emerged with Yun Po-sŏn as its president, advocating the promotion of democracy. In May 1965, however, it and the Democratic Party (formed in August by Pak Sun-ch'ŏn) were united into the Masses Party (Minjungdang). Eventually, in February 1967, the Masses Party and one other party were united, forming the New Democratic Party. *See also:* DEMOCRATIC PARTY, MASSES PARTY, NEW DEMOCRATIC PARTY.

CIVIL SERVICE. Korean government officials were classified into two main categories by the Law on Public Officials of 1949. A "special category" included military personnel, members of the National Assembly, cabinet ministers, presidential staffs, judges and senior diplomats. The "general category" included bureaucrats in various branches of the government who were classified into five ranks. All "general category" officials were appointed according to the results of a civil service examination which had two categories, the higher and the ordinary. Both were open to all who met certain required educational standards.

COALITION COMMITTEE FOR CO-OPERATION BETWEEN THE RIGHTISTS AND THE LEFTISTS. In October 1946, Kim Kyu-shik, representing moderate right-wing nationalists, and Yŏ Un-hyŏng, representing moderate leftists, organized this committee as the extreme rightists and the hardline leftists, including the Communists, were engaged in bitter controversy in connection with the implementation of the Moscow Agreement. The aims of this committee were to promote the strength of the moderates by unifying them, and to establish "a democratic transitional government" in Korea in accordance with the Moscow Plan of the Allies. Both Kim and Yŏ saw the inevitability of imposing the trusteeship of the Allies in Korea, and neither of them wished to see the establishment of absolute control over the government by either conservative rightists, or radical leftists. *See also:* KIM KYU-SHIK, MOSCOW AGREEMENT, YŎ UN-HYŎNG.

COMBINED ECONOMIC BOARD. An agency set up under the Economic Co-ordination Agreement signed between the Korean and U.S. governments in 1952 "to insure effective support of the military forces . . . to relieve the hardships of the people of Korea, and to establish and maintain a stable economy." Its membership included both Koreans and Americans. It was abolished in 1960.

COMMITTEE FOR THE PREPARATION OF NATIONAL RECONSTRUCTION. This committee known in Korean as Kŏnguk Chunbi Wiwŏnhoe was established on August 16, 1945 by Yŏ Un-hyŏng with An Chae-hong, a prominent moderate right-wing nationalist, as the vice-chariman, to function as a transitional government of all Korea. As soon as it was established, branches were organized throughout the country, functioning as local governmental units. Under these committees were formed security maintenance units, performing the role of the police. When the Korean People's Republic and its government were established by the "National Assembly" on September 6, 1945, the committee went out of existence.

COMMITTEE FOR THE THREE PEOPLE'S STRUGGLE. This committee known in Korean by its acronym, Sammint'uwi, was formed in the spring of 1985 by radical students. It adopted an anti-imperialist and antifascist line, advocating three struggles of the people, namely, national unification, people's liberation, and democratization. *See also:* STUDENT MOVEMENT.

COMMITTEE TO PROMOTE A DEMOCRATIC COALITION. This political organization whose Korean name is Minju Yŏnhap Ch'ujin Wiwŏnhoe, or commonly called Minyŏnch'u, was formed in April 1990 by leaders of the dissident forces who represented a broad national coalition composed of such radical groups as the National Association of Laborers (Chŏnnohyŏp, formed in January 1990), the National Federation of Farmers' Unions, the National Federation of Teachers' Unions (Chŏn'gyojo formed in May 1989), and the National Council of Representatives of University Students (Chŏndaehyŏp). The main purpose of the founder of this committee was to create a progressive party in cooperation with the Party for Peace and Democracy of Kim Dae-jung and the newly formed Democratic Party of Yi Ki-t'aek. Their aim was to establish a large, united opposition party of all dissidents. However, the leaders of the committee were split between those who advocated the creation of their own party and those who favored the formation of a united opposition party with other opposition parties. In the end, those who belonged to the former group set up their own Masses (People's) Party in November 1990. *See also:* MASSES (PEOPLE'S) PARTY.

CONFUCIANISM. A Chinese secular philosophy, which was introduced to Korea in the second century A.D., that gained strength during the Three Kingdoms period, exerting its influence on political, cultural, and social development. The Koryŏ dynasty maintained Confucian influence, but it did not strengthen it, other than its promotion of an educational system in Confucian tradition.

The Yi dynasty adopted the Chu Hsi school of Neo-Confucianism as a state creed, building a Confucian temple, establishing Confucian academies such as Sŏnggyunwan as a national university and other colleges collectively known as *Sahak* in Seoul. Along with the Confucian bureaucracy which the Yi dynasty strengthened, certain social institutions such as "ancestor worship" (*chesa*) were transplanted to Korea and became firmly entrenched there. Although only some 800,000 South Koreans now indicate they are "Confucianists," certain moral and ethical standards, educational philosophy, cultural patterns, and social institutions which developed in Korea under Confucian influence are still evident in South Korea.

CONSTITUENT ASSEMBLY. *See:* NATIONAL ASSEMBLY.

CONSTITUTION. The Constitution of the Republic of Korea was adopted on July 12, 1948 following a perfunctory debate by the Constituent Assembly, and it was promulgated on July 17. It showed traces of both the principles of responsible parliamentary democracy and of the American concept of an independent executive. While displaying the outward form of responsible parliamentary government, it provided much power to the presidency. While no constitutional provision was made for the dissolution of the National Assembly, Article 48 gave the president an extraordinary power, stating that "in time of civil war, or a dangerous situation arising from foreign relations, in case of a national calamity, or an account of a grave economic or financial crisis it is necessary to take urgent measures for the maintenance of public order and security, the President shall have a power to issue orders having the effect of law . . . if time is lacking for convening of the National Assembly."

The 103-article Constitution was divided into ten chapters, followed by a preamble which stated that "We the people of Korea at this time engaged in reconstructing a democratic and independent society," are determined to (1) "consolidate national unity by justice, humanity, brotherly love and the elimination of all kinds of social evils," (2) "offer equal opportunity to every person," (3) "provide for the fuller development of an equality of each individual in all the fields of political, economic, social and cultural life," (4) "permit every person to discharge his duties and responsibilities," and (5) "promote the welfare of the people, to maintain permanent internal peace, and thereby to assure Security, Liberty and Happiness of ourselves and our posterity."

Chapter I (Articles 1–6) included general provisions. It stated that Korea shall be a democratic republic (Article 1) and the territory of Korea shall consist of the Korean Peninsula and its accessory islands (Article 2). Chapter II (Articles 8–30) enumerated rights and duties of citizens; Chapter III (Articles

31–50) dealt with the National Assembly established on the principle of universal, direct, equal and secret votes; Chapter IV (Articles 51–75) dealt with the structure of the government, making the president the head of the executive branch. The president and the vice-president were to be elected by the National Assembly, and the prime minister was to be appointed by the president with the consent of the National Assembly. Under Articles 46 and 47 they, together with the members of the cabinet and judges, were subjected to impeachment by the National Assembly.

Chapter V (Articles 76–83) dealt with the judicial branch of the government. It specified that the chief justice and justices of the Supreme Court were to be appointed by the president with the consent of the National Assembly. Article 80 designated the Constitution Committee, consisting of the vice-president as its chairman and five members of the National Assembly, as having the power to determine the constitutionality of a law. Chapter VI (Articles 84–89) established the principle of the economic order of the nation, recognizing citizen's private ownership of property; Chapter VII (Articles 90–95) covered financial matters of the government; Chapter VIII (Articles 96–98) dealt with local autonomous organizations; Chapter IX (Article 98) spelled out the procedure for amendment to the Constitution, and Chapter X (Articles 99–103) included supplementary rules concerning the National Assembly and enactment of the special law dealing with the punishment of those who committed malicious antinational acts prior to August 15, 1948.

CONSTITUTION COMMITTEE. Under the Constitution of 1948, questions involving the constitutionality of laws were decided by this committee headed by the vice-president of the Republic. It included five justices of the Supreme Court and five members of the National Assembly.

Under the Constitution of 1960, the Constitution Court, consisting of three members of the National Assembly, three justices of the Supreme Court and three others appointed by the president, was set up, replacing the Constitutional Committee. The Constitution Court adjudicated (1) the constitutionality of laws (2) impeachment trials, (3) dissolution of a political party, and (4) litigation on election of the president, chief justice, and justices of the Supreme Court.

CONSTITUTION COURT. *See:* CONSTITUTION COMMITTEE.

CONSTITUTION REVISION DELIBERATION COUNCIL. Under great pressure, the government established this committee in March 1980. It consisted of 69 individuals drawn from political, academic, business, legal, journalistic and other circles, and chaired by the prime minister. The new constitution it drafted was approved in a national referendum on October 22, 1980 (promulgated on October 27), and it replaced the *Yushin* Constitution.

CONSTITUTIONAL AMENDMENTS. The Constitution has been amended nine times since its adoption. The first amendment made on July 4, 1952, which was forced upon the National Assembly by then President Rhee and his Liberal Party, instituted the system of a direct popular election of the president and vice-president. It also included the right of nonconfidence by the National Assembly against cabinet members and the decision (not carried out by the president) to establish a bicameral legislative body by adding the House of Councillors as upper house of the National Assembly. The lower house was to be named the House of Representatives.

The second amendment was voted on November 27, 1954, eliminating any limit on the term of office of the incumbent president. It received 135 votes, one vote short of the required two-thirds majority. Nevertheless, the Liberal Party declared it passed applying a dubious mathematical principle known as "Sa-sa o-ip," (round off) practice of knocking off fractions under 0.5. It instituted the system of national referendum on constitutional amendments, and abolished the office of the prime minister. The amendment was adopted by the National Assembly after the fall of the Rhee administration in April 1960. Adopted on June 15, 1960, the Constitution of the Second Republic strengthened fundamental civil rights and freedom of the press, and established a new Constitutional Court and a Central Election Management Committee. At the same time, it reinstalled the system of election of the president as a figurehead chief-of-staff by the National Assembly, eliminated the office of the vice-president, and established a responsible cabinet system, giving the prime minister full responsibility for the administration responsible to the National Assembly. It also created an upper house (House of Councillors) of the National Assembly.

The fourth constitutional amendment adopted on March 23, 1960 by both houses of the National Assembly provided for an exception to the principle of no retroactive punishment so that those involved in the rigging of the March 15 presidential and vice-presidential elections would be punished. The fifth amendment was adopted following the May 16 Military Revolution of 1960. For the first time, the amended constitution was put to a national referendum on December 17, 1960, and became the Constitution of the Third Republic in 1963. It revived the presidential power, abolished the upper house of the National Assembly, downgraded the cabinet to a consultative body, and authorized the president to appoint the prime minister without the consent of the National Assembly.

The sixth amendment was approved by a national referendum on October 17, 1969, eliminating the two-term restriction on the president. The amendment also authorized members of the National Assembly to concurrently serve as cabinet ministers and increased the membership of the National Assembly to no less than 150 and no more than 250. With the seventh amendment approved by a national referendum on November 21, 1972, the Constitution became known as the *Yushin* Constitution, which provided extraordinary power to the president. With the removal of the restriction on the term of office, the incumbent president was reelected on December 23, 1972, bringing the beginning of the Fourth Republic. The amended constitution introduced a new system of presidential election by establishing the National Conference for Unification (NCU), whose members were popularly elected, as an electoral college. It also authorized the president to recommend 73 members of the National Assembly form a new political society named Political Fraternal Society for Revitalizing Reform, to be appointed by the NCU as members of the

National Assembly. In February 1975, the voters confirmed the authenticity of the *Yushin* Constitution in a national referendum.

The eighth amendment was adopted on October 22, 1980 in a national referendum and was promulgated on October 27, ending the *Yushin* rule and laying the legal foundation for the launching of the Fifth Republic in 1981. The amended constitution strengthened parliamentary and judiciary branches and limited the term of office of the president to a single seven-year term. Upon its promulgation, the National Assembly and all existing political parties were dissolved, and the Legislative Council for National Security was set up to function as a legislative body.

The ninth amendment adopted by the National Assembly on October 12, 1987 and approved in a national referendum on October 28, limited the term of office of the president to a single five-year term, laying the foundation for the establishment of the Sixth Republic. Under the amended constitution, the system of a direct, popular election of the president was restored, civil rights and freedoms of the press and speech were expanded, and the power of the National Assembly was strengthened. *See also:* LIBERAL PARTY; POLITICAL FRATERNAL SOCIETY FOR REVITALIZING REFORM; PUSAN POLITICAL DISTURBANCE; *YUSHIN* RULE.

COUNCIL FOR THE PROMOTION OF DEMOCRACY. Organized by the opposition leaders in 1984 to promote a united movement of all dissident groups to bring about a constitutional reform and democratization, it was led by two co-chairpersons (Kim Young-sam and Kim Dae-jung). The organizers of the council were disillusioned when the two Kims failed to unify, making the council an almost meaningless entity. When the two Kims formed their own political parties in 1987, the council was virtually dissolved. *See also:* KIM DAE-JUNG, KIM YOUNG-SAM.

COUNCIL OF WOMEN COLLEGE STUDENT ORGANIZATION. *See:* WOMEN'S MOVEMENT.

-D-

DECEMBER 12, 1979 COUP. On December 12, 1979, Maj. Gen. Chun Doo-hwan, commander of the Defense Security Command, an army intelligence unit charged with preventing internal subversion in the army, carried out a coup with the aid of the 9th Army Division troops under Lt. Gen. Roh Tae-woo, with sufficient evidence of possible complicity of some senior army officers in the conspiracy against the late President Park. The outward purpose of the coup was to "insure a joint investigation into the assassination of the late President Park Chung-hee."

Gen. Chun arrested Gen. Chŏng Sŭng-hwa, Army Chief of Staff and the Martial Law Command, and several other generals, charging them with involvement in the death of the president, and Gen. Chun took control over the armed forces. The coup placed the real power in the hands of Gen. Chun and a small group of army officers who cooperated with him, and Acting President Ch'oe Kyu-ha became a puppet.

DECLARATION OF DEMOCRATIC NATIONAL SALVATION. This declaration was adopted by the opposition leaders, including Yun Po-sŏn, Kim Dae-jung, and Ham Sŏk-hŏn, on March 1, 1976 at the Myŏngdong Cathedral in Seoul, bringing about the so-called Myŏngdong Incident. Many dissident leaders were arrested following the issuance of this declaration. At this juncture, those who were dismissed from the Tong-A Daily Press formed the Tong-A Committee for the Struggle for Protection of Freedom of the Press and Speech.

DECONTROL OF THE PRESS. This policy adopted by the government in July 1988 lifted the ban on literary and artistic works by some 80 defectors to the north and liberalized the press. It allowed the circulation of books on Socialism and Communism, as well as North Korean publications, thereby encouraging the rise of studies on North Korea and other Socialist Countries.

DEFENSE SECURITY COMMAND. A military intelligence organization of the Ministry of Defense, it is primarily responsible for security within the armed forces. However, it was also empowered to deal with civilian subversive activities as a gendarmerie.

DEMILITARIZED ZONE (DMZ). With the signing of the Korean armistice on July 27, 1953, a 150-mile long zig-zagging military demarcation line that established a new boundary between North and South Korea was drawn across the central part of the peninsula. At the same time, the demilitarized zone (DMZ) was established along the military demarcation line. The DMZ is 2.5 miles (4 km) wide, 1.25 miles (2 km) on each side of the line. A 10-foot high fence, which is a counterpart of the Berlin Wall, was erected on each edge of the zone and guarded by heavily armed guards posted outside the zone. All civilian dwellings inside the DMZ were removed, but some farmers were allowed to farm there. Panmunjom is located at the point in the western DMZ where a main north-south highway meet. *See also:* PANMUNJOM; THE KOREAN ARMISTICE; THE KOREAN WAR.

DEMOCRATIC JUSTICE PARTY. In January 1981, the supporters of Gen. Chun Doo-hwan formed a new political party named Minju Chŏng'ŭidang, with Gen. Chun as its president. It became the ruling party in the National Assembly. In April 1988, Roh Tae-woo replaced Chun as its president. In February 1990 it merged with the RDP and the NDRP, becoming the Democratic Liberal Party (Minju Chayudang). *See also:* DEMOCRATIC LIBERAL PARTY.

DEMOCRATIC KOREA PARTY. In January 1981, a group of dissidents formed a new political party named Minju Han'guk Tang, or Minhandang, with Yu Ch'i-song as its president. In 1984, it was absorbed into the New Korea Democratic Party.

DEMOCRATIC LIBERAL PARTY. The merger of the ruling Democratic Justice Party (DJP) and two minor parties—the Reunification Democratic (RDP) and the New Democratic Republican (NDRP) parties—brought about this new party whose Korean name is Minin Chayudang. The agreement to form a "grand alliance" of these three parties was announced on January 22, 1990. The formal decision to form a new party was made on Feb. 9. By doing so, the new party secured an absolute majority by including 127 lawmakers of the former DJP, 54 lawmakers of the former RDP, and 56 lawmakers of the former NDRP, having 18 more seats to pass any bills at the National Assembly. Only five lawmakers of the former RDP refused to join the new party.

Key elements of the five-point merger plan were as follows:

1. The DJP, the RDP and the NDRP will unconditionally merge into a new political party. Presidents of the three parties will serve as co-leaders until there is a national convention.

2. The new party will be a national party open to all moderate, middle-of-the-road democratic forces aimed at national reunification, welfare and justice, and promotion of national culture.

3. Registration of the merger will be done by the end of February and a national convention will be held by the end of May.

4. A committee composed of five persons from each of the three parties will be established to work out details of the merger.

5. The three parties will cooperate with other political forces which do not join the new party as long as they believe in parliamentary democracy.

When the representatives of the three parties met on February 9 and made a formal decision to form a new party, they chose Roh Tae-woo, Kim Young-sam, and Kim Jong-pil as supreme representatives of the new party, forming the party leadership of a troika.

DEMOCRATIC NATIONALIST PARTY. In February 1949, the Korean (Han'guk) Democratic Party merged with several other conservative groups, forming an anti-Rhee political party named Minju Kungmindang under the leadership of Shin Ik-hŭi. Its leadership group boasted many prominent individuals, including Cho Pyŏng-ok. It failed to prevail in its opposition to constitutional amendments in 1952 and 1954. Many of its members suffered in the Pusan Political Disturbances of 1952. Among its aims was to institute a responsible cabinet system in order to strengthen parliamentary democracy. After suffering much under the repressive measures of the government, it was reorganized into Democratic Party in September 1955. *See also:* DEMOCRATIC PARTY.

DEMOCRATIC PARTY. Shortly after the constitutional revision in November 1954, the members of the Democratic Nationalist Party formed the Society of the Comrades for the Protection of the Constitution, and solicited a wider support of the people. In order to strengthen their antiautocracy struggle, in September 1955 they reorganized their party in an enlarged Democratic Party (Minjudang) with Shin Ik-hŭi, Cho Pyŏng-ok and Chang Myŏn as its supreme committee members. It became the majority party in the aftermath of the fall of the First Republic, and its leaders Yun Po-sŏn and Chang Myŏn were elected by the National Assembly as the president and prime minister respectively of the Second Republic.

The party was badly split into the "old" and the "new" factions, and when the new faction gained prominence under Chang Myŏn's leadership, the old faction broke away, forming the New Democratic Party (Shin Minjudang, or Shinmindang) in October 1960. The Democratic Party, along with others, was dissolved in May 1961 when the military revolution came. However, as a dozen new political parties emerged in the spring and summer of 1963, Pak Sun-ch'ŏn established a new Democratic Party in July, and in May 1965 it and the Civil Rule Party were united into the Masses Party. In order to strengthen the opposition group, in February 1967, the Masses Party and the New Korea Party (formed in May 1966) were united into another New Democratic Party, which became the main opposition party under the leadership of Yu Chin-o. The third Democratic Party was formed in June 1990, by Yi Ki-t'aek and others who refused to follow Kim Young-sam, who united his Reunification and Democracy Party with the Democratic

Justice Party and the New Democratic Republican Party to form the Democratic Liberal Party in February 1990. In September 1991, Yi Ki-t'aek of the Democratic Party and Kim Dae-jung of the New Democratic Party agreed to merge their parties, bringing the fourth Democratic Party into existence with Kim and Yi as co-presidents. *See also:* CIVIL RULE PARTY; DEMOCRATIC LIBERAL PARTY; MASSES PARTY; NEW DEMOCRATIC PARTY; NEW KOREA PARTY.

DEMOCRATIC REPUBLICAN PARTY. A political party established in February 1963 by the leaders of the May 16th Military Revolution of 1961, with Gen. Park Chung-hee as its president. With its Korean name Minju Konghwadang, it became the ruling party, remaining as such until 1979. It was dissolved along with other political organizations in May 1980, but in 1981 it was revived as the New Democratic Republican Party under Kim Jong-pil's leadership.

-E-

EAST BERLIN, CASE OF. On July 8, 1967 the Korean CIA announced that some 107 Koreans had been arrested in connection with an antistate espionage (pro-North Korean) team based in East Berlin. Seventeen leaders of the East Berlin-based spy ring were abducted to Seoul via West Germany, and they, along with those who were arrested in South Korea, were tried under the Anti-Communism Law. This was known as "Case of East Berlin."

Of 34 of those who were indicted, two were given the death sentence, one life term, and the rest received various prison terms. Five of those who were abducted from East Berlin were allowed to return to West Germany in March 1969. The death sentence given to two was later commuted to life imprisonment. *See also:* ANTI-COMMUNISM LAW; NATIONAL SECURITY LAWS.

EC 121, DOWNING OF. On April 15, 1969, an American reconnaissance plane with 31 crew on board was shot down by

North Korean MIG fighter planes over the Sea of Japan at some 95 miles south of the North Korean port of Ch'ŏngjin on the east coast. This U.S. plane had been engaged in reconnaissance activity along the eastern coast of North Korea with its home base at Atsuki, Japan.

ECONOMIC DEVELOPMENT. South Korea was a poverty-stricken nation when Korea was divided into two zones of the Allies occupation. Most of the mineral deposits were located in North Korea, which also had most of the heavy industries established by the Japanese. South Korea had mostly light industries, depending entirely on North Korea's supply of electric power (95%) and chemical fertilizers (100%), as well as fuel (coal) and timber. The supply of these vital commodities was cut off in 1948, with devastating economic consequences. Almost all industrial establishments were forced to close down due to the shortage of electric power, and food production was sharply reduced due to the shortage of fertilizers. A World Bank report of 1948 indicated that the South Korean economy was "close to the bottom of the international economic scale and without the benefit of sufficient supply of natural resources."

South Korea had virtually no highly trained scientists, technicians, economic experts, or managerial personnel as a result of the Japanese policy which did not allow Koreans to be trained in these fields, and the American military government had done virtually nothing to bring about economic improvement.

With a meager American economic aid ($110 million for 1949 and 1950), the South Korean government made various efforts to improve economic conditions. The economic reconstruction program began with the land reform which was carried out in June 1949, when all farmlands (excluding fields where special crops such as tobacco and ginseng were grown) not cultivated by the owners, and holdings of more than 7.5 acres of farmlands owned by owner-cultivators were purchased by the government. The government, in turn, sold these lands to the farmers, charging lower prices than it had paid to the former owners, and providing the buyers the opportunity to pay the price in a long-term installment scheme. Around 1.5

million farmers acquired some 1.2 million acres of land. With this the system of absentee landlordism was abolished, and the amount of grain produced rose from 4.6 million tons in 1948 to 5.2 million tons by 1950. The construction of three new railroads and the development of the coal industry helped manufacturing industries to operate their factories as the per capita gross national product (GNP) grew to $68 in 1950.

The Korean War (1950–1953) not only negated the economic improvement which South Korea had made, but created a worse situation. Most of South Korea's industrial facilities, railways and roads, and an enormous amount of farmlands and irrigation system were destroyed or badly damaged. The war damage was estimated at $5 billion. In 1953, the country's gross national product (GNP) was $13.5 billion with per capita GNP of $58.

The post-Korean War economic recovery that began with $2.7 billion in U.S. economic aid, along with sizeable U.N. grants given between 1954 and 1969, brought about the gradual improvement of economic conditions as new railroads, highways and roads, and power plants were constructed and the fertilizer supply was increased. The annual GNP growth rate between 1953 and 1962 was 4.1%, bringing the GNP to $12.7 billion and per capita GNP to $74. However, South Korea remained an economically underdeveloped country with rampant inflation, a high rate of unemployment, and a huge amount of imports.

The government maintained the free enterprise system until 1962 when the military junta adopted various economic development plans and increased its control. Significant economic growth began following the implementation of the first Five-Year Economic Development Plan (1962–66) by the military junta, accompanying sustained expansion of exports with large U.S. grants and foreign loans. South Korea's GNP grew by 7.4% per year between 1962 and 1981, during which period the second Five-Year Economic Development Plan (1972–76), the third Five-Year Economic Development Plan (1977–81), and the fourth Five-Year Economic and Social Development Plan (1977–81) were successfully completed, bringing the nation's GNP to $66.2 billion with per capita GNP of $1,605 by 1981. The high rate of increase in GNP and personal income was accompanied by rising ratios of investment savings, exports, and by a basic structural change. Whereas the first Plan promoted import-substitution industries, the second Plan laid the foundation for a modern industrial structure, promoting exports; and the third Plan, achieving between 8.6% and 10.1% annual GNP growth, brought about the rise of a high state of industrial structure, facilitating heavy industry and modernization of farm villages and rural areas with the New Community Movement. Finally, the fourth Plan established the foundation of a self-reliant growth structure and the advancement of high technology.

The share of agriculture/fisheries in the GNP decreased from 36.6% in 1962 to 18% in 1981 while that of mining and manufacturing industries increased from 16.2% to 30.9% during the same period. The manufacturing industry's share rose from 14.2% to 29.5%, and while the share of light industry decreased from 73.2% in 1962 to 44.6% in 1981, that of heavy industry and chemical industry increased from 26.8% to 55.3% during the corresponding period. The social service industry's share in the GNP also grew.

All but the fourth Plan achieved the planned goals. The actual growth rate during this period of the fourth Plan was 5.8% per year. Among the factors responsible for the setback were: substantial increase in the price of imported petroleum and raw materials, a worldwide recession, the rise of protectionist sentiments in the advanced countries, strong inflationary pressures, rising wage rates, and the chaotic situation that developed in South Korea following the assassination of President Park in 1979.

The fifth Economic and Social Development Plan (1982–86), which accompanied the liberalization of the domestic market and the strengthening of exports, was highly successful as South Korea attained a GNP growth rate of 10% per year during the period, the GNP reaching the $95.1 billion mark in 1986 with the per capita GNP of $2,300, despite the population increasing to 41 million. For the first time, South Korea's exports ($34.715 million) exceeded its imports ($31.584 million).

In 1986, some 5,300,000 acres of farmlands were cultivated by 8.2 million owner-cultivators. Of the total farmlands, 3,260,000 acres, or 62.1% were paddy fields where rice was grown and 1,740,000 acres, or 37.9% were dry fields where soya beans, wheat, barley, potatoes, and other beans were grown. The production of rice increased from 3 million tons in 1962 to 5.6 million tons in 1986, achieving near self-sufficiency in food supply. The total amount of grain production increased from 6.5 million tons in 1961 to 8.5 million tons in 1986, thanks to modernization of farming, the introduction of a new variety of high-yield rice, the cooperative spirit promoted by the New Community Movement, and an abundant supply of fertilizer. Other important accomplishments in the agriculture and forestry sector were the implementation of a ten-year Resources Development Plan (1972–81), which included the planting of 186.6 million trees in 51,000 acres of land, rejuvenating hills and forest lands.

The most significant economic achievement of South Korea was industrialization of the nation with the increasing production of anthracite, electric power, cement, chemical fertilizer, textiles, and the training of scientists and skilled workers. Along with these industries, South Korea developed new industries such as automobile, electronics, iron and steel, petrochemical, oil refinery, and shipbuilding. The production of anthracite rose from a meager 3 million tons in 1962 to 24 million tons in 1985, and that of cement increased from 790,000 tons in 1962 to 16.5 million tons in 1986. While increasing power production from 1,789 million kwh in 1962 to 67,639 million kwh in 1986, South Korea's chemical fertilizer production increased from 83,000 tons in 1966 to 3.5 million tons in 1986. The automobile manufacturing and shipbuilding industry which began in the early 1970s made remarkable progress as South Korea became one of the world's largest shipbuilders and automobile exporters.

The carefully formulated economic development plans brought about the rise of many industrial centers (tax-free industrial zones included), beginning at Kumi. Such industrial centers as shipbuilding at Ulsan and on Kŏje Island; iron-steel and petrochemical works at Pŏhang; cement, coal and fertilizer manufacturing at Samch'ŏk; and automobile manufacturing, electronics plants, and textile factories located at Inch'ŏn and other places had revolutionary effects on the Korean economy, increasing exports and changing the social life of the people.

In 1987, the sixth Five-Year Economic and Social Development Plan (1987–91) began with the aim to increase the GNP by 7% and exports by 13.3% per year. In 1987 alone, the GNP grew to 128.4 billion with per capita GNP of $3,110, and South Korea's exports ($47.2 million) remained greater than its imports ($41 million). In this way, South Korea managed to reduce its foreign debts from $45 billion in 1986 to $35.5 billion in 1987 as it showed its capacity to bring about continuous economic growth, despite many problems. The GNP growth rates were 13% in 1987, 12.2% in 1988, and 6.5% in 1989. In 1991, the GNP growth rate rose to 8.6%, with the GNP of $284.8 billion and per capita GNP of $6,498. *See also:* LABOR MOVEMENT.

EDUCATION LAW. Promulgated on December 31, 1949, the law set forth the basic direction and objectives of education and delineated the fundamental policy directions for education in the country. Education, according to the law, was to inculcate in everyone a sense of national identity and respect for national sovereignty. The law emphasized the development of the spirit of universal fraternity and ability to work for the common prosperity of all humankind.

EDUCATIONAL DEVELOPMENT. Korea's educational development began with the introduction of Confucianism in the second century A.D. and Buddhism in the fourth century A.D. Since then, Confucian learning, along with studies in Chinese culture, developed rapidly under state sponsorship, particularly during the Yi period. Buddhism also contributed toward the development of scholarship.

Modern education began in 1883 when a modern private school was established in Wŏnsan by a Korean, followed by the establishment of schools by foreign missionaries in 1885 and 1886, and a palace school by the government in 1886. The establishment of girls schools by foreign missionaries from 1886 was significant, for it was the first time in Korean history that Korean girls were given an opportunity to receive formal education. A large number of private schools were established in the 1890s and up to 1906, increasing educational opportunity for young Koreans.

When Japan annexed Korea in 1910, the Japanese educational system was imposed, and public primary and secondary schools, as well as professional schools were established, although the number of these schools was small. Meanwhile, four colleges were established by foreign mission boards. However, educational development was restricted due to the Japanese colonial policy, and only a small number of Koreans were able to receive modern education. The illiteracy rate of the Koreans at the end of Japanese colonial rule was a staggering 75%.

Korea's liberation from Japan in 1945 provided a turning point for educational development although the progress was slow due to the shortage of funds and trained teachers. Those Korean colleges which had been closed down by the Japanese were reopened, and private schools began to appear slowly. The American military government, while maintaining the centralized national education system which the Japanese had established, brought the American school system of 6-3-3-4, published new textbooks, and trained teachers at various institutes.

When the Republic was inaugurated, the American system was kept and the Constitution of 1948 guaranteed equal opportunity for education, making elementary education compulsory and free. The Education Law of December 1949 laid the new cornerstones of national education as it proclaimed the purpose of education. Whereas all public primary schools were coeducational, separate public middle and high schools were established for boys and girls.

The implementation of the six-year plan for compulsory education, originally planned to begin in 1950, was delayed until 1954 due to the Korean War. By the end of 1959, 95% of all school-age children were enrolled in primary schools which operated in two shifts. Meanwhile, a five-year plan for vocational education was implemented in 1958, and it was followed by the implementation of the Industrial Educational Promotion Law of 1963. A significant step in education was taken in 1969 to extend compulsory education to the 9th grade, and abolish the entrance examination for middle schools. With this, the ratio of primary school graduates advancing to middle schools reached 98.7% in 1987. In that year, 91.9% of middle school graduates advanced to both academic and vocational high schools.

The government paid particular attention to the promotion of secondary vocational and technical schools, as well as higher education. Meanwhile, many private colleges and universities were established along with primary and secondary schools of various kinds, contributing toward rapid educational development and increase of skilled workers. In April 1974, two years after a nongovernmental Korean Educational Development Institute (KEDI) was founded in 1972, the government established the National Institute of Education to carry out comprehensive research for the development of educational theories and practice in the sociocultural context of Korea and improvement of educational programs.

In March 1985, the Presidential Commission for Educational Reform was formed, and it was given a mandate to formulate a comprehensive set of reform measures for educational policy and administration to promote education for the 21st century.

Educational Growth in South Korea, 1945–1991
(1945 figures include both North and South Korea)

Number of Schools

	1945	1960	1970	1980	1991
Primary Schools	2,834	4,496	8,961	6,487	6,245
Middle Schools	166	1,054	1,608	2,121	2,498
High Schools*	640	889	1,353	1,624	1,730
Colleges/ Universities**	19	85	168	236	244

*Includes vocational/technical high schools such as agricultural, commercial, fishery and marine, and technical high schools.

All secondary schools were middle schools in 1945.

**Includes private, national universities, national teachers colleges, junior and senior colleges.

Number of Students

	1945	1960	1970	1980	1991
Primary Schools	1,366,024	3,622,685	5,739,301	5,658,002	4,758,505
Middle Schools	80,828	528,593	1,318,808	2,476,997	2,232,330
High Schools		273,434	590,382	1,696,792	2,233,894
Colleges/ Universities	7,819	101,041	201,436	501,994	1,427,208

Aside from formal education, nonformal education also developed, first under the sponsorship of the government and then under various social organizations. Until the early 1960s, nonformal education consisted of literacy campaigns, civil education, agricultural extension, and adult education. These programs not only reduced the rate of illiteracy among the adult population, especially in rural areas, but also provided practical knowledge and technology for life in a rapidly changing world.

Rapid cultural, economic, and social transformation of Korean society after 1963 increased the need for a more organized and systematic form of continuing or lifelong education to prepare individuals to cope with the modern pace of life. As a result, after adding the Non-formal Education Division in the Bureau of Social and International Education of the Ministry of Education, the government expanded and strengthened nonformal educational programs. Civic schools were established for the youth who had not completed a primary school education, and civil high school for those who were unable to attend formal middle and high schools. Trade schools of primary and secondary levels were also established for those who had primary education but did not go to secondary schools. In 1972, the Air (radio-TV) and Correspondence High School system was adopted to provide educational opportunity to those who had to start making their livelihood early. In 1974, junior college level courses were added when the Korean Air and Correspondence University was established, offering 12 bachelor's programs in 13 departments.

After inaugurating in 1977 the program of special evening classes for the working youth, as well as establishing evening secondary schools attached to industry, in 1982, the open college programs were initiated. These national and private open colleges offered opportunity to industrial workers with high school education to earn a college degree while working. Some 28,823 students were enrolled at six open colleges as of 1987.

EMERGENCY DECREES. President Park issued a series of Emergency Decrees (Nos. 1–3) in January 1974, banning criticism against the *Yushin* rule. The Decree No. 1 prohibited any agitation for constitutional revision, Decree No. 2 established an Emergency Court Martial, Decree No. 3 was concerned with security of lives, and Decree No. 4, issued in April, prohibited activities of Democratic Youth and Student Federations.

These decrees were cancelled in August 1974, following the death of Madam Yuk Yŏng-su, wife of President Park, by pistol shots fired on August 15 by a would-be assassin whose aim was to kill the president. But new Emergency Decrees Nos. 5–9 were proclaimed in April and May of 1975, dealing with campus unrest and the growing demand for constitutional revision. *See also: YUSHIN* RULE.

EQUAL LAW OF MALE AND FEMALE EMPLOYEES. *See:* LABOR MOVEMENT.

EXCHANGE OF HOMETOWN VISITORS. According to the agreement reached in August 1985 between the Red Cross societies of North and South Korea, on September 20 visiting groups and folk art troupes numbering 151 members from each country arrived in Seoul and Pyongyang, respectively, for four-day visits.

-F-

FAMILY COURT. *See:* WOMEN'S MOVEMENT.

FAMILY LAW. *See:* WOMEN'S MOVEMENT.

FARMERS DEMONSTRATION. The Korean farmers were not happy with the farm policy of the government, but they carried out no public demonstrations until the wind of democracy grew strong after 1987. Thus, on February 13, 1989, some 15,000 farmers from various parts of the country held a violent rally in front of the National Assembly building, clashing with riot police. It was led by the Preparation Committee for the Federation of Farmers Movement, a branch of the National

Coalition for a People's Democratic Movement (Chŏnminyŏn) which includes many dissident groups.

FEDERATION OF KOREAN EDUCATION ASSOCIATIONS (FKEA). This federation of primary and secondary school teachers known in Korean as Taehan Kyoyuk (Yŏnmaeng, or simply Kyoryŏn, was established in the spring of 1947 for the purpose of promoting welfare, unity, and friendship among the members. Later on, college professors became its members. The principal activities of the Federation include: the improvement of teachers' economic livelihood and welfare, the protection and extension of teachers' rights, and the securing of professional competence of teachers and promotion of educational development.

Although it is not a labor union as such, it represents the interests of the educators to the Ministry of Education and the National Assembly. In 1987, its membership included 90.4% of primary school teachers; 78.7% of secondary school teachers; 31.5% of college professors; and 2,270 administrators and school staff. While publishing its journals and the *Education Yearbook,* it adopted the Charter for Teachers and the Code of Ethics for Teachers.

In December 1989, it was renamed the General Federation of Korean Teachers' Associations (Han'guk Kyowŏn Tanch'e Ch'ongyŏnhaphoe, or Han'guk Kyoch'ong). *See also:* KOREAN FEDERATION OF TEACHERS' LABOR UNIONS; LABOR MOVEMENT; NATIONAL TEACHERS' UNION.

FOREIGN AFFAIRS. When the Republic was inaugurated, the United States and other democratic countries extended their recognition of the new nation and established diplomatic relations with it. However, none of the Soviet bloc nations, or most of the Middle Eastern and African states had done so. Even after the U.N. General Assembly in December 1948 recognized the South Korean government as the only legitimate government in Korea, South Korea was unable to obtain U.N membership, and her diplomatic ties with the nations of the world were limited.

Although South Korea signed a mutual defense treaty with the United States in October 1953 and strengthened its ties with the United States, the efforts it made with Japan to establish normal relations with that country brought no results. However, South Korea secured membership in the World Health Organization (WHO); the Food and Agricultural Organization (FAO); the Universal Postal Union (UPU) in 1949; the U.N. Educational, Scientific and Cultural Organization (UNESCO); the U.N. Children's Fund (UNICEF) in 1950; and other international agencies after 1953, including the International Monetary Fund (IMF) and the Asian Development Bank (ADB).

During the 1960s, South Korea's diplomatic relations expanded following the adoption of a positive foreign policy. As a result, the number of countries with which South Korea maintained diplomatic ties increased from 22 to 93; the number of resident missions abroad rose from 17 to 97; membership in international organizations increased from 26 to 476, and the number of international agreements signed grew from 127 to 598. The president of South Korea made only four state visits (mainly to the U.S.) up until 1961, but between 1961 and 1970, 13 such visits were made, followed by many more in the 1980s. The foreign policy goals of South Korea were to improve her image in the international community and gain a greater share of the world markets through a program of modernization, thereby strengthening her own economic position.

One of the most significant achievements in foreign relations was the conclusion on June 22, 1965, of the South Korean-Japan Basic Treaty, establishing a new diplomatic relationship between the two, and in which Korea secured a large loan and a large sum of monetary reparations from Japan. Other major achievements were the conclusion on July 9, 1966, of a Status-of-Forces Agreement with the United States, the strengthening of ties with the U.S. by dispatching South Korean troops to South Vietnam to cooperate with the U.S., and the establishment of the Asian and Pacific Council (ASPAC) in 1966 on the initiative of South Korea to promote cultural ties with Asian nations.

In the 1970s, South Korea continued to expand its diplomatic ties with other nations, particularly with those in Africa, Latin America, and the Middle East. Hoping to establish relations with the Soviet bloc nations, on June 3, 1973, President Park issued a statement and said, among other things, that South Korea "will open its doors to all the nations of the world on the basis of the principle of reciprocity and equality," and he urged those countries whose ideologies and social institutions were different from South Korea's "to open their doors" to it. Efforts made by the Seoul government to establish diplomatic relations with Socialist countries did not bring any results until late in the 1980s, but it increased the number of other countries which established diplomatic ties with South Korea to more than 103, including 50 full members of the group of nonaligned nations, and the Holy See.

South Korea supported all those countries which had been struggling for independence, the elimination of racial discrimination, and national sovereignty and territorial integrity. Meanwhile, South Korea concluded bilateral cultural treaties with 35 countries (28 between 1965 and 1977) and multilateral cultural agreements with several consortiums. As of July 1988, South Korea maintained a network of embassies, consulates and other diplomatic missions in 127 countries, having diplomatic ties with 17 Asian, 33 African, 19 European, 14 Middle Eastern, 33 North and South American, and 11 Oceanic countries.

Although cordial and amicable relations developed between South Korea and many countries, particularly with Japan, the United States, and West Germany, some incidents created friction. The relationship between South Korea and Japan was strained when Kim Dae-jung was kidnapped from Tokyo to Seoul in August 1973 by the Korean CIA agents, and when the Japanese government revised high school history textbooks, white-washing Japanese aggression in Korea. Korean-American relations were strained by the May 1961 Military Revolution and subsequent suppression of civil liberties by the South Korean government, together with U.S. criticism against it, President Jimmy Carter's plan to withdraw all American ground troops from South Korea, the investigation of the House of Representatives of the U.S. Congress of the so-called "Koreagate," and Gen. Chun Doo-hwan's coup in December 1979. The abduction of an East Berlin-based pro-North Korean espionage team of the Koreans from West

Germany to Seoul by Korea's CIA agents in 1967 likewise created some diplomatic problems between Seoul and Bonn.

In the 1980s, South Korea continued its efforts to improve ties with its allies and friends while expanding its diplomatic relations with others. Thus, after visiting the U.S. in January 1981, President Chun made state visits to Southeast Asian nations in June 1981, holding summit meetings with the heads of the states in the Association of Southeast Asian Nations (ASEAN). Following these first-time state visits for a South Korean president, President Chun also visited African nations in August 1982. After that, he made the first official state visit of the South Korean president to Japan in September 1984, strengthening ties with that country. President Chun visited the U.S. again in April 1985, improving ties with South Korea's closest ally.

The Soviet Union's permission for South Korean diplomats to participate in the UNESCO conference in Moscow in 1976, and the participation of the Soviet Union, Hungary, East Germany and Yugoslavia in the International Athletic Association Federation (IAAF) meeting in Seoul in 1978, paved the way for the establishment of new relations between South Korea and these Socialist countries.

After the adoption of the policy of perestroika by Mikhail Gorbachev, South Korea increased commercial and cultural ties with the Soviet Union. At the same time, South Korea increased its cultural and economic contacts with the People's Republic of China and East European countries. Hungary was the first Socialist country to open a trade office and mission in Seoul in March 1988, followed by those of the Soviet Union and China. After the 1988 Seoul Olympic Games, South Korea's foreign relations with Socialist countries grew rapidly.

In February 1989, following the establishment of trade offices in Seoul by the Soviet Union and China in late 1988, South Korea established diplomatic relations first with Hungary and then with Poland. Yugoslavia agreed to do so as South Korea and the Soviet Union concluded an agreement to establish consular relations in early December. Meanwhile, South Korea established new trade relations with Vietnam, looking forward to establishing diplomatic ties.

In November 1989, President Roh Tae-woo strengthened

new ties with Hungary by his state visit. It was the very first time that a South Korean president had made an official state visit to a Socialist country, marking a significant turning point in South Korea's foreign relations. After visiting Hungary, Roh also made state visits to England, France, Switzerland and West Germany in late November and early December of that year.

Following the meeting between President Roh and Soviet President Mikhail Gorbachev in San Francisco on June 4–5, 1990, on September 30 Soviet Foreign Minister and South Korean Foreign Minister who met in New York announced the establishment of full diplomatic relations between the two nations. After that, President Roh made a state visit to Moscow in December, and in April 1991 President Roh and President Gorbachev held a summit meeting in Cheju Island of Korea. *See also:* SOUTH KOREA-JAPAN NORMALIZATION TREATY; U.S.-SOUTH KOREAN MUTUAL DEFENSE TREATY; U.S.-SOUTH KOREAN STATUS-OF-FORCES AGREEMENT.

-G-

GENERAL ALLIANCE OF LABORERS FOR RAPID REALIZATION OF KOREAN INDEPENDENCE. This alliance was formed in March 1946 by the right-wing labor leaders to combat the leftist labor movement, with Dr. Syngman Rhee as its honorary president and Kim Ku as its honorary vice-president. It was renamed the General Federation of Korean Labor Union (Taehan Nodong Chohap Ch'ongyŏnmaeng, or Taehan Noch'ong for short) when the Republic was inaugurated, becoming a political front of the conservative regime of President Rhee. *See also:* GENERAL FEDERATION OF KOREAN LABOR UNIONS; LABOR MOVEMENT; NATIONAL COUNCIL OF LABOR UNIONS.

GENERAL FEDERATION OF KOREAN LABOR UNIONS. In November 1960, the National Council of Labor Unions joined the General Federation of Korean Labor Unions forming the new General Federation of Korean Labor Unions (Taehan Nodong Chohap Ch'ongyŏnmaeng, or Taehan Noryŏn for short), claiming a total membership of three million. However, it was disbanded by the military revolutionaries in May 1961, only to be reestablished in August as Han'guk Nodong Chohap Ch'ongyŏnmaeng, or Han'guk Noryŏn (General Federation of Korean Labor Unions). *See also:* GENERAL ALLIANCE OF LABORERS FOR RAPID REALIZATION OF KOREAN INDEPENDENCE; LABOR MOVEMENT; NATIONAL COUNCIL OF LABOR UNIONS.

GENEVA POLITICAL CONFERENCE. A conference of 19 nations was held in April-June 1954 at Geneva to deal with Korean and Vietnamese questions. Whereas it divided Vietnam into two nations, it failed to solve the Korean problem when the North Korean delegation rejected proposals made by the South Korean government and the United States to bring about a peaceful unification of Korea. Following the conference, the 16 nations which fought in the Korean War issued a declaration stating that the United Nations was fully empowered to take collective action to repel aggression, to restore peace and security, to extend its good offices, and to seek a peaceful settlement in Korea, and that genuinely free elections should be held in Korea under United Nations supervision to unify the country. In addition to the 16 nations, North Korea, China and the Soviet Union participated in the conference. *See also:* KOREAN ARMISTICE AGREEMENT; KOREAN WAR.

GOVERNMENT-GENERAL OF KOREA. When the Japanese annexed Korea in August, 1910, Chosen Sotokufu, or the Government-General of Korea, was established as the Japanese colonial government in that country. The government seat was in Seoul, renamed Keijō by the Japanese. Korea was called Chosen. The colonial government was headed by a Governor-General of Korea (Chōsen Sōtoku) who was assisted by the Director-General of Administration (Seimu Sokan). All the governors-general were Japanese army generals on active duty. The one exception was a retired Japanese admiral.

The Governor-General was appointed by the Japanese Emperor himself and was directly responsible to the Emperor as well as to the Japanese prime minister. He also exercised military power and was authorized to mobilize Japanese armed forces in Korea. All chiefs of bureaus and sections in the Government-General were Japanese, as were most of the top-ranking officials. The Governor-General appointed provincial governors as well as provincial police superintendents.

The Government-General of Korea was abolished when Japan surrendered to the Allies on August 15, 1945.

-H-

HAM SŎK-HŎN (1901–1989). A 1924 graduate of Tokyo High Normal School, Ham joined the Korean Quaker Church in 1960, becoming the voice of Korean pacifists and a champion for peace and democracy. He published a monthly named *Voice of a Prayer,* became an uncompromising crusader for human rights, and played the role of spiritual leader, gaining the respect and love of the people until his death. He was arrested, tried, and imprisoned many times in the 1970s.

HAMP'YŎNG-KŎCH'ANG INCIDENTS. These two separate bloody incidents refer to the massacre of villagers in the Hamp'yŏng and Kŏch'ang areas by South Korean troops. Both of these incidents, involving the 9th Regiment of the 11th Division of the South Korean Army, occurred during the mopping-up campaign following the beginning of the counterattack of the U.N. forces in October 1950.

The first of these incidents took place in the Hamp'yŏng area in South Chŏlla Province between December 1950 and early January 1951, in the aftermath of an attack on the local police station by Communist guerrillas. The incident was created when the troops of the 5th Battalion launched an antiguerrilla assault. In doing so, they killed some 500 villagers in several villages in the Hamp'yŏng area, charging them with collaboration with the enemy.

The second incident took place in the Kŏch'ang area in South Kyŏngsang Province, from February 9th to 11th of 1951, when troops of the 3rd Battalion launched their mopping-up campaign, killing some 700 villagers and burning down over 700 houses in several villages, charging them with harboring fugitives.

HIJACKING OF SOUTH KOREAN AIRPLANES. The first hijacking of a South Korean plane took place in February, 1958, when a passenger plane belonging to the Korean Air Lines, on its way to Seoul from Pusan, was hijacked to North Korea. All passengers and crew were returned to South Korea in March. The second hijacking took place in December, 1969, when a passenger plane belonging to the Korean Air Lines was hijacked en route from Kannŭng to Seoul and diverted to North Korea. Of the 47 passengers on board, 35 were returned to South Korea in February, 1970 along with four crew members.

HŎ CHŎNG (1896–). A graduate of Posŏng College (now Korea University), he joined the ranks of the nationalists. Elected to the National Assembly in 1948, he served as minister of transportation (1948–50), minister of social affairs (1950–59), acting premier (1950–51); and minister of foreign affairs (April–Aug. 1960). He became acting president following the fall of the First Republic in April 1960, bringing in the Second Republic in August 1960. After 1961, he served as adviser to the National Unification Board (1969–84), was a member of the Advisory Council on State Affairs (1980–88), and chairman of the National Unification Advisers' Conference (1980–84).

HOMELAND RESERVE FORCES. The 2.5 million (191 reserve battalions with 2,018 companies) Homeland Reserve Forces were established in April 1968. The reservists were under the operational control of the regular army and they received part of their training at regular military installations. All veterans remained in the reserve units until the age of 35 in the case of enlisted men, and until 45 in the case of officers. In June 1975, a Combat Land Reserve Corps was set up under the Homeland Reserve Forces.

HONG SUK-CHA (1933–). A graduate of Ewha Woman's University and holder of a doctoral degree, she served as assistant to the minister of foreign affairs in 1959, vice counsel in New York in 1965, and chairman of the Korean National Council of Women (1980–87). In the 1987 presidential election, she ran as a candidate for the presidency for the Social Democratic Party, but she withdrew from the race in favor of the DJP candidate, Roh Tae-woo.

HOUSE OF COUNCILORS. Under the revised Constitution of 1952, the Election Law for the upper house named House of Councilors (Ch'amŭiwŏn) was promulgated in January 1958 after a long period of bickering among the lawmakers. According to this law, each city and province constituted an election district, between two and eight councilors were to be elected from each district, each representing 600,000 constituents, and that the total number of the councilors was to be not more than 70. The elections for the upper house were to be held within a year after the promulgation of the law, but President Rhee failed to implement the law.

When the First Republic fell, and the constitution was amended in June 1960, it was decided that the upper house be established according to the previous Election Law for the House of Councilors, which was modified. According to the new law, only the city of Seoul and each province would constitute an election district, each electing between two and eight councilors to serve a three-year term.

In June 1960, 58 Councilors were elected from ten election districts (Seoul plus nine provinces). However, in May 1961, when the military revolution came, the National Assembly was abolished, and the House of Councilors was never reestablished afterward. *See also:* NATIONAL ASSEMBLY.

HOUSE OF REPRESENTATIVES. The National Assembly which was established in 1948 had one house until the upper house, named the House of Councilors, was established in July 1960 under the revised Constitution of that year. At that time, the lower house was designated as the House of Representatives (Minŭiwŏm). As before, each member of the lower house represented 100,000 constituents, serving a four-year term.

Under the new National Assembly Election Law of 1962, the country was divided into 131 single-member districts and 44 additional at-large districts. Each single-district representative was elected by popular vote, and at-large seats were distributed to each party according to the percentage of popular votes it received. When the unicameral legislative system was restored under the Constitution of 1963, the South Korean legislature was simply called the National Assembly. Currently, the total number of seats is 299, of which 224 are elected from single-member electoral districts, and 75 are national constituency seats which are distributed to four major political parties. All members of the National Assembly are elected for four-year terms of office. *See also:* NATIONAL ASSEMBLY.

-I-

INFILTRATION TUNNELS. The underground infiltration tunnels which the North Koreans built under the DMZ were discovered by U.N. troops. The first two of these tunnels were discovered in 1974, the third one in 1975, and the fourth one in 1989. The U.N. Command charged North Korea with digging these and other tunnels, (it was suspected that at least ten more such tunnels have been dug by the North Koreans) for the purpose of invading South Korea on a large scale. Three of these tunnels were found in the western zone of the DMZ and the fourth in the eastern zone.

-J-

JOINT DECLARATION OF THE NON-NUCLEARIZATION OF THE KOREAN PENINSULA. This Declaration was initialed by the representatives of North and South Korea on December 31, 1991. The Declaration* reads as follows:

> In order to eliminate the danger of nuclear war, to create an environment favorable to peace and peaceful unification of our homeland and to contribute to peace and security in Asia and other parts of the

world by securing a nuclear-free Korean Peninsula, the South and the North declare as follows:

The South and the North will not test, manufacture, produce, accept, possess, store, deploy or use nuclear weapons.

The South and the North will use nuclear energy solely for peaceful purpose.

The South and the North will not possess nuclear reprocessing and uranium enrichment facilities.

The South and the North, in order to verify the denuclearization of the Korean Peninsula, will implement inspections of installations selected by the other side and agreed upon by both sides, in a manner and procedures to be specified by the South-North joint committee for nuclear control.

The South and the North will form and operate a South-North Joint Committee for nuclear control within one month after this declaration goes into effect, in order to implement this declaration.

This declaration will take effect as of the day when the South and the North exchange texts after going through the necessary formalities.

Note: This Declaration was approved by South Korean President Roh Tae-woo on January 17, 1991, and by North Korean President Kim Il-sung on January 18, 1991. The signed document was exchanged at the sixth round of talks between the premiers of two Koreas held in Pyongyang, February 18–21, 1992.

JOINT U.S.-SOVIET COMMISSION. Under the Moscow Agreement of the foreign ministers of the U.S., Great Britain and Russia in December 1945, the occupation authorities of the Allies in Korea were mandated to form this commission to establish a Korean national government to end the Allied occupation of Korea.

The Joint Commission was formed in January 1946. The Soviet delegation was headed by Colonel General Terenti Shtykov, and the American delegation was headed by Major General A.V. Arnold. The first meeting of the Joint Commission was held in March-May, briefly interrupted in April, but on May 8 the Joint Commission was adjourned *sine die,* without reaching any accord regarding the establishment of the new Korean government. The second commission meeting was held in June-August, and the third commission meeting was held in May-August 1947, without achieving its primary goals. This was the last meeting of the commission.

The Joint Commission was virtually dissolved when the U.N., requested by the American government, took over the Korean question in November 1947.

JUDICIARY. The judicial branch of the government is headed by the Supreme Court, whose Chief Justice is appointed by the President with the consent of the National Assembly. The Supreme Court justices are appointed by the President on the recommendation of the Chief Justice and with the consent of the National Assembly. Below the Supreme Court are the High (Appellate) Courts, District Courts, and a Family Court.

As of December 31, 1987, there were 877 judges, including 11 in the Supreme Court, 118 in the High Courts, and 509 in the District Courts.

All judges of the High Courts, District Courts, and the Family Court are appointed by the Chief Justice of the Supreme Court.

JULY 4TH STATEMENT REGARDING KOREAN UNIFICATION. On July 4, 1972, following a series of secret negotiations that began in May between the director of the Korean CIA and its North Korean counterpart, the governments of North and South Korea each issued an identical statement announcing an historic agreement to end hostility and work together toward peaceful unification of the country without outside interference.

The seven-point statement included the following three principles for national unification: (1) "unification shall be achieved through independent Korean efforts without being subjected to external imposition or interference; (2) unification shall be achieved through peaceful means, and not through the use of force against each other; and (3) as a homogeneous people, a broad national unity shall be sought above all, transcending differences in ideas, ideologies, and systems."

The statement pledged "to ease tension and foster an atmosphere of mutual trust between the south and the north." Both sides agreed not to "slander or defame each other" or "undertake avowed provocative measures to prevent inadvertent military incidents," and that each side would carry out "various exchanges in many fields" to restore severed ties, promote mutual understanding and to expedite independent peaceful unification."

In order to achieve these objectives, the statement said that a political dialogue between Seoul and Pyongyang would begin. *See also:* NORTH-SOUTH POLITICAL COORDINATING COMMITTEE.

JUNE 29TH DEMOCRATIZATION DECLARATION, THE. Issued in 1987 by Roh Tae-woo, then chairman of the ruling Democratic Justice Party and its presidential candidate, it included the following points.

1. The constitution should be expeditiously amended to adopt a direct presidential election system, and presidential elections should be held under a new constitution to realize a peaceful transfer of power in February 1988.
2. The Presidential Election Law should be revised so that freedom of candidacy and fair competition are guaranteed.
3. Antagonisms and confrontations must be resolutely eradicated not only from our political community, but also from all other sectors to achieve grand national reconciliation and unity. Kim Dae-jung should be given amnesty and his civil rights restored, and all those who are being detained in connection with the political situation should also be set free, except those who have committed treason.
4. Human dignity must be respected even more greatly and the basic rights of citizens should be promoted and protected to the maximum.
5. The freedom of the press and the relevant systems and practices must be drastically improved.

6. Freedom and self-regulation must be guaranteed to the maximum. . . . Colleges and universities . . . must be made self-governing and educational autonomy in general must be expeditiously put into practice.
7. A political climate conducive to dialogue and compromise must be created expeditiously, with healthy activities of political parties guaranteed.
8. Bold social reform must be carried out to build a clean and honest society.

At the end of his speech, Roh Tae-woo said he was confident that President Chun and the DJP members would accept his proposals. But he added: "If they fail to be accepted, however, I want to make it very clear that I will resign from all public duties, including the presidential candidacy and the chairmanship of the Democratic Justice Party."

-K-

KANG YOUNG-HOON (1922–). Born in Ch'angsŏng, North of P'yŏngan Province, Kang graduated from the Manchukuo National University. Returning home at the end of the Pacific War, he joined the Korean army. Rising in rank during the Korean War, he served as a division commander in 1953. In 1958, he studied at the U.S. Army Command and General Staff College.

In 1959, he became a corps commander, becoming the Commandant of the Korean Military Academy in 1960. He was critical of the military revolutionaries who brought about the May Military Revolution, and retired from the army as Lt. General in 1961, and came to the United States for graduate studies, receiving a doctoral degree in political science from the University of Southern California. He established the Research Institute on Korean Affairs in Silver Spring, Maryland.

Returning to Korea in 1976, Kang became dean of the graduate school of Hanguk University of Foreign Studies in 1977, and from 1978 to 1981 he served as director of the Institute of Foreign Affairs and National Security. He was ambassador to the United Kingdom (1981–84) and to the Holy See (1984–87), and after leaving the Foreign Ministry he was elected to the National Assembly in 1988 as a member of the DJP. In December 1988, he was appointed prime minister, serving in that office until December 1990.

KIM DAE-JUNG (1925–). Born in Kwangju, South Chŏlla Province, Kim graduated from Kŏnguk University in 1953, and earned graduate degrees from Korea and Kyunghee Universities. After that, he became president of a daily newspaper in Mokp'o in 1950, and elected to the National Assembly in 1960 he became spokesman of the Democratic Party in 1963. Reelected to the National Assembly in 1963, he became spokesman for the newly formed Masses Party in 1965, and when the DP and the Masses Party merged into the New Democratic Party in 1967, he became its spokesman.

Kim ran for the presidency in 1971 as the nominee of the NDP, narrowly losing the election. After visiting the United States, where he organized his supporters, in Japan he formed his support groups and bitterly criticized the South Korean government. Then on August 8, 1973 he was abducted by the agents of the Korean CIA to Seoul from Tokyo.

Although he was released from prison, he was arrested many times for his antigovernment activities, and in 1979 he was given the death sentence for his alleged espionage activity. His death sentence was reduced to life term, but he was purged in May 1980, put on trial, and again given the death sentence, this time for his alleged instigation of the Kwangju Uprising. His sentence was reduced to life term, and he was allowed to travel to the United States ostensibly for medical treatment in December 1982.

Returning home in February 1985, he served as co-chairman of the Council for the Promotion of Democracy, and after a brief period of collaboration with Kim Young-sam as a member of the Reunification Democratic Party, he organized his own Party of Peace and Democracy in 1987, becoming its head as well as its presidential candidate. After losing the election, he successfully ran for the National Assembly in 1988, becoming a lawmaker representing the interests of the people in the dissident groups. In the spring of 1991, he brought about merger of his party with the Democratic Party, forming the New Democratic Party. In September of that year, his party merged with the Democratic Party, becoming the new Democratic Party. In May 1992, he was nominated by his party as its presidential candidate. *See also:* COUNCIL FOR THE PROMOTION OF DEMOCRACY; NEW DEMOCRATIC PARTY; PARTY FOR PEACE AND DEMOCRACY; REUNIFICATION DEMOCRATIC PARTY.

KIM HWALLAN (1899–1970). Born to a Christian family, in Inch'ŏn, Kyŏnggi Province, her childhood name was Kidŭk, and she was better known among the Westerners in Korea as Helen Kim. Educated at Ewha Girls' School and becoming a nationalist in 1919, she received higher education in the United States. Receiving her doctoral degree from Columbia University in 1931, she became the first Korean woman to earn a doctorate.

She taught at Ewha Woman's College (now Ewha Woman's University) while promoting Korean women's modernization and nationalist movement during the 1920s and 1930s, and in 1939 she became president of her alma mater in Seoul, serving in that position until 1961.

Kim was a cofounder of the Korean YWCA (founded in 1922), a dedicated educator, a devout Christian, as well as a social reform advocate. After retiring from her presidency of Ewha Woman's University, she devoted her life for Christian and social reform movement, receiving five honorary doctorate degrees. She was the recipient of the Magsaysay Prize of 1963.

KIM JONG-PIL (KIM CHONG-P'IL, 1926–). Popularly known as J.P., he was born in Kongju, South Ch'ungch'ŏng Province. After graduating from Seoul National University in 1947, he enrolled at the Korean Military Academy, graduating as a member of the "8th graduating class" in 1949. Rising in rank to Lt. Colonel, he served in the Army Headquarters G-2 Intelligence Section, and married a niece of Major General Park Chung-hee.

In December 1960, he and other rebellious army officers, who had been contemplating a military *coup* for some time since early 1960, advocated the purification of the army, and he was forced to retire from active military service for his insubordination to his superiors. After that he became a more determined plotter of a military *coup,* bringing about the May 16, 1961 Military Revolution.

Following the military revolution, he established the Korean Central Intelligence Agency, becoming its first director, and when he and his comrades in arms established the Democratic Republican Party in early 1963, he became one of its key leaders. He was elected to the National Assembly in 1963 as chairman of the DRP. Reelected to the National Assembly in 1967, he served as senior adviser to President Park Chung-hee, who was also president of the Democratic Republican Party. Kim himself became vice-president of the DRP in 1971. Appointed to premiership in June 1971, he carried out various programs of the Third Republic until December 1975.

In March 1973, when he and his close associates formed a new political party named the Political Fraternal Society for Revitalizing Reform, Kim became one of its key leaders. Reelected to the National Assembly in 1979, he became the president of the DRP when President Park was assassinated in October. However, he was purged in May 1980, and was often under house arrest.

De-purged in 1987, he reconstructed the then defunct DRP into the New Democratic Republican Party, becoming its head as well as its presidential candidate. He lost the election in December 1987, but in 1988 he was elected to the National Assembly once again. When the party merged with the Democratic Justice and the Reunification Democratic parties, forming the Democratic Liberal Party in February 1990, he became one of its three supreme leaders.

KIM KU (1876–1949). Born in Haeju, Hwanghae Province, he joined the Tonghak movement in 1893. Fleeing to Manchuria in 1895, he joined the contingent of the Righteous Armies unit there, but he returned to Korea to fight the Japanese. Imprisoned for his killing of a Japanese army officer in 1895, he managed to escape from the prison in 1898. He was briefly a Buddhist monk until he joined the Christian church in 1903, teaching at a mission school. In 1911, he was arrested in connection with the so-called 105 Persons Incident, serving a prison term until 1914. After that he was involved in the Rural

Enlightenment Movement until he joined the March First Movement in 1919. (See the Introduction, pages 13–14.)

Fleeing from Korea to Shanghai in 1919, he became one of the founders of the Provisional Government of Korea in exile, serving as its chief of security, minister of home affairs, and then premier. In 1930, he and others formed the Korean Independence Party and directed terroristic activities against the Japanese. In 1935, he established the Korean National Restoration Army in China, and he served as the president of the Provisional Government in Chungking from 1944.

Returning to Korea in October 1945, as head of the Provisional Government with his Korean Independence Party, he and Dr. Syngman Rhee collaborated as leaders of the rightist movement for a while. Kim served as vice-president of the National Council for Rapid Realization of Korean Independence, and vice-chairman of the Representative Democratic Council.

As the controversy grew over the implementation of the U.N. plan to establish a Korean government by having general elections only in the south, he opposed the U.N. plan, as well as that of Dr. Rhee, becoming a bitter political rival and critic of Dr. Rhee. He and others made vain efforts to solve the Korean question by Koreans themselves and prevent the permanent division of Korea. Kim and others even went to Pyongyang and met the North Korean Communists, but they were betrayed by the North Koreans.

Kim refused to take part in the founding of the Republic of Korea, and he was assassinated on June 26, 1949 by an army officer. *See also:* KOREAN INDEPENDENCE PARTY; NATIONAL COUNCIL FOR RAPID REALIZATION OF KOREAN INDEPENDENCE; REPRESENTATIVE DEMOCRATIC COUNCIL.

KIM KYU-SHIK (1881–1950). Born into a poverty-stricken family near Pusan, he became an orphan at the age of nine when his widower-father died. With the help of Dr. Horace G. Underwood, an American Presbyterian educational missionary, he was able to study at Roanoke College in Virginia from 1896. Returning home in 1904, he worked as Dr. Underwood's private secretary while teaching at the Korean YMCA in Seoul and at a mission school.

He became an elder in a Presbyterian church in Seoul, and worked for Korean independence while teaching English at Paejae College in 1911–1912. Fleeing from the Japanese police, in 1912 he went to Manchuria, ending up in Shanghai in 1918 where he met many Korean nationalists and became one of the leaders of the Korean Independence Movement.

In Paris in January 1919 as a representative of the Korean YMCA, he solicited the help of Western powers for the Korean cause, and when the Provisional Government of Korea in exile was established in April he was appointed as foreign minister, continuing his work for Korea in Paris. In May 1919, he presented the "Petition of the Korean People and Nation for Liberation from Japan and for the Reconstitution of Korea as an Independent State" and the "Claims of the Korean People and Nation" to the Paris Peace Conference. When the Provisional Government of Korea was reorganized, he was named the minister of education and was sent to Washington as chairman of the Korean Commission to work with Dr. Syngman Rhee, who as president of the Provisional Government of Korea created the Korean Commission in Washington in 1919. Kim Kyu-shik arrived in Washington in September 1919 and remained in the United States until early 1921.

After his return to Shanghai, he served in the Provisional Government of Korea in various capacities while endeavoring to bring about the unity of the Korean nationalists. In 1930, he and his colleagues formed the Anti-Japanese United League of the Koreans in China, and in 1935 they organized the Nationalist Revolutionary Party to lead the united anti-Japanese struggle of the Koreans. In 1944, he became vice-president of the Provisional Government of Korea in Chungking, China.

Kim Kyu-shik and other members of the Provisional Government returned to Korea in November 1945. A moderate nationalist, Kim and a moderate liberalist leftist formed the Coalition Committee for Cooperation Between the Rightists and the Leftists. When the American occupation authorities established the SKILA in 1946, Kim was appointed its chairman. Meanwhile, his opposition to Dr. Syngman Rhee's plan to establish a separate government in South Korea, when it became apparent that the U.N. plan would not work in all Korea, led to the growing antagonism between him and Dr. Rhee.

Kim, along with others who were determined to prevent the permanent partition of Korea, visited Pyongyang in April 1948 to solve the Korean question in cooperation with the North Korean Communists, but they failed to achieve their aims. During the Korean War he was abducted by the North Koreans and taken to the north where he died in 1950.

KIM SANG-HYŎP (1920–). A graduate of Tokyo Imperial University in 1942, he taught at Korea University (1957–62, 1963–70, 1972–82). He served as the minister of education (1962), and president of Korea University (1970–75). Elected to the National Assembly in 1980, he was named prime minister in 1982, resigning in 1983. He served as the president of the Korean Red Cross Society in 1985.

KIM SŎNG-SU (1891–1955). Born into a wealthy landlord family in Koch'ang, North Chŏlla Province, he graduated from Waseda University, Tokyo, in 1914. In 1915, he took over a secondary school for boys (Chung'ang) in Seoul, becoming its principal in 1917. He and his brothers established a textile firm named Seoul Spinning and Weaving Company in 1919, contributing to the development of nationalistic entrepreneurial ventures.

In 1920, he established a new Korean-language daily newspaper press, publishing the *Tong-a Daily* and other Korean-language materials for the purpose of maintaining Korean nationalistic spirit. After taking over Posŏng College in 1932, Kim became its president, training Korean youths in modern law and commercial studies.

In 1947, he and other right-wing political leaders established the Korean (Han'guk) Democratic Party. He served as vice-president of the National Council for Rapid Realization of Korean Independence, and when his party and another party merged into the Democratic Party in 1949, he became one of its top leaders.

In May 1951, Kim was elected by the National Assembly as vice-president of the Republic, replacing Vice-President Yi Si-yŏng who resigned after bitter disputes with Dr. Rhee, but he too resigned from the position in May 1952 after bitterly criticizing the autocratic rule of Dr. Rhee. After that he served as adviser to the Democratic Nationalist Party, championing democracy. *See also:* DEMOCRATIC NATIONALIST PARTY; KOREAN (HAN'GUK) DEMOCRATIC PARTY; NATIONAL COUNCIL FOR RAPID REALIZATION OF KOREAN INDEPENDENCE.

KIM YOUNG-SAM (1927–). Born in Pusan, South Kyŏngsang Province, he graduated from Seoul National University in 1951. He was a progressive element within the Liberal Party, serving as secretary to the prime minister in 1951. Deserting the Liberal Party, he joined the Democratic Party and was elected to the National Assembly in 1954 and 1960. He was reelected to the National Assembly in 1963 as a member of the Civil Rule Party, and in 1967 as a member of the New Democratic Party, serving in the National Assembly until 1980.

Kim served as co-chairman of the Council for Promotion of Democracy in 1984, and when the New Korea Democratic Party was established in 1986 he became its adviser. In 1987, he founded the Reunification Democratic Party, becoming its president, as well as its candidate in the 1987 presidential election. He lost the election, but was elected to the National Assembly in 1988. In June 1989, he visited the Soviet Union, contributing to the development of Seoul-Moscow ties. In February 1990, when his party merged with the Democratic Justice and the New Democratic Republican parties, forming the Democratic Liberal Party, he became one of the three supreme leaders of the new party first, and then its Executive Chairman. In March 1990, he made another visit to Moscow, increasing the ties between Seoul and Moscow. In May 1992, he was nominated by his party as its presidential candidate. *See also:* COUNCIL FOR THE PROMOTION OF DEMOCRACY; NEW DEMOCRATIC PARTY; REUNIFICATION DEMOCRATIC PARTY.

KŎCH'ANG INCIDENT. *See:* HAMP'YŎNG-KŎCH'ANG INCIDENTS.

KOREA ADVANCED INSTITUTE OF SCIENCE AND TECHNOLOGY. Under the agreement signed in 1965 between the American and South Korean governments, a nonprofit research organization named the Korea Institute of Science and Technology (KIST) was established in 1966 for the promotion of science and technology through the conduct and encouragement of scientific research and development. A major portion of the KIST funds was provided by the U.S. government, and with a large number of well-trained scientists and technicians, most of whom were educated abroad, the KIST contributed much toward South Korea's industrial development through its research and technology transfer in cooperation with the United States.

In 1970, the South Korean government, feeling the acute need for a pool of experts in the field of science and technology, reorganized the KIST as the Korea Advanced Institute of Science and Technology (KAIST). The KAIST, while expanding its research programs, established a graduate school exclusively for physical science and engineering, training a large number of high-level scientists and engineers.

KOREA DEVELOPMENT INSTITUTE. A private think tank, funded by the government but with considerable independence in operation, was established in 1970 under a charter to conduct research and analysis on a systematic basis on matters relating to the national economy as a whole and to specific problems of particular sectors. While making studies on past performances of the economy, the KDI provides professional advice to the Economic Planning Board of the government and makes economic forecasts.

With a large number of foreign-trained, economic specialists on its staff, the KDI publishes various reports on the economic performance of the nation, and it is expected to play an even larger role in the future.

KOREA INSTITUTE OF SCIENCE AND TECHNOLOGY. *See:* KOREA ADVANCED INSTITUTE OF SCIENCE AND TECHNOLOGY.

KOREA TRADE PROMOTION ASSOCIATION (KOTRA). A government agency established in 1962 for the purpose of promoting exports. It participates in international trade fairs, sends trade missions overseas, provides information to foreign businesspeople and firms, and displays Korean products at the World Trade Center in Seoul. It has 90 branch offices around the world.

KOREAN ARMISTICE AGREEMENT. An agreement signed on July 27, 1953 between the U.N. Command and North Korean and Chinese representatives, ending the fighting in Korea. However, South Korea refused to sign the agreement which established the then existing battle line as a cease-fire (military demarcation) line and designated a 1-1/2 mile area on each side of the line as a demilitarized zone (DMZ). The cease-fire line is some 150 miles long, zig-zagging from sea to sea. *See also:* DEMILITARIZED ZONE (DMZ); KOREAN WAR; MILITARY DEMARCATION (CEASE-FIRE, TRUCE) LINE; NEUTRAL NATIONS SUPERVISORY COMMISSION.

KOREAN COMMUNIST PARTY. In September 1945, Pak Hŏn-yŏng and others reconstituted a Communist party named Chosŏn Kongsandang, which had been broken up by the Japanese soon after it emerged in 1925. On its revival, it formed many of its subordinate labor and social organizations to promote Socialism in South Korea.

In November 1946, the Korean Communist Party was reorganized into the South Korean Workers' Party (Namchosŏn Nodongdang) by uniting two other leftist parties under the leadership of Hŏ Hŏn and Pak Hŏn-yŏng. This occurred after the North Korean Bureau of the Korean Communist Party and the New People's Party in North Korea merged to form the North Korean Workers' Party in July. In 1947, following the crackdown of the American military government against the South Korean Workers' Party (SKWP) and its affiliated organizations, which came about because of their illegal activities—including the printing of counterfeit money by the press (Chŏngp'ansa) of the SKWP—the leadership group of the party fled to the north and many of its members went underground in the south in order to continue their activity. Their subversive actions led to the rebellion on Cheju Island and the Yŏsu-Sunch'ŏn Rebellion.

Under the control of Korean Communist Party (later SKWP) were: the National Council of Labor Unions, the General

League of Korean Women, the National Federation of Farmers' Unions, and the General Federation of Democratic Korean Youth.

In October 1949, the South Korean government outlawed the SKWP and its subordinate organs. However, many Communists, who went underground, continued their subversive activities. *See also:* CHEJU REBELLION; NATIONAL ASSEMBLY SPY RING CASE; YŎSU-SUNCH'ŎN REBELLION.

KOREAN DEMOCRATIC PARTY. In September 1945, the right-wing nationalists in North Korea formed the party whose Korean name was Chosŏn Minjudang, and they struggled against the Communists there, maintaining an antitrusteeship stand under the leadership of Cho Man-shik, an elder in the Presbyterian church in Pyongyang.

When the Soviets put Cho under house arrest and cracked down on the rightist organizations, because of their opposition to the Moscow Agreement, its leaders brought the party to the south. Eventually it was broken up as its members joined other opposition parties in South Korea. *See also:* MOSCOW AGREEMENT.

KOREAN EDUCATIONAL DEVELOPMENT INSTITUTE (KEDI). Established in 1972 as an autonomous educational research and development organization its purpose was the development of high-quality education in South Korea by undertaking comprehensive and systematic research and development activities on educational goals, content, and methodology, and formulating education policies and recommending them to the Ministry of Education.

KOREAN FEDERATION OF TEACHERS' LABOR UNIONS (KFTLU). Following the fall of the First Republic, labor unions of all kinds were formed. In May 1960, some 300 primary and secondary school teachers and college professors formed this federation in order to launch a more aggressive movement to promote the welfare of the teachers and protect their rights. The Ministry of Education immediately outlawed these unions and their federation, but it was not until May 1961 that these unions together with their federation were dissolved by the military junta. *See also:* FEDERATION OF KOREAN EDUCATION ASSOCIATIONS; LABOR MOVEMENT; NATIONAL TEACHERS' UNION.

KOREAN (HAN'GUK) DEMOCRATIC PARTY. In September 1945, conservative right-wing leaders in South Korea formed a political party called Han'guk Minjudang in Korean under the leadership of Song Chin-u, Chang Tŏk-su, and Kim Sŏng-su. The list of its leadership included nearly all prominent right-wing leaders in the south. After Song was assassinated in 1945 and Chang in 1947, Kim led the party as the major opposition party in 1948. In February 1949, it merged with another party, forming the Democratic Nationalist Party. *See also:* DEMOCRATIC NATIONALIST PARTY.

KOREAN HISTORY RESEARCH SOCIETY. Founded in September 1988 by new generation historians who desire to throw off the restraints imposed by a conservative view of Korean history, it advocates the study of Korean history based on a "scientific methodology" and sees the masses (*minjung*) as the agents of social transformation and progress.

KOREAN INDEPENDENCE PARTY. An extreme right-wing political party formed in China by Kim Ku in 1930, advocating violent struggle for Korean independence against the Japanese. It relocated to South Korea when Korea was liberated, but after the assassination of Kim Ku in June 1949, its party members abandoned it and joined other parties. The party was reorganized in October 1963, but it failed to become a dynamic and popular party. *See also:* KIM KU.

KOREAN NATIONAL COUNCIL OF WOMEN (KNCW). *See:* WOMEN'S MOVEMENT.

KOREAN NATIONAL WRITERS' UNION. Formed in September 1987 by some 500 liberal playwrights, novelists, and poets, its aim is to promote what it called people's (*minjung*) literature to bring about national unification.

KOREAN NATIONAL YOUTH CORPS. An ultra-rightist youth organization, known in Korean as Chosŏn Minjok

Ch'ŏngnyŏndan, or Chokch'ŏng for short, was organized in October 1946 by Gen. Yi Pŏm-sŏk, a military leader who returned from China in 1945. Its primary aim was to combat the Communists and other leftists who supported the Moscow Agreement. Dr. Syngman Rhee and Kim Ku were its honorary chairmen, and at one point, the corps claimed over one million members. When the Republic of Korea was inaugurated, it changed its name to Taehan Minjok Ch'ŏngnyŏndan, and rendered strong support to Dr. Rhee until 1956 when Yi Pŏm-sŏk withdrew from the Liberal Party. *See also:* YI PŎM-SŎK.

KOREAN NATIONALIST PARTY. (Party of the Moderate Nationalists) In September 1945, An Chae-hong and other moderate Nationalists brought several small political parties together and formed a party whose Korean name was Chosŏn Kungmindang. It was a party of moderate nationalists who broke away from the Committee for the Preparation of National Reconstruction. However, gradually, the members of the party withdrew their support, joining other parties, and when An became the Civil Administrator of the South Korean Interim Government in July 1947, the party was virtually dissolved. *See also:* AN CHAE-HONG; SOUTH KOREAN INTERIM GOVERNMENT.

KOREAN NATIONALIST PARTY. (Party of Right-Wing Politicians) In November 1949, several small groups of politicians who supported President Rhee formed a new political party named Taehan Kungmindang in Korean, creating intense rivalry with the Democratic Nationalist Party. It was a party of the right-wing politicians led by Yun Ch'i-yŏng. It was dissolved in March, 1952, when the Liberal Party was formally established. *See also:* LIBERAL PARTY.

KOREAN PEOPLE'S PARTY. Following the outlawing of the Korean People's Republic by the American occupation authorities in October 1945, in November Yŏ Un-hyŏng and other moderate leftists organized the Korean People's Party (Chosŏn Inmindang) by uniting several small moderate left-wing political and social groups, advocating socialistic economic reform, and supported the Moscow agreement of the Allies.

After joining the Coalition Committee for Cooperation Between the Rightists and Leftists in May 1946, in October the Korean People's Party and two other moderate leftist parties were united into the Socialist Labor Party (Sahoe Nodongdang), pursuing democratic socialism. When the Korean Communist Party was expanded into the South Korean Workers' Party in November by incorporating two other radical leftist parties, many of the members of the Socialist Labor Party deserted, joining the radical Communist party. Consequently, Yŏ and other moderate leftists reorganized their party into the Working People's Party (Kŭllo Inmindang) in May 1947, pursuing the middle-of-the-road policy and seeking cooperation with the moderate rightists. With the death of Yŏ Un-hyŏng in July 1947 the party collapsed. *See also:* COALITION COMMITTEE FOR CO-OPERATION BETWEEN THE RIGHTISTS AND THE LEFTISTS; KOREAN COMMUNIST PARTY; YŎ UN-HYŎNG.

KOREAN PEOPLE'S REPUBLIC. This republic and its government were established on September 6, 1945 by the "National Assembly," which was convened under the auspices of the Committee for the Preparation of National Reconstruction. The "National Assembly" appointed Dr. Syngman Rhee, who was still in the United States, as chairman of the republic, and Yŏ Un-hyŏng as vice-chairman. It elected Hŏ Hŏn, a prominent leftist, as premier, and it named cabinet ministers. The key cabinet members were: Kim Ku (Internal Affairs), Kim Kyu-shik (Foreign Affairs), Cho Man-shik (Finance), Kim Sŏng-su (Education), Kim Pyŏng-no (Justice), Ha P'il-wŏn (Commerce), and Shin Ik-hŭi (Communications). Its main program included: the establishment of a politically and economically independent nation, the elimination of Japanese collaborators, the realization of a democracy based on fundamental human rights, implementation of social and economic reforms, and maintenance of international peace in close cooperation with friendly nations. However, the republic and its government were outlawed by the U.S. occupation authorities in the south.

KOREAN WAR. This war came when, on June 25, 1950, North Korea launched a well-prepared invasion against South Korea.

Kim Il-sung, premier and chairman of the Korean Workers' Party of North Korea, had been scheming to overthrow the government of the Republic of Korea and annex South Korea ever since the establishment of the two Korean states. In early 1949, Kim Il-sung proposed to Stalin of the Soviet Union an aggressive war against South Korea, but it was only when he realized that Communist uprisings and other subversive activities failed to topple the South Korean government that he finally decided to launch war against South Korea and asked Stalin in February 1950 for his permission to do so. After receiving a green light from Stalin, sometime in March or April, 1950, and new Soviet military advisors arrived, Kim proceeded to start the war with massive Soviet military aid.

The North Korean Communists called their aggression the "war to liberate the southern half of the Republic from American imperialists and their puppets." Initially some 80,000 of 165,000 North Korean troops, supported by Soviet-built tanks, crossed the 38th parallel. Shortly after that, more troops of the People's Army of North Korea crossed over. Three days later, on June 28, the North Koreans captured Seoul, the South Korean capital, forcing the South Korean government to flee first to Taejŏn and then to Taegue and finally to Pusan. North Korean troops pushed southward, encountering minor resistance.

When South Korea, which was taken by surprise with only 67,000 ill-equipped and poorly trained troops and faced with the threat to its very existence, requested military assistance of the United States, the American government ordered U.S. troops in Japan to go to Korea in support of South Korean troops. The U.S. forces that arrived on July 1 could not stop the southward push of North Korean troops, and both South Korean and U.S. troops took up their defense positions in the southeastern corner of the peninsula known as "the Pusan perimeter."

In response to the North Korean attack, the U.N. Security Council condemned North Korea as an aggressor and mounted a collective defense action in support of South Korea. When sixteen U.N. member states, including Britain, France, Australia, New Zealand, Greece and Turkey, in addition to the United States, provided military forces, the U.N. Command was set up and American General Douglas MacArthur was named Supreme Commander of the U.N. Forces. The South Korean government put its defense forces under his command as U.N. troops arrived in growing numbers.

Following seaborne landing by the U.N. forces at Inch'ŏn on September 15, on September 26 Seoul was recovered from the North Korean forces, and in early October the U.N. forces moved across the 38th parallel in pursuit of the fleeing enemy, capturing Pyongyang, the North Korean capital, on October 20 as U.N. troops reached the Yalu River. At this juncture, troops of the Chinese Liberation Army, which had been prepared to enter Korea from Manchuria for some time, joined the North Korean forces in combat, bringing "an entirely new war" as Gen. MacArthur called it. Initially some 250,000 Chinese troops entered North Korea in mid-October, but soon after that over one million Chinese troops were engaged in military actions in the Korean War. A recently published report in Russia revealed that some 70,000 Russian airmen were involved in the Korean War from November 1950, flying MIG-15 and other Soviet planes, wearing Chinese uniforms, and with their air bases in Manchuria.

The massive counter-attack launched by the Chinese forces around October 25 against the U.N. forces brought about the withdrawal of the U.N. forces from the Yalu River region as well as other areas. As U.N. troops withdrew southward, the Communist forces came across the 38th parallel. Seoul fell for the second time on January 4, 1951, as the U.N. forces set up their defense line just south of the city of Wŏnju, some one hundred miles south of Seoul.

The counterattacks launched by the U.N. forces in February pushed the enemy northward, and on March 15, Seoul was recovered and the U.N. forces crossed the 38th parallel once again in early April. However, a stalemate developed as see-saw battles ensued. Meanwhile, Lt. Gen. Matthew B. Ridgway was appointed Supreme Commander of the U.N. Forces, replacing Gen. MacArthur who was dismissed by President Truman.

In April 1951, the Chinese launched a ferocious attack as a means to end the war, but it failed to achieve its objective. Meanwhile, the United States, which was unwilling to invite the Soviet Union and China into the Korean conflict directly, wished to end the fighting somehow despite the South Korean president's wish to destroy North Korea completely and unify Korea. Thus, when on June 23, Yakov Malik, the Soviet ambassador to the United Nations, called for a cease-fire, and when the Chinese voiced their desire for a cease-fire two days later, the U.S. government welcomed the opportunity to initiate truce talks, and instructed Gen. Ridgway to arrange meetings with the Communists to achieve this.

Armistice negotiations began on July 10, 1951, at Kaesŏng, a South Korean city taken over by North Koreans, but the talks dragged on until on August 23 the Communists suspended negotiations. Talks were resumed at Panmunjom on October 25, but various issues prevented any progress toward an armistice. Meanwhile, fighting continued as issues related to Communist prisoners-of-war and the location of a truce line troubled both sides. As the United States was anxious to end the "wrong war at the wrong place," President Rhee expressed his strong feelings against a cease-fire, advocating a complete victory against the Communists. Such a stand by President Rhee led the U.S. government even to contemplate his removal from the presidency by a military coup.

Gen. Dwight Eisenhower who assumed office as the new president of the United States in January 1953 was anxious to end the fighting, but he was not in favor of the U.S. taking drastic action against Rhee. As a result, he agreed with Rhee to sign a mutual defense treaty between the United States and South Korea and that the Korean question be solved by political means at a conference at Geneva at a later date. Despite such an agreement, in June 1953 President Rhee ordered South Korean guards at Communist prisoner-of-war camps at Pusan and other places to release North Korean prisoners-of-war who did not wish to be repatriated. Some 25,000 of them were freed without the knowledge or approval of the U.N. Commander. Such an action not only angered the Americans, but also the North Koreans. However, the threat made by President Eisenhower that the United States might use atomic weapons to end the war, together with the death of Stalin in March 1953, led the Communists to resume cease-fire negotiations.

The Korean armistice was signed on July 27, 1953, by Gen.

William K. Harrison, representing the U.N. Command, Gen. Nam Il, representing North Korea, and Gen. Peng Te-huai, representing the "volunteers" of the Chinese People's Liberation Army. South Korea refused to sign, however. With the signing of the truce, the 150-mile-long zig-zagging truce (military demarcation) line was established, and on each side of the line a mile-and-half (two kilometers) wide demilitarized zone (DMZ) was set up. At the same time, Panmunjom, where the truce was signed, was designated as a neutral zone where the Neutral Nations Armistice Supervisory Commission and the Military Armistice Commission established their headquarters. Whereas the Neutral Nations Armistice Supervisory Commission, composed of those U.N. member nations which did not take part in the Korean War, was established to supervise observance of the terms of the armistice by the former belligerents, the Military Armistice Commission, composed of the representatives of North Korea, China, and the U.N. Command, was established to deal with any problems rising between the two former belligerents.

With the armistice, North Korea lost a sizeable amount of mountainous area in the east while gaining a small but fertile rice growing area in the west, including the city of Kaesŏng. When the truce was signed, the sixteen U.N. member states which fought the war declared that they would fight again if the Communists renewed their aggression.

Exchange of prisoners-of-war was carried out under supervision of the U.N. Neutral Nations Repatriation Commission in the name of "Operation Big Switch" that began on August 5. It saw the handing over of 75,823 Communist prisoners-of-war (5,640 were Chinese) who wished to be repatriated. The Communist side turned over 12,773 U.N. prisoners-of-war (3,597 American, 7,862 South Koreans, and 1,112 other U.N. troops). The remaining 22,606 prisoners-of-war were held under the custody of the Neutral Nations Repatriation Commission pending their decision on repatriation. Of these, some 22,118 Communists (mostly Chinese) who did not wish to be repatriated elected to settle either in South Korea or Taiwan. Of the U.N. prisoners-of-war, only 349 refused repatriation while only 137 Communists wished to be repatriated. The Chinese People's Liberation Army troops withdrew from

North Korea toward the end of 1953 while a sizeable number of U.N. troops (mainly American) remained in South Korea.

The Korean War caused heavy property damage and a large number of casualties on both sides. Of some 1.3 million U.S. troops who served in the Korean War, 33,625 were killed, 105,785 were wounded, and several hundred were reported missing. The South Korean Army lost 225,784 men and 717,170 were wounded. Some 2,186 other U.N. troops were killed and 10,117 were wounded. In South Korea, some 373,500 civilians were killed, more than 225,600 wounded, and over 387,740 were listed as missing. The war produced some one million orphans and 600,000 war widows in South Korea alone. During the Communist occupation of Seoul, 128,936 civilians were massacred by the Communists and 84,523 were taken captive to North Korea. When the Communists retreated from Seoul, a large number of artists and writers who were pro-North Korean defected to the North.

The casualties on the part of North Korean troops was established to be 294,151 dead, 229,849 wounded, and 91,206 missing. It was estimated that some 900,000 Chinese troops were either killed or wounded. Some 406,000 North Korean civilians were reported to have been killed, 1,594,000 were wounded, and 680,000 were missing. Over 1.5 million North Koreans fled to the South during the war.

The Korean War was a national tragedy of the Korean people. It achieved nothing other than causing property destruction, loss of life, and great human suffering. It made peaceful settlement for Korean unification more difficult as it fostered deep roots of hatred between the north and the south. *See also:* DEMILITARIZED ZONE (DMZ); GENEVA POLITICAL CONFERENCE; THE KOREAN ARMISTICE; U.S.-SOUTH KOREA MUTUAL DEFENSE TREATY; U.S.-SOUTH KOREA STATUS-OF-FORCES AGREEMENT.

KOREAN WOMEN'S ASSOCIATION OF WOMEN'S STUDIES. *See:* WOMEN'S MOVEMENT.

KOREAN WOMEN'S NATIONALIST PARTY. *See:* WOMEN'S MOVEMENT.

KOREAN WOMEN'S SOCIETY. *See:* WOMEN'S MOVEMENT.

KOREAN YOUTH CORPS. *See:* KOREAN NATIONAL YOUTH CORPS.

KWANGJU UPRISING. Following the violent student demonstrations in Seoul on May 14, 1980 the government extended martial law which had been declared on October 26, 1979 to the entire country on May 17, 1980, banned all political activities, and arrested many leading political leaders, including Kim Dae-jung. Kim Dae-jung was charged with the crime of inciting the students. Angered by such government action, the dissident groups in the city of Kwangju in South Chŏlla Province rose in violent protests, clashing with the police.

When the situation in Kwangju got out of control and demonstrations against the government spread into other nearby cities and towns, troops were sent in to crush what the government regarded as a rebellion, only provoking the people in Kwangju more. A violent protest movement became an open uprising as the demonstrators attacked police stations, other government buildings, and small military units, confiscating weapons. A bloody rebellion ensued.

A special paratrooper unit was sent in to put down the rebellion, causing many deaths. Although the official estimate of the number of people killed was around 200, the local people claimed that more than 2,000 were killed. The Kwangju Uprising ended on May 27, 1980.

On April 1988, following the fall of the Fifth Republic, the government of the Sixth Republic redesignated the 1980 Kwangju Uprising as a "part of the democratization efforts of the students and citizens in Kwangju," and publicly apologized for failing to provide a satisfactory solution for the Uprising. In June, the National Assembly set up a Special Committee for the Investigation of the Kwangju Incident, and eventually the government agreed to provide monetary compensation to the families of the victims and erect a proper monument in honor of the dead.

-L-

LABOR MANAGEMENT COUNCIL. *See:* LABOR MOVEMENT.

LABOR MOVEMENT. The organized labor movement, which was developed in the mid-1920s by the leftists, was crushed by the Japanese colonial regime after 1931. When Korea was liberated from Japan, the leftists quickly took the initiative in developing the labor movement by forming labor unions, and in November 1945 they established the National Council of Labor Unions (Chŏn'guk Nodong Chohap P'yŏngyŭihoe, or Chŏnp'yŏng). In order to combat the leftist labor movement, the right-wing labor unions were organized, and in March 1946 the General Alliance of Laborers for Rapid Realization of Korean Independence (Taehan Tongnip Ch'oksŏng Nodong Ch'ongyŏnmaeng, or Taehan Noch'ong) was formed with Dr. Syngman Rhee as its president and Kim Ku as its vice-president.

The Korean labor movement was highly politicized due to the colonial situation in which Korea was placed during the Japanese colonial period, the partition of Korea, and the growing antagonism between the rightists and the leftists. The Moscow Agreement of the Allies only made the labor movement more political with the rightists opposing it and the leftists supporting it.

As the leftists brought about a general railway workers' strike in the fall of 1946, bloody clashes took place between the members of the Taehan Noch'ong and the Chŏnp'yŏng throughout the fall and winter of 1946 and in the spring of 1947. It was followed by a nationwide railway, factory, and communication workers' strike sponsored by the Communists in March 1947.

Following the emigration of the leaders of the South Korean Workers' Party to the north in the fall of 1947, and the implementation of antileftist measures by the new government after August 1948, the leftist labor movement was drastically weakened, but the rightist labor federation became badly split between those who were allies of the Rhee administration and those who advocated a pure labor movement. The conflict between these two groups grew more vicious when the head of the Taehan Noch'ong became minister of social affairs in 1948 and the top leadership of the Taehan Noch'ong consisted of pro-Rhee elements. Meanwhile, the name of the Taehan Noch'ong changed to the General Federation of Korean Labor Unions, claiming over 3 million membership. The Taehan Noch'ong had become a tool of the government first, and then that of the Liberal Party after 1952, playing more of a political role rather than promoting the welfare of the laboring class.

The labor strikes of the workers at Chosŏn Spinning and Weaving Company in Pusan in March 1952, followed by the dock workers' strike in Pusan in July, led the National Assembly to enact four labor laws: a labor standard law, a labor dispute mediation law, a labor commission law, and a labor union law. But labor strikes and labor unions entering into separate negotiations with the management were banned. Nonetheless, the growing labor unrest brought about the strikes of the workers at Taehan Spinning and Weaving Company in Taegu in May 1955 and February 1956, the cement factory workers in Samch'ŏk in December 1956, the workers at Chosŏn Spinning and Weaving Company in Pusan in January 1958, and the workers at Taehan Shipbuilding Corporation in November 1958.

In October 1959, those who advocated the development of a pure and democratic labor movement formed a new National Council of Labor Unions (Chŏn'guk Nodong Chohap Hyŏpŭihoe, or Chŏn'guk Nohyŏp) in Pusan, and brought about a labor strike at Chosŏn Spinning and Weaving Company in Pusan in March 1960. It was followed by the emergence of the Korean Federation of Teachers' Unions (dissolved in May 1961), of primary and secondary school teachers and college professors in May 1960, and the establishment of the National Labor Union of Bank Employees in July. In order to unify the labor movement and strengthen it, in November 1960 the Taehan Noch'ong and the Chŏn'guk Nohyŏp merged into the General Federation of Korean Labor Unions (Han'guk Nodong Chohap Ch'ongyŏnmaeng, or Han'guk Noryŏn), which included 1,000 labor unions. It was dissolved in May 1961 when the military revolution took place, but it was reestablished in August as a new federation of labor unions commonly known as Han'guk Noryŏn, composed of some 1,035 separate trade unions. Meanwhile, in August 1961, the government established the Association of Agricultural Cooperatives (Nongŏp Hyŏptong Chohap, or Nonghyŏp).

The Supreme Council for National Reconstruction revised the labor union law in December 1963, making labor unions self-supporting and restricting their activity. Labor strikes were banned as before. South Korean labor laws prohibited the development of a true labor movement, and as a result many unions went out of existence, reducing the number of trade unions to 420 and the membership to 260,000 by 1965. The government tightened its control over the labor movement even more after 1965, further weakening it following the protest made by the Han'guk Noryŏn against the labor law and a wage dispute of the employees at government monopoly industries (ginseng and tobacco) in December 1963.

The leaders of the Noryŏn made various efforts to bring about the revision of the labor law without much success. In November 1970 a labor leader demanding higher wages and improvement of working conditions in a dramatic gesture of protest set himself afire and died. The incident was followed by violent labor strikes at Hyundai shipyard in September 1974, that of the Tongil Spinning and Weaving Company in Pusan of February-March 1978, and that of the female workers of the YH Trading Company in Seoul in August 1979. Then in April 1980, some 700 coal mine workers at Sabuk and over 1,000 workers at Tongguk Steel Works in Pusan carried out violent strikes, demanding higher wages. Subsequently, some 500 labor disputes erupted until martial law of May 17, 1980 was proclaimed and a large number of labor union leaders were purged.

During the Fifth Republic (1981–88), the government continued its suppressive measures against the labor movement, but beginning with the labor strike of the workers at Kuro Industrial Estate in 1985, labor unrest continued to grow with an increasing number of wage disputes including that of the taxi drivers in Seoul in the spring of 1987.

The watershed in the labor movement came in July and August, 1987, immediately following the publication of the statement concerning domestic reforms by the then presidential candidate Roh Tae-woo on June 29. The labor strike which began at Hyundai Motors at Ulsan on July 5, 1987, was followed by some 3,200 labor strikes that occurred during the months of July and August. The largest-ever number (3,749) of labor strikes occurred in 1987, some 3,500 of them after June 29. This represented 18 times as many labor disputes as there had been in the 12 years since 1975. After June 29, 1987, the number of labor unions increased from 2,658 to 4,086 in 1987, 6,142 in 1988 and 7,500 in 1989. The number of labor union members increased from 900,000 before 1987 to 1,800,000 in 1989.

The major issues in the labor disputes were those of wage and working conditions. In order to deal with the rapidly growing labor problems, the National Assembly adopted the new Labor Standard Law, the Labor Union Law, and other laws concerning labor in October 1987. These laws allowed the formation of labor unions and simplified the procedures for establishing a union. With this, the new General Federation of Korean Trade Unions (Han'guk Nodong Chohap Ch'ongyŏnmaeng, or Noch'ong) was established.

Meanwhile, the government of the Fifth Republic at its twilight encouraged the establishment of labor-management councils for the betterment of the relations between the two. As a result, a total of 6,596 such councils were established by the end of November 1987, reducing the number of labor disputes to 1,686 in 1988 and 1,560 in 1989 following the establishment of the Sixth Republic in 1988. In order to reduce the labor problems, the National Assembly adopted a two-tiered Minimum Wage Law in January 1988 and the Equality Law of Male and Female Employees, effective April 1, to ensure equal opportunity and equal treatment for female workers. At the same time, labor wages rose by 10.1% in 1987, 15.5% in 1988 and 18.8% in 1989.

The radical labor leaders, who advocated the development of a genuine labor union movement, regarded the General Federation of Korean Trade Unions as a government-manipulated organization. Consequently, they launched a "democratic labor movement," and supported the establishment of a new National Teachers' Union in 1989 despite the government ban against the organization of labor unions by school teachers. The radical labor leaders formed a new federation tentatively named National Council of Labor Unions (Chŏn'guk Nodong Chohap Hyŏpŭihoe, or Chŏnnohyŏp) in January 1990 and some 400,000 workers were reported to have joined the new Council.

LAND REFORM LAW. Promulgated on June 12, 1949, the law provided for government purchase of all (except half an acre) of farmlands not cultivated by the owners themselves and all holdings of more than 7.5 acres, irrespective of whether they were cultivated by the owners or not. Certain lands (special crop-growing areas such as orchards, sapling gardens, and mulberry trees) were exempt from the 7.5 acre limitation as were lands cultivated by religious and educational institutions.

The government paid 150% of the current market price to the sellers, and sold the lands to farmers at 125% of the current land price. Those who could not pay for the land could purchase on an installment plan, paying in cash or in crops. The land reform program was interrupted by the Korean War, but it was completed in 1964. Some 25 million acres of farmlands were sold to the farmers who had little or no land. Whereas small farmers who sold land to the government received an additional 30% compensation, poor farmers who bought the land were given a 30% subsidy by the government. With the implementation of this law, traditional absentee landlordism was abolished.

LAW CONCERNING EXTRAORDINARY MEASURES FOR NATIONAL RECONSTRUCTION. This law, divided into four chapters and 22 articles followed by a supplementary provision, was promulgated on June 6, 1961 for the purpose of national reconstruction.

Chapter I dealt with the establishment of the Supreme Council for National Reconstruction "for the reconstruction of the Republic of Korea as a genuine, democratic republic, in order to safeguard the Republic of Korea against Communist aggression, and to overcome the national crisis resulting from corruption, injustices, and poverty." It defined the Supreme Council for National Reconstruction as having the status of the supreme ruling organ of the Republic, pending the establishment of a civilian government following the recomposition of the National Assembly. The basic rights of the citizens were allowed only when they did not have any conflict with the fulfillment of the tasks of the revolution.

Chapter II dealt with the composition of the Supreme Council, Chapter III dealt with the authority of the Supreme Council, and Chapter IV covered "miscellaneous provisions," including the methods of amendment to this law.

LAW CONCERNING LABOR UNIONS. *See:* LABOR MOVEMENT.

LAW CONCERNING PUNISHMENT OF THOSE WHO COMMITTED CRIMES AGAINST THE PEOPLE. Commonly known as the anti-traitor law, it was promulgated in September 1948 to punish those who committed crimes against the people in collusion with the Japanese between 1910 and 1945. Under the law, the Special Investigation Committee for Acts Against the People was established. After much debate and haphazard endeavors to punish traitors (*minjok pan'yŏkcha*), the law and the committee were abolished in August 1949.

LAW CONCERNING THE LABOR COMMISSION. *See:* LABOR MOVEMENT.

LAW CONCERNING THE LABOR STANDARD. *See:* LABOR MOVEMENT.

LAW CONCERNING THE MEDIATION OF LABOR DISPUTES. *See:* LABOR MOVEMENT.

LAW CONCERNING THE RESTRICTION OF THE CIVIL LIBERTIES OF THOSE WHO COMMITTED ANTI-DEMOCRATIC ACTS. This law No. 587, dated December 31, 1960, was adopted by the National Assembly to deprive of civil rights those who performed "notably anti-democratic acts" prior to April 26, 1960. Many political leaders (most of whom were members of the Liberal Party), police officers, and high military personnel who were investigated, lost their civil rights under this law.

LEAGUE FOR THE PROTECTION OF WOMEN'S RIGHTS. *See:* WOMEN'S MOVEMENT.

LEGISLATIVE COUNCIL FOR NATIONAL SECURITY (LCNS). Shortly after the public referendum on a new constitution in October 1980, the National Assembly was replaced by the 81-member Legislative Council for National Security, whose members were appointed by President Chun. It served as the legislative arm of the Special Committee for National Security Measures, and after adopting various crucial laws, including the revised National Security Law which incorporated the Anti-Communism Law, and following the general elections for the National Assembly on March 25, 1981, the LCNS was dissolved on March 31.

LIBERAL PARTY. Two of pro-Rhee conservative political groups emerged in December 1951, each calling itself Liberal Party. One belonged to the National Assembly members, and the other belonged to those who were not. However, in March 1952, these two were united into a single Liberal Party, exercising enormous power in collusion with the Rhee administration. The united party elected Dr. Rhee as its president and Yi Pŏm-sŏk as its vice-president.

The Liberal Party was crippled when the April Student Uprising occurred, and after the fall of the First Republic it barely maintained its existence. It was dissolved in May 1961 by the military revolutionaries, but in January 1963 it was reestablished under the leadership of Chang T'aek-sang. It made no attempt to win the presidency in the 1963 and 1967 presidential elections. Its members ran for the National Assembly, but all failed to win seats. *See also:* CHANG T'AEK-SANG; APRIL STUDENT UPRISING; SYNGMAN RHEE; YI PŎM-SŎK.

LOCAL AUTONOMY. Although Articles 96 and 97 of the Constitution enacted on July 12, 1948 stated that local autonomy would be operated under local assemblies, the Rhee administration was either unwilling or reluctant to proceed with its implementation. It was President Rhee's determination to appoint all provincial governors and the mayor of the Special City of Seoul. However, on June 17, 1949, the National Assembly adopted the local autonomy bill (revised in December), and elections for the establishment of local governments and their councils were to be held in December 1950. The 1949 law governing local autonomous organizations specified that the mayor of Seoul and provincial governors were to be appointed by the president; mayors of other cities, chiefs of towns and townships were to be elected by respective local councils; and provincial councils, those of Seoul and other cities, and towns and townships were to be established by direct elections of the inhabitants. County chiefs were to be appointed by governors in the respective provinces. However, because of the war that broke out in June 1950, it was not until April and May 1952 that elections for autonomous organizations of provinces, cities, towns and townships were held in South Korea, except in Seoul and one other city, three towns, and 140 townships in northern districts. In these elections conducted in 1950, 378 councilmen of 17 municipal councils, 1,115 councilmen of 272 town councils, 16,051 councilmen of 1,308 township councils were elected.

The local autonomy law was revised twice in 1956 abolishing the previous system of indirect election of mayors of cities, towns, and chiefs of townships. However, it retained the system of appointment of the mayor of Seoul and provincial governors. Under the revised law, elections were held in August to elect new councilmen of all municipalities, including Seoul, provinces, towns, and townships as well as heads of local governmental units, except the mayor of Seoul.

Fearful of the election of his opponent in the forthcoming local elections in August 1960, in December 1958 the Rhee administration and its ally, the Liberal Party, engineered the railroading of the amendment to the local autonomy bill whereby provincial governors, mayors of municipalities and towns, as well as chiefs of townships were to be appointed by the central government. With this, any chance for the development of bona fide local autonomy was destroyed.

The amended local autonomy law went into effect in January

1959, and in February and May the central government appointed all provincial governors, the mayor of Seoul and other cities, and county chiefs. The county chiefs in turn appointed township heads while mayors of cities appointed ward chiefs. Only the chiefs of the precincts in small cities, towns, and townships were elected by their local councils. Under such a system, local government bodies enjoyed little or no autonomy as their financial situation did not allow them to promote local autonomy while the control of the central government increased. The Bureau of Political Affairs of the Ministry of Home Affairs controlled virtually all local affairs, including the allocation of grants in aid, the collection of local taxes and fees, as well as other affairs of local governments.

The Second Republic took measures to establish meaningful local autonomy under the amended Constitution. Thus, it enacted in November 1960 a new local autonomy law, and in early December elections for new councils of Seoul, provinces, cities, towns and townships were carried out. The elections for mayors of cities, excluding Seoul, and chiefs of towns and townships were carried out, followed by the elections for the mayor of Seoul and provincial governors at the end of December.

The May 16, 1961, military revolution "temporarily" suspended the local autonomy law, abolishing all local councils. However, Article 110 of the Constitution amended in 1963 to be that of the Third Republic stated that "The local government authority shall have a council," and Article 109 stated that "The local government authorities shall deal with matters pertaining to the welfare of local residents, manage properties, and may establish, within the limit of laws and ordinances, rules and regulations regarding local government." Nevertheless, the central government of the Third Republic steadfastly refused to reestablish local councils and hold elections to elect local government heads on the grounds that the local areas in South Korea did not have financial self-sufficiency to institute true local autonomy. The doubtless reason of the central government was its unwillingness to decentralize power as President Rhee had been doing during the First Republic. Chapter X of the Constitution amended and approved in a national referendum in November, 1972, to be that of the

Fourth Republic, retained those features regarding local autonomy included in the Constitution amended in 1963, but it decided to postpone the restoration of local autonomy "until reunification" was achieved. Be that as it may, until the collapse of the Fourth Republic in 1979, its central government failed to restore local autonomy for one reason or another. Likewise, the Fifth Republic made no attempt to restore local autonomy.

It was the Sixth Republic that reestablished local autonomy when, in December 1990, the National Assembly enacted three laws related to local autonomy. Accordingly, President Roh announced in early March 1991 that elections for councils of small districts (small cities, counties, towns and townships, and wards in cities) would be held in late March, and that elections for councils of large districts (six special cities and nine provinces) would be held in June.

In the elections for small district councils which were held on March 26, 1991, 10,102 candidates from 3,562 electoral districts ran for 4,304 council seats. In these elections, the new ruling Democratic Liberal Party (the united party of the Democratic Justice, the Unification and Democracy, and the New Democratic Republican parties) won a total of 2,142 seats whereas its major opponent, the Party of Peace and Democracy won only 785 seats, and another minor Democratic Party won only 33 seats. Some 1,343 seats were won by Independents. All small district councils were opened on April 15. In the large district council elections conducted on June 20, 2,873 candidates ran for 866 seats in six special cities and nine provincial councils. As was in the case of small district council elections, the ruling DLP won the victory when 564 of its candidates were elected while only 165 of the New Democratic Party (a new party that emerged in April when the PPD and the New Democratic Alliance were united) won. Only 21 of the Democratic Party, and one of the Masses Party won. Some 115 Independents won council seats in all areas, except Seoul and Pusan.

In both these elections, the voters showed their skepticism for true local autonomy, or their disinterest. In the small district council elections, 13.2 million (55.9%) of 24 million eligible voters cast their ballots. Only 42.3% of eligible voters in Seoul cast their ballots in ward council elections. In the elections for large district councils (municipal councils of the special cities of Seoul, Pusan, Taegu, Kwangju, Inch'ŏn, and Taejŏn and nine provincial councils), 16.5 million (58.9%) of 28 million eligible voters cast their ballots. In Seoul 52.4% of the eligible voters participated in the elections for the Seoul Municipal Council.

Complete local autonomy was not achieved, however, as in May 1992, mayoral and gubernatorial elections to be held sometime in mid-1992 were postponed until 1995 because of "financial constraints."

-M-

MARINE CORPS. Established in April 1949 and patterned after that of the United States, it played a crucial role in the May Military Revolution of 1961. In October 1973, it was disbanded and incorporated into the Navy. In November 1987, the Marine Corps regained its former status as a separate entity within the South Korean armed forces. *See also:* NATIONAL DEFENSE FORCES.

"MASSACRES OF THE MASS MEDIA." In October-November 1980, under pressure exerted by the Defense Security Command, the Special Committee for National Security Measures forced the publishers of newspapers and magazines to dismiss 298 journalists and bring about "voluntary resignation" of some 635 others who have defied the ruling party and the government. It was at that time that the *Tong-a Daily Press* was taken over by the pro-government *Kyonghyang Daily Press,* and the government-run KBS Radio-TV absorbed the Tongyang and the Tong-a radio-TV broadcasting systems as well as three others, leaving only two (KBS and the MBC) radio-TV broadcasting systems and one (Christian) radio broadcasting system in operation. Several local newspapers were either abolished, or forced to merge with other pro-government presses.

MASSES PARTY. In May 1965, the Democratic Party of Pak Sun-ch'ŏn and the Civil Rule Party merged, forming the Masses Party (Minjungdang), playing a key role as an opposition party. In February 1967, it united with the New Korean Party to form the New Democratic Party (Shin Minjudang) with Yu Chin-o as its president. *See also:* NEW DEMOCRATIC PARTY; PAK SUN-CH'ŎN; YU CHIN-O; YUN PO-SŎN.

MASSES (PEOPLE'S) PARTY. This left-of-the-center party whose Korean name is Minjungdang was formed in November 1990 with Yi Wu-jae as its leader. It was organized by former members of the Committee to Promote a Democratic Coalition who refused to become associated with the regionally-based PPD of Kim Dae-jung when the leaders of the committee advocated its merger with the PPD. *See also:* COMMITTEE TO PROMOTE A DEMOCRATIC COALITION (MINYŎNCH'U).

MILITARY ARMISTICE COMMISSION. This Commission was established shortly after the Korean armistice was signed on July 27, 1953. It was composed of a half-dozen representatives of North Korea and China and those of the U.N. Command to deal with any issues related to violation of the neutrality of the Demilitarized Zone (DMZ) or territorial rights of North and South Korea by another party.

A conference building of the Military Armistice Commission was built in Panmunjom where the armistice was signed and it was designated as a free zone. The conference building was constructed in such a way that half of it is located in the northern side and the other half is located in the southern side of the military demarcation line. A table covered with green cloth in the center of the conference room straddles the border.

The Chinese representatives left the Commission and made arrangements for the North Koreans to deal directly with the U.N. Command. In March 1991, a South Korean general replaced the American military officer as head of the U.N. Command members on the Commission. However, North Korea refused to recognize such a change, charging that South

Korea had no right to represent the U.N. Command because it did not sign the armistice. Thus, the 460th meeting that was to take place on May 29, 1992 failed to materialize. *See also:* DEMILITARIZED ZONE (DMZ); KOREAN WAR.

MILITARY DEMARCATION (CEASE-FIRE, TRUCE) LINE. A new boundary between the north and the south was drawn up along the battle front when the Korean armistice agreement was signed in July 1953. The 150-mile-long line runs a course from sea to sea. A 1-1/2 mile (2 kilometers) wide demilitarized (neutral) zone (DMZ) was established on each side of the line, and a hitherto unknown hamlet named Panmunjom on the line was designated as a "truce village" where the Korean Armistice Commission meets on an irregular basis. *See also:* KOREAN ARMISTICE; KOREAN ARMISTICE COMMISSION.

MILITARY REVOLUTION OF MAY 16, 1961. As early as February 1960, young army officers, under the leadership of Major General Park Chung-hee, then logistic base commander in Pusan, formulated a plan to carry out a coup. This group included Major General Yi Chu-il, chief of staff of the Second Army, Major General Kim Tong-ha, commander of the Marine Corps, Lieutenant Colonel Kim Chong-ch'ŏl, commander of the 33rd Anti-Aircraft Artillery Battalion, and Lieutenant Colonel Kim Jong-pil of the Army Headquarters G-2. They decided to stage the coup on May 8, 1960, three days after the scheduled departure of Army Chief of Staff General Song Yo'ch'an for a U.S. visit.

The plan adopted by this disgruntled and rebellious group, which was dominated by the 8th graduating class of the Korean Military Academy (1949), included the following:

1. Punishment of top military officers who collaborated with the Liberal Party in rigging the 1960 presidential elections.

2. Punishment of military officers who amassed wealth illegally.

3. Elimination of incompetent and corrupt commanders.

4. Establishment of political neutrality of the armed forces and elimination of factionalism within the armed forces.

5. Improvement of treatment for military servicemen.

The planners were particularly unhappy with three things: (1) politicization of the armed forces, particularly the army, (2) incompetent generals who occupied top army posts and blocked the advancement of younger (mostly in the rank of colonel) army officers, and (3) corrupt and illegal means with which these top-ranking army generals enriched themselves.

The April Student Uprising interrupted their plan. After the fall of the First Republic, the group decided to wait and see how the new president and the new Chang administration would handle domestic problems, including the problem that existed within the military establishments. They were disappointed, although they were able to pressure Army Chief of Staff Gen. Song to resign in May 1960, as well as obtain the resignation of the new Army Chief of Staff Lt. Gen. Ch'oe Yŏng-hŭi, who had replaced Gen. Song. The appointment of Lt. Gen. Chang To-yŏng in early 1961 as Army Chief of Staff did not fully satisfy the core group of revolutionaries whose number had grown to some 250 officers. The planners of the military revolution succeeded in securing the pledge of many commanders of various units of the Army, as well as those of the Marine Corps before they launched the revolution.

In the pre-dawn hours of May 16, 1961, some 1,600 troops, spearheaded by the Marines, struck and seized key government buildings, banks, the Metropolitan Police headquarters, and communications centers. Some 2,000 more troops entered the city, putting Seoul under siege. On May 16, the Military Revolutionary Committee (MCR) consisting of a handful of generals, which was quickly formed, declared martial law, along with a 7 p.m. to 5 a.m. curfew. It froze all banks, closed airports and harbors, placed the press under strict censorship, and forbade assembly. At the same time, it dissolved both houses of the National Assembly as well as provincial councils.

Although both President Yun and Gen. Chang were urged by

the Americans to launch a counterrevolution in cooperation with U.S. troops, they did not wish to bring about possible large-scale bloodshed by doing so, for they believed that many army commanders were behind the revolution. They were also keenly mindful of the ever-present threats of the North Korean Communists. Moreover, it was the opinion of President Yun that, although a military revolution was not desirable, it was perhaps inevitable in view of the domestic situation. Had they followed American advice, there is no doubt that it would have resulted in a civil war. Gen. Yi Han-lim, commander of the First Army Corps, which was stationed near Seoul, could have mobilized at least three divisions under his command against the revolutionaries, but he did not, although he himself was not a member of the core group of the revolutionaries, and in the late afternoon of May 17, his headquarters announced that Gen. Yi supported the revolution.

The revolutionaries succeeded in persuading President Yun to remain in office and approved the martial law which was declared. At the same time, they persuaded Gen. Chang to join and lead the revolution. Gen. Chang, with the idea of controlling and leading the revolutionaries so as to preserve the constitutional system, accepted the chairmanship of the Military Revolutionary Committee on May 18.

On May 18, Premier Chang returned to Seoul from his hiding place, and held the last cabinet meeting, submitting the resignation of cabinet members *en masse,* ending the Second Republic. Meanwhile, on May 18, the Military Revolutionary Committee issued its six pledges of military revolution.

Efforts made by Gen. Chang brought about the American recognition on May 19 of the military takeover as a *fait accompli,* as well as its acquiescence for its aims. Following this, on June 6, the revolutionaries promulgated the Law Regarding Extraordinary Measures for National Reconstruction, and next day renamed the MRC the Supreme Council for National Reconstruction (SCNR) as the nation's supreme governing organ. All administrative, judicial and legislative functions were now in the hands of the 30-member SCNR. It appointed the head of the cabinet (prime minister), who in turn appointed cabinet members with the approval of the SCNR. The judicial branch was also placed under the control of the members of the SCNR, as were the armed forces. The SCNR functioned as a legislative organ as well. Thus the junta rule began. *See also:* APRIL STUDENT UPRISING, CHANG TO YŎNG; KIM JONG-PIL; PARK CHUNG-HEE; SUPREME COUNCIL FOR NATIONAL RECONSTRUCTION.

MILITARY REVOLUTIONARY COMMITTEE. *See:* SUPREME COUNCIL FOR NATIONAL RECONSTRUCTION.

MONETARY SYSTEM. Japanese monies were replaced by the new monies issued by the Bank of Korea in 1948. The smallest unit was a copper penny called *chŏn,* and 100 *chŏn* was called *wŏn* (paper money). There were five *chŏn,* ten *chŏn,* and fifty *chŏn* coins. In February 1953, when a monetary reform was carried out, the *won* currency was replaced by the *hwan* currency at the rate of 100 *wŏn* to one *hwan.* In June 1962, the second monetary reform was implemented, returning to the *wŏn* system at the rate of 10 *hwan* to one *wŏn,* and new paper monies of larger monetary units were issued by the Bank of Korea.

MOSCOW AGREEMENT. To deal with the postwar problems among the Allies, the foreign ministers of the United States, the United Kingdom, and USSR met in Moscow from December 16 to 26, 1945. Regarding Korea, they agreed on the following matters, and made it public on December 28: (1) to set up a provisional Korean democratic government, (2) in order to do so, a Joint Commission consisting of representatives of the U.S. and the Soviet occupation authorities in Korea be established, and it, in consultation with the Korean democratic parties and social organizations, establish a provisional Korean government, and (3) a four-power trusteeship of the United States, China, Great Britain and the Soviet Union be imposed on Korea for a period of up to five years following the establishment of the Korean government and the national independence of Korea. *See also:* JOINT U.S. SOVIET COMMISSION.

MURDER OF RIOT POLICE. On May 3, 1989, when the riot police invaded the campus of Tongŭi University in Pusan to break up a large, violent, antigovernment student demonstration, the rioting students confined some police in a corridor, then doused them in inflammable liquid which they set on fire. Seven police officers died and six others were badly burned. Seventy-one students were arrested, and in October one was sentenced to life-imprisonment, and thirty others were given various prison terms. About half of them were released on suspended sentences.

-N-

NATIONAL ALLIANCE FOR DEMOCRACY AND UNIFICATION. This alliance of radical opposition groups was organized on December 1, 1991. Its Korean name was Minjujuŭi Minjok T'ong'il Chŏn'guk Yŏnhap, or Chŏn'guk Yŏnhap, and it included some 21 radical organizations such as Chŏnminyon, Chŏnnong, Chŏngyojo, and Chŏndaehyŏp. It advocated "the rejection of interferences of outside (foreign) powers, the winning of the autonomy of the people, and the establishment of a democratic government." *See also:* NATIONAL COALITION FOR A PEOPLE'S DEMOCRATIC MOVEMENT; NATIONAL COUNCIL OF FARMERS' UNIONS; NATIONAL COUNCIL OF REPRESENTATIVES OF UNIVERSITY STUDENTS; NATIONAL TEACHERS' UNION.

NATIONAL ASSEMBLY. The National Assembly of the Republic of Korea emerged as a unicameral Constituent Assembly in June, 1948, following the May 10th general elections under the supervision and sponsorship of the UNTCOK. Of the 300-member assembly, 198 were elected from mainland South Korea, each representing 100,000 constituents. Two more members were elected from Cheju Island later in May 1949 when the rebellion on that island was subjugated. One hundred seats allocated for the north were left vacant.

The members of the Constituent Assembly, who were elected for a two-year term of office, inaugurated the assembly on May 31, elected Dr. Syngman Rhee as chairman, and on July 12, it adopted the Constitution of the Republic of Korea.

In accordance with the constitution, Dr. Rhee was elected president and Yi Si-yŏng was elected as vice-president for four-year terms of office. Thus, the Constitutent Assembly acted as a legislative assembly, as well as an electoral college.

In May 1950, the second general elections were held, a new legislative National Assembly of 210 members was established, and the term of office of each assemblyman was extended to four years. It remained a single-house legislature until July 1960, when, with a constitutional amendment, a bicameral legislature was established with the House of Councillors as an upper house and the House of Representatives as a lower house. When the May 16 Military Revolution of 1961 took place, it was dissolved, only to be reestablished in November 1963 as a unicameral legislative assembly.

The seventh constitutional amendent of 1972 introduced a new system of legislative assembly, whereby 73 of its 219 members, or one-third of its total membership were appointed by the newly established National Conference for Unification upon the nomination made by the president. Thus, the 9th, 10th and 11th National Assemblies had one-third of the total number of seats occupied by members of the Political Fraternal Society for Revitalizing Reform (Yujŏnghoe), a sister political group of the ruling Democratic Republican Party. With the fall of the Fourth Republic in 1979, this system was abolished. In October 1980, the National Assembly was again dissolved, replaced by the Legislative Council for National Security whose members were appointed by the president.

When the Fifth Republic emerged in March 1981, the new National Assembly Election Law stipulated that 184 of the 276-member National Assembly were to be popularly elected from 184 electoral districts, and the remaining 92 seats (proportional representation) were to be distributed among parties winning five seats or more in the National Assembly according to the percentage of the number of candidates each party elected in the direct election.

The National Assembly Law was revised after the proclamation of the Constitution of the Sixth Republic. According to the new law, 224 members of the 299-member National Assembly were to be elected through popular vote, and the remaining 75 seats were to be proportionally distributed among parties winning five or more seats. The 14th National Assembly elections were held on March 24, 1992.

The National Assembly has one speaker, two vice-speakers, sixteen standing Committees, and a secretariat. It holds one regular session per year (up to 100 days), extraordinary sessions (up to 30 days), and occasional special sessions requested by the president. *See also:* HOUSE OF COUNCILLORS; HOUSE OF REPRESENTATIVES; LEGISLATIVE COUNCIL FOR NATIONAL SECURITY; YUJŎNGHOE.

NATIONAL ASSEMBLY SPY RING CASE. In May-June 1949, Kim Yak-su, No Ik-hwan, and eight other National Assembly members were arrested in connection with an alleged conspiracy in collaboration with the Communists, most of whom were underground members of the South Korean Workers' Party. Their conspiracy was suspected by the government when they proposed the withdrawal of U.S. troops and negotiations with the north for national reunification. They were tried, and on February 10, 1950, they were given four-to-twelve year prison terms for violating the National Security Law.

NATIONAL COALITION FOR A DEMOCRATIC CONSTITUTION. An alliance of the dissidents which was formed in early 1987. As an umbrella organization of the opposition intellectuals and religious leaders, it provided a leadership for popular opposition outside the established opposition parties.

NATIONAL COALITION FOR A PEOPLE'S DEMOCRATIC MOVEMENT. Formed in January 1989 by some 200 dissident social, labor and religious organizations, it launched a new grass-roots democratization movement and struggle against dictatorship and foreign influence under the slogan "Social Movement in an Age of Masses."

NATIONAL CONFERENCE FOR UNIFICATION. An electoral college established in December 1972 under the revised constitution of 1972. Its members, not less than 2,000 and no more than 5,000 were to be popularly elected. In 1972, 2,359 members were popularly elected.

It was replaced in February 1981 under the revised constitution of 1980 by a new 5,278-member Presidential Electoral College. When the revised constitution was approved in a national referendum in October 1987, its existence was terminated as the system of the direct presidential election went into effect in December. *See also:* YUSHIN RULE.

NATIONAL COUNCIL FOR RAPID REALIZATION OF KOREAN INDEPENDENCE. On October 25, 1945, some 50 right-wing political and social organizations formed this council known in Korean as Tongnip Ch'oksŏng Kungmin Hyŏpŭihoe, or Tokch'ok for short, and after setting up its central committee they named Dr. Syngman Rhee as its head. Its purpose was to launch a united movement to end the Allied occupation as quickly as possible and restore Korean national independence. However, many moderate nationalists, as well as moderate and radical leftist organizations declined to join the council.

NATIONAL COUNCIL OF KOREAN WOMEN'S ORGANIZATIONS. *See:* WOMEN'S MOVEMENT.

NATIONAL COUNCIL OF LABOR UNIONS. (of the Leftists) Chŏn'guk Nodong Chohap P'yŏngŭihoe, or Chŏnp'yŏng was formed in November 1945 by the leftists following the emergence of various labor unions after August 1945. It included some 500,000 members belonging to various trade unions. Following the railway labor strike in October 1946 and a general strike of laborers in November 1947, its movement declined under the suppressive measures taken by the USAMGIK against violent, illegal labor movements, and its existence was terminated in June 1948. *See also:* LABOR MOVEMENT.

NATIONAL COUNCIL OF LABOR UNIONS. (of the Moderates) In October 1959, the progressive labor leaders formed this council known in Korean as Chŏn'guk Nodong Chohap Hyŏpŭihoe for the purpose of promoting a more efficient and "true" labor union movement in South Korea. However, in

November 1960 it was forced to be merged with the General Federation of Korean Labor Unions, forming the General Federation of Korean Labor Unions (Han'guk Nodong Chohap Ch'ongyŏnmaeng, or Han'guk Noryŏn for short). *See also:* GENERAL FEDERATION OF KOREAN LABOR UNIONS; LABOR MOVEMENT.

NATIONAL COUNCIL OF LABOR UNIONS. (of the Progressives) This organization of radical labor unions known by its Korean names of Chŏn'guk Nodong Chohap Hyŏpŭihoe, or simply Chŏnnohyŏp, was formed in late January 1990. Some 190,000 members belonging to 600 local chapters of various labor unions joined the new group. The organizers of this radical labor council charged that the existing Federation of Korean Trade Unions was "pro-government" and "pro-management" rather than working for the rights of the workers. The government immediately declared that the council was an illegal body. *See also:* LABOR MOVEMENT.

NATIONAL COUNCIL OF REPRESENTATIVES OF UNIVERSITY STUDENTS. A national federation of radical university students, commonly called Chŏndaehyŏp, was established in June 1988. Spearheaded by the Federation of Seoul Student Association, its member groups numbered some 115, and it promoted socialistic democratization, an anti-U.S. national reunification movement, and North-South student talks. *See also:* STUDENT MOVEMENT.

NATIONAL COUNCIL OF TEACHERS' LABOR UNION. Shortly after the formation of the Secondary School Teachers' Labor Union in Seoul, on May 1, 1960 some 300 elementary and secondary teachers, as well as college professors, met in Seoul and established the National Council of Teachers' Labor Unions. The government immediately declared that it was an illegal body (violation of the Public Employees Law). It was dissolved in late May 1961, when the Military Revolutionary Committee dissolved all political and social organizations under its Decree No. 6. *See also:* LABOR MOVEMENT; NATIONAL TEACHERS' UNION.

NATIONAL DEFENSE FORCES. On August 29, 1948, the Law on Organization of the National Defense was promulgated, and with this the Korean Constabulary and the Coast Guard which the American military government had established in January and September 1946, respectively, were reorganized into the Army and the Navy, and the Army and the Navy chiefs of staff were installed on November 30, 1948. The Marine Corps was established in April 1949, followed by the establishment of the Air Force in October. In 1981, the Marine Corps was absorbed into the Navy, but it was separated from the Navy in 1983.

Up to September 1952, members of the armed forces consisted of volunteers. However, in September 1952 a military conscription law was implemented, and all able-bodied men between the ages of 20 and 40, except students and only sons, were obligated to serve in the armed forces for two years in the Army or the Navy and three years in the Air Force. *See also:* CIVIL DEFENSE CORPS; HOMELAND RESERVE FORCES; STUDENT NATIONAL DEFENSE CORPS.

NATIONAL DEMOCRATIC FRONT. This front known in Korean as Minjujuŭi Minjok Chŏnsŏn was organized in February 1946 by Yŏ Un-hyŏng, Hŏ Hŏn, Pak Hŏn-yŏng and other leftists in order to counter the rightists and establish a socialistic Korean nation. However, Yŏ withdrew from the front, leaving it in the hands of more radical leftists. It collapsed when Hŏ and Pak fled to North Korea in 1947.

NATIONAL DEVELOPMENT PLANS. Five Five-Year Economic Plans have been completed between 1962 and 1986, and the sixth national development plan was implemented in 1987. The First Five-Year Plan (1962–66) was aimed at developing social overhead capital, such as electricity, railroads, ports, and communications in order to build a firm basis for subsequent economic development.

In the Second Five-Year Economic Development Plan period (1967–71), the government sought to upgrade industrial structures by developing electronic and petrochemical industries while promoting exports and increasing farm income. The Third Five-Year Plan (1972–76) marked a turning point in the expansion of heavy industries such as shipbuilding, iron and steel production, and petrochemical manufacturing. During this period, the New Community Movement played an important role in modernization of the rural environment and reconstruction of farm economy.

The Fourth Five-Year Plan (1977–81) included both economic and social development plans. It paid particular attention to the development of technology and skilled labor-intensive industries such as machinery and electronics. Shipbuilding was stressed and industrial consolidation was carried out. At the same time, urban renewal accompanied a comprehensive and systematic social development plan.

After suffering a sharp economic decline in 1980, the Fifth Economic and Social Development Plan (1982–86) was implemented with the basic goal of achieving stability, efficiency, and balance in economic growth. During this period, the GNP growth rate rebounded from -3.7% in 1980 to 12.9% in 1986 with the GNP increase from $60.5 to $102.7 billion.

In 1987, the Sixth Economic and Social Development Plan (1987–91) was launched with the aim of achieving an average GNP growth of 7.2% and raising the GNP to $166 billion and per capita GNP to $3,800. Despite the many negative factors which emerged in South Korea, the plan moved ahead, achieving the GNP growth of 13% in 1987, 12.2% in 1988, and 6.6% in 1989. In 1989, the GNP reached the $204 billion mark and per capita GNP increased to $4,830.

NATIONAL FEDERATION OF STUDENT ASSOCIATIONS. *See:* STUDENT MOVEMENT.

NATIONAL FEDERATION OF STUDENTS FOR PEOPLE'S DEMOCRACY. *See:* STUDENT MOVEMENT.

NATIONAL INSTITUTE OF EDUCATION (NIE). Created in 1974 as an organic body of the Ministry of Education, its main functions are to conduct basic research concerning the policy and administrative aspects of education, to develop and distribute educational materials, and to elevate the quality of the teachers.

NATIONAL INSTITUTE OF EDUCATIONAL EVALUATION (NIEE). Established in August 1985 as a government organ under the Ministry of Education, its primary function is to evaluate educational achievement. However, it also strives to improve the quality of Korean education.

NATIONAL INSTITUTE OF EDUCATIONAL RESEARCH AND TRAINING (NIERT). Established in 1970 as an in-service training organization of the Ministry of Education named the National Institute for Training of Educational Administrators, it was reorganized into the NIERT in 1981. Its educational evaluation function was handed over to the NIEE in 1985. Today, it concentrates on developing competent educational leadership with a strong sense of mission.

NATIONAL LABOR FEDERATION OF BANK EMPLOYEES. *See:* LABOR MOVEMENT.

NATIONAL SECURITY LAWS. The first National Security Law was enacted by the Constituent Assembly in November 1948, making it a crime to betray the Constitution by posing as a government or "in collusion with a betrayer" to seek to consolidate or group together with the purpose of disturbing the tranquility of the state. The second National Security Law was promulgated on December 26, 1958. It was aimed at punishing those individuals, associations, groups or organizations "which seek to overthrow the state in violation of the national constitution and the activities for the realization of their objectives." The law declared that anyone who detected or gathered "national secrets" or aided and abetted such acts for the purpose of "benefitting the enemy" would be punished by the death penalty or penal servitude for life.

Article 22 of the new National Security Law stated that "anyone who had openly impaired the prestige of a constitutional organ by holding a meeting or by publishing documents, tape-recorded materials, drawings and other materials of expression . . . shall be punished by penal servitude for not more than ten years." The constitutional organ stated in Article 22 included the president, the speaker of the National Assembly and the Chief Justice of the Supreme Court. The law provided that military intelligence agencies may conduct investigations of civilians who were suspected of having violated the National Security Law.

The enforcement of the National Security Law was enhanced when, at 3 A.M. December 28, 1971, the ruling party rammed through the National Assembly the Special Measures Law for National Security and Defense, (known in Korean as Kokka Powipŏp). In addition to imposing economic controls, the law empowered the president to curtail the freedom of the press, to issue national mobilization decrees, to prohibit outdoor assemblies and demonstrations, to restrict labor union activities, and to alter the national budget, when necessary to cope with emergency conditions.

In December 1980, the Anti-Communism Law was consolidated with the National Security Law. *See also:* ANTI-COMMUNISM LAW.

NATIONAL TEACHERS' UNION (NTU). The first teachers' labor unions were formed in 1960 following the fall of the First Republic, and the Korean Federation of Teachers' Labor Unions of primary and secondary school teachers emerged in May. However, these unions and the federation were first declared by the government as illegal organizations, and then in May 1961, when the military revolution came, they were dissolved.

Riding the new tide of democratization that developed in 1987, and despite the law against the formation of labor unions by educators, in May 1989 radical teachers reestablished the National Teachers' Union known as Chŏn'guk Kyowŏn Chopha, or Chŏn'gyojo, increasing the total membership in the National Teachers' Union to 14,000. However, the Ministry of Education refused to recognize its legitimacy, and dismissed thousands of teachers who joined the organization. *See also:* EDUCATIONAL DEVELOPMENT; KOREAN FEDERATION OF EDUCATION ASSOCIATIONS; LABOR MOVEMENT.

NATIONAL YOUTH CORPS. *See:* KOREAN NATIONAL YOUTH CORPS.

NEUTRAL NATIONS SUPERVISORY COMMISSION (NNSC). This commission was established immediately after the signing of the Korean Armistice in July 1953. It consisted of Swedish, Swiss, Czechoslovakian, and Polish representatives, and its primary function was to supervise the observation of the Korean armistice agreement by its signatories, and to bar any new arms build-up in North and South Korea. *See also:* KOREAN ARMISTICE; PANMUNJOM.

NEW COMMUNITY MOVEMENT. The New Community Movement, or *Saemaŭl undongs,* was launched in 1972 by President Park. The movement started as a rural modernization program intended to galvanize the tradition-bound and poverty-stricken rural society into participating actively in the national development. To this end, three main goals were adopted: improvement of the living environment, spiritual enlightenment, and income enhancement. The three methods adopted to achieve these aims were the fostering of a spirit of self-help, development of diligent habits, and promotion of mutual cooperation.

In the initial stage of the movement, the main emphasis was placed on environmental improvement with such projects as village clean-up, sanitation projects, housing renovation, and reconstruction of roads and waterways. After 1973, the emphasis was shifted to the promotion of income-generating enterprises. In 1974, the movement spread nationwide to include the urban sector and schools in a comprehensive national regeneration reform movement. Between 1972 and 1984 an aggregate of 24 million persons from 36,000 villages took part in a total of 18,600 projects. By the end of 1987 some 4,350 miles of rural roads were rebuilt or repaired and 800 miles of canals, irrigation dykes and other waterways were reconstructed.

NEW DEMOCRATIC PARTY. There were three political parties by the same name of Shin Minjudang, or New Democratic Party. The first one was formed in February 1961 by the "old faction" members of the Democratic Party who defected from it under the leadership of Kim To-yŏn. It said that its aim was to promote liberal democracy. However, it was dissolved in May 1961 when the military revolution came.

The second New Democratic Party was organized in February 1967 when the Masses and the New Korea parties merged to form the New Democratic Party, advocating progressive reforms under the leadership of Yu Chin-o. It was at this juncture that younger leaders such as Kim Dae-jung, Kim Young-sam and Yi Ch'ŏl-sŭng rose within the party.

In 1967, its presidential candidate, Yun Po-sŏn ran, but failed, and in the 1971 presidential election Kim Dae-jung lost by a narrow margin. In 1973, Kim Young-sam became its president. However, it became the major opposition party, winning more urban votes in the National Assembly elections. The third New Democratic Party emerged in the aftermath of defeat suffered by the Party of Peace and Democracy (PPD) that won only 785 seats in the March 1991 elections for local councils. In April, Kim Dae-jung brought about the merger of his PPD and the New Democratic United Party of Yi Wu-jŏng to form the New Democratic Party. It was a centralist reformist party with the collective leadership of Kim and Yi, with Kim as its president. In September 1990, it merged with the Democratic Party. *See also:* DEMOCRATIC PARTY; KIM DAE-JUNG; KIM YOUNG-SAM; LOCAL AUTONOMY; NEW DEMOCRATIC PARTY; PARTY OF PEACE AND DEMOCRACY; YU CHIN-O.

NEW DEMOCRATIC REPUBLICAN PARTY. In October 1987, Kim Jong-pil reconstituted the Democratic Republican Party, which had been defunct in 1980, naming it the New Democratic Republican Party (Shin Minju Konghwadang). Kim became its president and it won 35 seats in the 1988 National Assembly elections, becoming the third opposition party. *See also:* DEMOCRATIC REPUBLICAN PARTY; KIM JONG-PIL.

NEW DEMOCRATIC UNITED PARTY. When in February, 1990, Kim Young-sam, president of the Reunification Democratic Party, joined the leaders of the Democratic Justice Party and the New Democratic Republican Party to form a united party named the Democratic Liberal Party, Yi Wu-jŏng, a female professor who became a politician, and others who did not follow Kim's plan formed their own party named the New Democratic United Party (Shin-minju Yŏnhap in Korean). However, in April 1991, it merged with the Party of Peace and Democracy of Kim Dae-jung, forming the New Democratic Party. *See also:* DEMOCRATIC PARTY; NEW DEMOCRATIC PARTY: PARTY OF PEACE AND DEMOCRACY.

NEW KOREA DEMOCRATIC PARTY. This party, known in Korean as Shin Han'guk Minjudang, was formed in January 1985 by those politicians who regained their civil rights. In November 1984, all but 19 former political leaders were freed from the political blacklist, and they immediately launched a new party movement in order to promote their democracy drive. Yi Min-woo was named its president, and among its key leaders were Kim Young-sam and Yi Ch'ŏl-sŭng. Kim Dae-jung who returned from his self-imposed exile in the United States in February 1985 did not join the party immediately, but he agreed to serve as adviser to the president of the party.

The New Korea Democratic Party became the main opposition party, struggling against the Democratic Justice Party and the government of President Chun and launching a nationwide movement for constitutional revision in 1986. However, it suffered badly when, in May 1987, Kim Young-sam broke away from the NKDP and formed his own Reunification Democratic Party, and Kim Dae-jung joined the new party in August. As many National Assembly members of the NKDP left it and joined first the RDP, and then the Party for Peace and Democracy (PPD) which Kim Dae-jung formed in November, the party became virtually dissolved. *See also:* PARTY FOR PEACE AND DEMOCRACY; REUNIFICATION DEMOCRATIC PARTY.

NEW KOREA PARTY. (Saehandang) This party whose Korean name is Saehandang, was formed in January 1992 by Professor Kim Tong-gil. A long-time critic of then existing parties, as well as the government since the late 1960s, Kim had formed the Asia-Pacific-Era Committee, promoting a "new politics." The New Korea Party was a transformed body of the Asia-

Pacific-Era Committee. Shortly after its emergence, in February 1992 it merged first with the New Democratic Party, and then with the Unification National Party. *See also:* UNIFICATION NATIONAL PARTY.

NEW KOREA PARTY. (Shinhandang) In May 1966, Yun Po-sŏn formed this party known in Korean as Shinhandang, but in February 1967 it and the Masses Party were united, forming the New Democratic Party.

NORDPOLITIK. *Nordpolitik,* or Northern Policy, was advanced in June 1973 by then President Park Chung-hee when he announced that his government was willing to establish ties with countries having ideological and political systems different from South Korea's. His new foreign policy would free South Korea from the Cold War mold and establish balance in South Korea's relations with all of its neighbors, regardless of ideology. South Korea had been obliged to rely almost exclusively on the Free World, particularly the United States and Japan, and it was cut off completely from China, the Soviet Union, and other Socialist countries. The other aim of President Park was to weaken the ties between North Korea and the Soviet Bloc countries by establishing diplomatic and commercial ties with as many Socialist nations as possible.

It was the Sixth Republic which implemented the Northern Policy, taking advantage of the 1988 Summer Olympics in Seoul. President Roh Tae-woo capitalized on this golden opportunity, bringing cultural exchanges with Hungary, Poland, and the Soviet Union, as well as China, before the Seoul Olympics. The participation of sports teams from China, the Soviet Union, and other Socialist countries (except Albania, Cuba, and North Korea) in the Seoul Olympics paved the way for diplomatic and commercial relations of South Korea with them.

For implementation of Northern Policy and its result, see Foreign Policy and Diplomacy, pages 47–55.

NORTH-SOUTH POLITICAL COORDINATING COMMITTEE. After the issuance of the statement concerning peaceful reunification of Korea by both Seoul and Pyongyang on July 4, 1972, the Political Coordinating Committee of North and South Korea was established, and it held its preliminary meeting at Panmunjom in August 1972. After that, a total of six rounds of the full-dress meetings were held in Seoul as well as in Pyongyang between October 1972 and July 1973. These meetings were designed to discuss and settle various procedural steps necessary for the achievement of peaceful reunification of the country in accordance with the July 4th statement.

However, in August 1973, Pyongyang unilaterally suspended the dialogue between the north and the south in the wake of the kidnapping of Kim Dae-jung from Tokyo to Seoul. Since then, efforts made by the South Korean government to bring about the resumption of the dialogue have been unsuccessful. *See also:* JULY 4TH STATEMENT REGARDING KOREAN REUNIFICATION; KIM DAE-JUNG.

NORTH-SOUTH RED CROSS TALKS. On August 12, 1971, the president of the Red Cross Society of South Korea proposed to the North Korean Red Cross to initiate talks to discuss ways to ease the sufferings of dispersed families in both the north and the south and ultimately arrange their reunion. Specifically, he proposed that both Red Cross societies launch a movement to search for separated family members, arrange exchange of letters between them, and bring about their reunion.

The North Korean Red Cross promptly accepted the proposal on August 14, and Red Cross talks began in September, but without satisfactory results. The only two memorable events which they brought about were (1) the exchange of a 151-member group comprising hometown visitors and folk art troupes in late September 1982, and (2) the offering of relief goods (food and clothing) by the North Korean Red Cross Society to the flood victims in the south in September, 1984, which the South Korean Red Cross promptly accepted.

The working-level meetings of the representatives were held in 1989 to arrange another exchange of hometown visitors and performing art troupes, but they failed to reach an agreement.

-P-

PAK SUN-CH'ŎN (1898–1983). Born in Tongnae, South Kyŏngsang Province, she received a modern education, and became a teacher in Masan. In 1919, she was imprisoned in connection with her direct involvement in the independence movement in that city. Released from prison, she went to Tokyo to study, graduating from Nihon Women's College in 1926. Returning to Korea, she became an educator and a leader in the nationalist women's movement, and in 1940 she established the private Kyŏngsŏng Academy.

She became a dynamic woman politician after Korea's liberation. Elected to the National Assembly in 1950, she became one of the most influential politicians and a leading opposition member in the National Assembly until 1971. In 1966, she formed her own Masses Party, but in 1967 she and Yun Po-sŏn brought about the formation of the New Democratic Party, which became the main opposition party.

After retiring from politics in 1972, she became head of a girls' school, and served as a member of the State Advisory Council from 1980.

PANMUNJOM. Formerly a hamlet located some 35 miles from Seoul on the 38th parallel, this became a neutral area where truce negotiations have been held since September 1951 and where the Korean Armistice was signed in July 1953. The headquarters of the Neutral Nations Supervisory Commission is located there and the Korean Armistice Commission holds its meetings there. It is a joint security area under the U.N. Command and North Korean guards.

PANMUNJOM INCIDENT. On August 18, 1976, two U.S. Army officers and nine others were killed by North Korean soldiers in the joint security area when the American soldiers were involved in a tree-trimming operation. The following day, the Commander of the U.N. Forces sent a strong protest to North Korea's Kim Il-sung through its representatives at the meeting of the Military Armistice Commission held at Panmunjom. North Korea offered no apologies. Instead, Kim

Il-sung ordered all North Korean military units into full combat readiness. Neither the United States nor South Korea advocated drastic measures against North Korea at that time. On August 21, a U.N. Command work group cut down the tree instead of pruning it.

PARK CHUNG-HEE (1917–1979). Born as the youngest of seven children in a poor farm family in Sŏnsan, North Kyŏngsang Province, he graduated from Taegu Normal School and became a primary school teacher in 1937. After a fight with a Japanese teacher, he resigned from the school and went to Manchuria, enrolling at the Manchukuo Military Academy in 1942. After completing a two-year course there, in 1944 he enrolled at the Japanese Military Academy. Upon graduation from this school, he was commissioned as a second lieutenant in the Japanese Imperial Army and was assigned to the Kantō Army in Manchuria.

When the Pacific War ended, he returned to Korea, and in 1946 he enrolled at the military academy which the American military government established. Completing a short (three months) training course, he was commissioned as a captain in the Korean Constabulary.

When the Korean armed forces were formed, he remained in the military. He fought in the Korean War, and rose to the rank of brigadier general in 1953. After studying at the War College in 1957, he was promoted to the rank of major general in 1958. In 1960, at the time he formulated a plan for a military coup, he was commander of the Logistic Base Command in Pusan.

In May 1961, he brought about the May Military Revolution, overthrowing the Second Republic and becoming the vice-chairman of the Military Revolutionary Committee. He served as chairman of the Supreme Council for National Reconstruction from July 1961, and upon the resignation of President Yun in March 1962, Gen. Park became acting president. He retired from the army as lieutenant general in 1963.

Elected in October 1963 as the president of the Third Republic, he was reelected in 1967, 1971, 1972, and 1978. During his presidency, he carried out a series of five-year economic development plans, instituted the *Yushin* reform, launched the New Community Movement, and contributed to the modernization and industrialization of South Korea. He was shot to death by the then director of the Korean CIA on October 26, 1979. *See also:* ECONOMIC DEVELOPMENT; MILITARY REVOLUTION OF MAY 16, 1961; NEW COMMUNITY MOVEMENT; NATIONAL DEVELOPMENT PLANS.

PARTY FOR NEW POLITICAL REFORM. When the New Korea Party of Kim Tong-gil merged with the Unification National Party, those former members of the New Korea Party who opposed the merger formed their own party named the Party for New Political Reform (Shinjŏngdang) in late February 1992 under the leadership of Pak Ch'an-jong. *See also:* NEW KOREA PARTY: UNIFICATION NATIONAL PARTY (UNITED PEOPLE'S PARTY).

PARTY FOR PEACE AND DEMOCRACY. This political party known in Korean as P'yŏnghwa Minjudang, (or P'yŏngmindang for short) was formed in November 1987 by Kim Dae-jung, who became its president as well as its presidential candidate in the 1987 election. Bowing to mounting public criticism by his continuing rivalry with Kim Young-sam and his failure to unite with him to present a single candidate in the December 16, 1987 presidential election, Kim Dae-jung resigned the party presidency in March 1988, only to return to it in May following the National Assembly elections held in April in which his party became the first opposition party by winning the second largest number of seats. *See also:* KIM DAE-JUNG; REUNIFICATION DEMOCRATIC PARTY.

PEACE DAM. A dam constructed in Yanggu County, Kangwŏn Province, for the purpose of neutralizing a possible North Korean water offensive. The construction of the dam began in 1986 and was completed in 1988. It was designed to contain a large amount of water which could be released by the North Koreans from their own dam suspected of having been built for military purposes.

PEACE LINE. *See:* RHEE LINE.

PEACEFUL UNIFICATION FOREIGN POLICY. One of many policies enunciated by the South Korean government, this one was announced in the "June 26 Declaration" of 1973 by President Park regarding the new policy of the South Korean government for peaceful unification of Korea in conjunction with the North-South political dialogue that began in 1972. The seven-point foreign policy statement included the following:

1. The peaceful unification of Korea is the supreme task of the Korean people, and South Korea will continue to exert every effort to accomplish this task.

2. The south and the north should neither interfere with each other's internal affairs, nor commit aggression against each other.

3. South Korea would continue to make efforts with sincerity and patience to secure concrete results from the north-south dialogue based on July 4, 1972 statement.

4. South Korea would not oppose North Korea's participation with it in international organizations.

5. South Korea would not object to its admittance into the United Nations together with North Korea.

6. South Korea would open its doors to all the nations of the world, and it urged those countries whose ideologies and social institutions were different from it to open their doors to South Korea.

7. Peace and good-neighborliness were the firm basis of the foreign policy of South Korea.

PEOPLE'S REVOLUTIONARY PARTY CASE. In August 1964, the Korean CIA announced the arrest of a large espionage group of the People's Revolutionary Party which included radical college professors and students, as well as newspaper reporters. The group was allegedly involved in an organized revolutionary movement to overthrow the Republic in collusion with the North Korean Communists. In 1965, fourteen of them were given prison terms under the Anti-Communism Law.

POLITICAL ACTIVITIES PURIFICATION LAW. Enacted on March 16, 1962, by the Supreme Council, the law was aimed at banishing until August 1968, "old and corrupt politicians" and others, including the members of the Liberal Party, the Democratic Party, the New Democratic Party, and leaders of progressive organizations. Under the law, the Political Purification Committee was established to screen those individuals to be banned. Some 4,369 were put on the purge list of which 1,336 were cleared. President Yun resigned on March 22, 1962, protesting against the law.

POLITICAL FRATERNAL SOCIETY FOR REVITALIZING REFORM. A political society named Yushin Chŏng'uhoe, or Yujŏnghoe which was formed in March 1973 mostly by those who had been connected with the May Military Revolution of 1961. It was a sister political organization of the ruling Democratic Republican Party, and 73 of its members were appointed to the National Assembly, becoming a progovernment floor group, supporting President Park's *Yushin* rule. It was abolished in 1980. *See also:* MILITARY REVOLUTION OF MAY 16, 1961; *YUSHIN* RULE.

POLITICAL PARTIES. *See:* Individual entries for political parties.

POLITICAL PARTY LAWS. The first of this kind was promulgated on December 26, 1962, reviving organized political activities of politicians and bringing about the formation of four political parties. The law was promulgated in order to restore a civilian government. The second political party law was promulgated on December 30, 1972 for the purpose of reviving political party activities which had been curtailed in

October. In similar manner as with the first law, this one also saw the rise of new political parties.

POLITICAL REFORM COMMITTEE. A committee established by the Special Committee for National Security Measures in November 1980 to screen and purge undesirable politicians. It put 835 former politicians on the blacklist, barring them from playing any political role. *See also:* SPECIAL COMMITTEE FOR NATIONAL SECURITY MEASURES.

PRESIDENTIAL ELECTIONS. *See:* APPENDIX C.

PRESIDENTIAL ELECTORAL COLLEGE. Under the revised constitution approved in the national referendum on October 22, 1980, a new presidential electoral college composed of "no less than 5,000 popularly elected delegates" was created, replacing the National Conference for Unification. On February 11, 1981, elections were held to choose 5,278 members of the electoral college. When the revised constitution was approved in a national referendum on October 27, 1987, the electoral college was abolished, restoring the system of popular election of the president. *See also:* NATIONAL CONFERENCE FOR UNIFICATION.

PRESS CODE OF ETHICS. In April 1957 the Korean Newspaper Editors Association was established, and it adopted the press code of ethics primarily to protect national security and strengthen an anti-Communist stand. The self-imposed censorship for the press remained in force until 1988.

PROGRESSIVE PARTY. This party known in Korean as Chinbodang was formed in November 1956 by Cho Pong-am, a progressive socialist who had served as the minister of agriculture and forestry under President Rhee from August 1948 to February 1949, and ran for the presidency in the 1952 presidential election. When Cho was executed for his alleged antistate activity in July 1959 his party collapsed. *See also:* CHO PONG-AM.

PU-MA DISTURBANCES. This refers to antigovernment student demonstrations which took place in the Pusan and Masan area, accompanied by bloody clashes between the demonstrators and the riot police in October 1979. These violent demonstrations brought about the declaration of garrison law, preluding the fall of the Fourth Republic. The news from Pusan and Masan provoked the students in Seoul and elsewhere to prepare for large antigovernment demonstrations similar to those of April 1960.

PUSAN POLITICAL DISTURBANCE. This event, known in Korean as *Pusan chŏngch'i p'adong,* took place in the latter part of May 1952 in connection with the controversy surrounding the constitutional revision proposed by the Rhee administration. When the opposition lawmakers refused to pass the constitutional revision bill and Chang Myŏn, the opposition leader, resigned from his prime ministership in mid-April, President Rhee appointed a new prime minister and declared martial law on May 25 in the Pusan area. The military police arrested some fifty lawmakers from the National Assembly building, charged some of them for having received political funds from "international Communist organizations," and finally forced the National Assembly to pass the bill at midnight on July 4, revising the constitution so as to institute the direct, popular election of the president and vice-president.

-R-

REBELLION ON CHEJU ISLAND. *See:* CHEJU REBELLION.

RELIGIONS. The traditional native religion of the Koreans was animistic Shamanism, which may have been brought in by the Neolithic people. It was joined by Buddhism, which was introduced to Korea in the 4th century A.D. from China and eventually became a state religion in Paekche and Shilla, flourishing after the unification of Korea by Shilla and during the Koryŏ period. Buddhism, which was rejected by the ruling class and the government of the Yi dynasty, became the religion of the rural population, but after 1900 it began to grow as religious toleration was practiced.

Catholicism, which was introduced in the 17th century also from China, and Protestantism, which arrived in the late 19th century, became two powerful Christian denominations in Korea. In fact, Christianity became a major religion in Korea, playing an influential role in political and cultural activities of the enlightened population.

Taejonggyo is another religion with a deity named Hanul (Heaven), a trinity of creator, teacher and temporal king who took the form of the person of Tan'gun, the mythical founder of the first Korean nation. This religion became virtually extinct in the 15th century, but it revived with the resurgence of Korean nationalism and spirit of independence in the late 19th and early 20th centuries.

Tonghak ("Eastern Learning") was founded in 1860. It grew strong among the oppressed and mistreated population, becoming an antiforeign force in the late 19th century. Its influence declined sharply after the uprising (Tonghak "rebellion") which its followers had brought about in 1893–94. In 1906, it was renamed Ch'ŏndogyo ("Teachings of the Heavenly Way"), and survived.

There were a half dozen other minor religions which were Confucian in ethics, Buddhistic in rituals, and Taoistic in beliefs. After the liberation of Korea, both Buddhism and Christianity grew strong, while Ch'ŏndogyo and others maintained the status quo. Meanwhile, many new Christian sects emerged, one of the most successful being the T'ongilgyo, or the "Unification Church." Dozens of quasi-religious bodies (*yusa chonggyo* in Korean) of dubious nature emerged, attracting ignorant people by quaint doctrines and methods.

There were some 12 million, or 30% of the population, who were Christians in 1987, 9 million, representing some 21%, were Buddhists, and Ch'ŏndogyo had around 53,000 followers. Islam was introduced only in 1950, and its adherents formed the Federation of Korean Islamic Churches in 1966. *See also:* BUDDHISM; CH'ŎNDOGYO; CHRISTIANITY; TAEJONGGYO; T'ONGILGYO.

REPRESENTATIVE DEMOCRATIC COUNCIL. The 50-member advisory council, Minju Ŭiwŏn in Korean, was established on February 14, 1946 by Gen. John R. Hodge, commander of U.S. Forces in South Korea. With Dr. Syngman Rhee as its chairman, half of its members were appointed by the American occupation authorities, and the rest were selected by various Korean organizations. However, the leading liberals, as well as the leftists refused to serve in it. Not cooperating with the American military government, it was replaced by the South Korean Interim Legislative Assembly in December 1946.

REUNIFICATION DEMOCRATIC PARTY. This party, known in Korean as T'ongil Minjudang, was formed in May 1987 by the followers of Kim Young-sam who defected from the New Korea Democratic Party. Kim Young-sam became its president, and when Kim Dae-jung joined the party in May it gained a considerable amount of strength as many lawmakers who defected from the New Korea Democratic Party joined its ranks. However, when Kim Dae-jung left the party and formed his own Party for Peace and Democracy in November 1987, it was badly damaged as many of its lawmakers followed Kim Dae-jung. In the 1987 presidential election, the two parties failed to form a united front and present a single presidential candidate. In the 1988 National Assembly, the Reunification Democratic Party became the second major opposition party by winning the third largest number in the National Assembly. In February 1990, it merged with the Democratic Justice Party and the New Democratic Republican Party to form the Democratic Liberal Party. *See also:* DEMOCRATIC LIBERAL PARTY; KIM YOUNG-SAM; NEW KOREA DEMOCRATIC PARTY; PARTY FOR PEACE AND DEMOCRACY.

REUNITING OF SCATTERED FAMILY MEMBERS. Virtually no attempts were made by the government to reunite family members who were separated during the Korean War. But it was a telethon which the state-run Korean Broadcasting System launched between June 30 and November 14, 1983 that brought about the reuniting of some 10,189 family members who had been separated and whose whereabouts were unknown.

RHEE (PEACE) LINE, THE. A maritime demarcation line, running on an average up to 60 miles from the Korean shores but 170 miles at its farthest point in the Sea of Japan, was imposed by Gen. Douglas MacArthur as a means of keeping Japan closely within his jurisdiction. It was reaffirmed by Gen. Mark Clark, who succeeded Gen. Ridgway—who had succeeded General MacArthur—as the head of the U.N. Command during the Korean War. This line was renamed the Rhee, or Peace Line, and was intended to conserve Korean fisheries' resources in the Sea of Japan. The line became a bone of contention between South Korea and Japan. In April 1978, the South Korean government proclaimed a 12-mile limit of territorial waters.

RHEE, SYNGMAN (1875–1965). Born as Yi Sŭng-man in P'yŏngsan, Hawanghae Province, he became a student activist as a member of a student society named Hyŏpsŏnghoe at a mission school (Paejae) in Seoul. He was an advocate of nationalism and cultural reform, joined the Independence Club when it was founded in 1896, and was imprisoned in 1898 for an alleged plot to overthrow the monarchy and establish a republic.

Released from prison in 1904, he traveled to the United States to study, earning a doctoral degree in political science in 1910 from Princeton University. He returned to Korea, but in 1912 he was forced by the Japanese to leave. Returning to the United States, he formed a nationalist society of the Koreans named Tongjihoe (Comrades Society), and in 1919 he was named premier of the Provisional Government of Korea, which was established by the Korean nationalists in Shanghai. Dr. Rhee served the Provisional Government as its president when its administrative structure was revised, remaining in that capacity until 1931. While in the United States, he fought for Korea's freedom in a variety of ways, always seeking the official recognition of the Provisional Government as a legitimate government of the Koreans in exile by the American government and others.

Returning to Korea in October 1945 following her liberation, he became the leader of a rightist National Council for the Rapid Realization of Korean Independence, which included some 50 political and social organizations. After serving as chairman of the Representative Democratic Council which the American occupation authorities had established in 1946, he was elected to the Constituent Assembly in May 1948, and he was elected by the Constitutent Assembly as the first president of the Republic of Korea. He was reelected in 1952, 1956, and 1960, becoming more and more autocratic. He was forced to resign from the presidency on April 26, 1960, marking the end of the First Republic. In late May, he left Korea in exile for Hawaii, and died there. His body was brought back to South Korea and buried at the National Cemetery.

ROH TAE-WOO (1932–). Born in a middle-class farm family in Talsŏng, North Kyŏngsang Province, he first attended Taegu Technical Middle School in 1945, and then transferred to Kyŏngbuk Middle School, graduating in 1950. He joined the army, and in 1951 he entered the Korean Military Academy to be a career military officer.

After graduating from the Korean Military Academy in 1955 he served in various positions in the army. In 1959, he studied at the U.S. Special Warfare School, and in 1968 he graduated from the Korean Army War College. As he rose in rank, he served as commander of the 9th Special Forces Brigade (1974–79), commander of the 9th Infantry Division (1979), commander of Capital Security Command (1979), and in December 1979, after taking part in the December coup engineered by Gen. Chun Doo-hwan, he became commander of the Defense Security Command in August 1980.

When the Democratic Justice Party was inaugurated, he joined it, and after retiring from the army as a four-star general in July 1981 he served as minister of state for political and security affairs (1981–83), minister of sports (1982), minister of home affairs (1982–83), and in July 1983 he was named president of the Seoul Olympic Organizing Committee, becoming president of the Korean Olympic Committee in October 1984.

Elected as a member of the National Assembly in 1985, he

served as chairman of the ruling Democratic Justice Party. On June 10, during the hectic period of 1987, he was nominated as presidential candidate by his party for the 1987 presidential election, and on June 29 he made a stunning announcement regarding his plan for democratic reform in his Special Declaration for Grand National Harmony and Progress Towards a Great Nation.

On August 5, 1987 Roh replaced President Chun as president of the ruling Democratic Justice Party, and in the December 16, 1987 presidential election, he won the election as the 13th president by 36.6% of the popular vote, defeating four other candidates.

On February 25, 1988, he took the oath of office, inaugurating the Sixth Republic.

-S-

SAENARA DATSUN AUTOMOBILE SCANDAL. In February 1964, the opposition party lawmakers brought charges against illegal stock market manipulation and dubious financial dealings by members of the Democratic Republican Party in connection with importation of Saenara Datsun automobiles from the Japanese Datsun Company in 1963. These cases, plus two other scandalous financial and business dealings of ruling Democratic Republican Party members, constituted the so-called "four great economic scandals."

SAMMINT'UWI. *See:* STUDENT MOVEMENT.

SEVEN-POINT CONDITIONS FOR DEMOCRATIZATION. Proposed on December 24, 1986 by the New Korea Democratic Party, they included: guarantee for freedom of speech, assembly, and the press, adoption of a new fair election law, inauguration of local self-rule, political neutrality of government officials, strengthening of party politics, release of political prisoners, and restoration of civil rights of all former political leaders.

SHAMANISM. One of the earliest religions of the inhabitants of the Korean peninsula recognizing a myriad of spirits which affect the well-being of the people directly or indirectly. According to this belief, these spirits must be pacified to avoid evil consequences and their favors solicited to ensure the safety and good fortune of both individuals and village communities. Shaman priests and priestesses, commonly called *mudang,* perform a variety of religious rituals to exorcise evil spirits. There are no specific temples or shrines for the spirits, as in the case of Buddhism and Confucianism, but Korean villages used to have their shaman shrines (usually huts) called *sŏnghwangdang* in remote locations near the villages.

Regarded as superstition, Shamanism was practiced mostly by the uneducated population, particularly by women. At one time, it was outlawed (banned), but in recent years its popularity has become noticeable.

SHIN IK-HŬI (1892–1956). Born in Kwangju, Kyŏnggi Province, he became a freedom fighter while studying at Waseda University in Tokyo. Graduating from that university in 1913, he returned to Korea and taught at secondary school first, and then at Posŏng College for Commerce and Law. In 1918, he became involved in the independence movement. In the spring of 1919, he fled to Shanghai where he participated in the establishment of the Provisional Government of Korea in exile there becoming vice-chairman of its legislative council in 1922. He served in various positions in the Provisional Government of Korea until he returned to Korea in 1945.

Returning home, he founded Kungmin University in Seoul and served as a member of the South Korean Interim Legislative Assembly in 1947 as he and Chi Ch'ŏng-ch'ŏn of the Taedong Youth Corps united their organizations into the Korean Nationalist Party. He was elected to the Constituent Assembly in May 1948, serving as its vice-chairman first, and then chairman, replacing Dr. Rhee who was elected president of the Republic.

In 1949, his party and the Korean (Han'guk) Democratic Party merged into the Democratic Nationalist Party. Elected to the National Assembly in 1950, he expanded his party into the Democratic Party in 1955, becoming its president. He was nominated by his party as a presidential candidate in the 1956 presidential election, but he died of a stroke during his heated campaign.

SIX PLEDGES OF THE MILITARY REVOLUTIONARY COMMITTEE. On May 18, 1961 the military revolutionaries who overthrew the Second Republic and established the Military Revolutionary Committee announced the six pledges to win the support of the people. They were:

1. Positive, uncompromising opposition to Communism is the basis of our policy.

2. We shall respect and observe the United Nations Charter, and strengthen our relations with the United States and other Free World Nations.

3. We shall eliminate corruption, and eradicate other social evils which have become prevalent in our country; we shall inculcate fresh and wholesome moral and mental attitudes among the people.

4. We shall provide relief for poverty-stricken and hungry people, and devote our entire energies toward the development of a self-sustaining economy.

5. We shall strengthen our military power and determination to combat Communism, looking forward to the eventual achievement of our unchangeable goal of national unification.

6. As soldiers, after we have completed our mission, we shall restore the government to honest and conscientious civilians, and return to our proper military duties. As citizens, we shall devote ourselves without reservation to the accomplishment of these tasks, and to the construction of a solid foundation for a new and truly democratic republic.

SIXTEEN NATIONS DECLARATION ON KOREA. On July 27, 1953, when the Korean armistice was signed, the sixteen nations whose troops composed the United Nations Forces and fought in the Korean War issued a Joint Policy Declaration Concerning the Korean Armistice, pledging that they would again unite to resist any renewed Communist aggression. On July 15, 1954 at Geneva, these sixteen nations also declared that further consideration and examination of the Korean question should be transferred to the United Nations. *See also:* GENEVA CONFERENCE; KOREAN WAR; U.N. COMMAND.

SOCIAL AND CULTURAL DEVELOPMENTS. The most significant social change was the rise of the middle class. The Japanese colonial rule had modernized the traditional social structure of Korea somewhat when it reduced the power and privileges of the upper class (*yangban*) and created new conditions which allowed the rise of the commoners. However, it was South Korea's rapid economic development which increased the number of professional and skilled people, enabling them to establish a solid and growing middle class. A recent poll indicated that some 65% of the population regarded themselves as "middle class."

As the economic structure changed, migration of the rural population into urban areas and new industrial centers took place. The urban population grew at an annual average rate of 5% after 1955, while the population in rural areas showed a commensurate decrease. The migration of rural population grew faster from the mid-1960s. The number of people engaged in agriculture, forestry, and fisheries declined from 9.1 million in 1966 to 3.6 million in 1985 while the number of industrial workers grew from 1.1 million in 1966 to 4.6 million, and the number of those who were engaged in the social services sector grew from 2.5 million in 1966 to 8.2 million in 1987. According to the 1985 census, the urban population stood at 26.5 million, or 66% of the total population of 40.5 million, and the rural population was 14 million, or 34% of the total population.

The urbanization of South Korea brought about an increase

in the population of many cities. For example, the population of Seoul grew from about one million in 1948 to 10 million by 1987, that of Pusan from 500,000 to 3.5 million, that of Taegu from 250,000 to 2.0 million, and those of Inch'ŏn, Taejŏn, and Kwangju grew a little over one million each.

With the improvement of living standards, the death rate and the rate of birth decreased. The percentage of the annual rate of birth declined from 3.0% in the 1950s to 1.3% in the 1980s, but the population grew from 21.5 million in 1955 to 42 million in 1987. This was due to the fact that the average life expectancy increased from 51.1 years for men and 53.7 years for women in 1960, and to 69.5 for men and 73.3 for women in 1987. The average Korean woman had 6.1 children in 1960, but this dropped to 4.2 in 1970, 2.8 in 1980, and 2.3 in 1987. The rate of population growth in the 1960–66 period was 2.7%, but it dropped to 2.3 in the 1966–70 period, 1.9% in the 1972–75 period, and in 1987 it was 1.37%.

The disappearance of the traditional social class structure, along with the rise of a new middle class and a new elite business community, contributed to the growth of social equality. Individual ability and educational background, rather than birthright, became the means by which to rise in social status. Although many leaders came from a formerly high social class, such as *yangban,* a majority of the new Korean leaders were from the commoner class. The economic development which affected the rural economy also closed the gap between the living standards of the urban population and the rural areas in conjunction with the New Community Movement.

Another important social change was the rise in social status of women. A growing number of women with higher education became professionals, and along with the increasing number of women wage earners they brought about a growing social equality with men, although there are many areas where considerable disparity still exists. The increase of the number of nuclear families and the commensurate decrease of the number of extended families constituted another important social change.

As the educated population grew, the number of newspapers increased to 31 by 1987. Of these, five were national papers, and others were local papers. Two of them were English-language dailies. The total circulation of daily newspapers surpassed the 15 million mark in 1987. Meanwhile, meeting the growing demands for more reading materials, hundreds of magazines and journals were published and the number of copies of books published reached the 65 million mark in 1987.

The radio broadcasting system which had existed was renamed the KBS-Radio, and in 1956 the KBS-TV began television broadcasting. Following this, private radio and television networks such as CBS, MBC, TBS and FEBC were established. However, in 1980, the state-owned KBS, and the MBC absorbed the private radio and television networks. As of 1989, the KBS-TV featured four channels and MBC-TV had one channel with 20 local stations. In 1987, nearly all Korean homes had radio and television sets, thanks also to electrification of the rural areas.

While reviving traditional national culture, especially music, dance, and painting, South Korea at the same time promoted modern culture, importing a variety of new foreign cultures, particularly in the area of music and art. Meanwhile, the traditional religions—Buddhism and Shamanism—remained strong while Christianity became the major religion. Confucianism is still practiced by a vast number of people as they maintain Confucian morality and ethics, rituals, and social values. The Confucian shrine in Seoul observes semiannual rituals in honor of the Chinese sage. *See also:* ECONOMIC DEVELOPMENT; EDUCATIONAL DEVELOPMENT; "MASSACRE OF THE MASS MEDIA"; NEW COMMUNITY MOVEMENT; RELIGIONS; TRANSPORTATION AND COMMUNICATIONS; WOMEN'S MOVEMENT.

SONG CHIN-U (1889–1945). Born to a well-to-do family in Tamyang, South Chŏlla Province, he received both traditional and modern education in Korea as a child, followed by secondary education in Japan. While studying at Meiji University from 1911, be became a student activist in the nationalist movement of the Korean students in Japan. Graduating from Meiji University in 1915, he returned to Korea and became the principal of a private Chung'ang School which his friend,

Kim Sŏng-su, established in Seoul, and promoted ethnic consciousness and patriotism among the students.

Arrested for his nationalistic activity in connection with the March First Movement of 1919, he was imprisoned for one and a half years. In 1920, when the Tong-a Ilbo Press was established, he was made its president, playing an important role as a nationalist leader during the Japanese colonial period.

Upon Korea's liberation, he and his childhood friends, such as Kim Sŏng-su, formed the Korean (Han'guk) Democratic Party, which represented a conservative, nationalist, propertied class, and became one of its key leaders. Although he opposed the leftists, his views regarding the Allied plan to impose a trusteeship in Korea alienated him from other right-wing leaders, for he was in support of such steps for Korean independence for practical reasons. Two days after his statement regarding his support for the trusteeship plan on December 28, 1945 was made public, he was assassinated by an ultra right-wing youth. *See also:* ASSASSINATION AND ASSASSINATION ATTEMPTS; KIM SŎNG-SU, KOREAN (HAN'GUK) DEMOCRATIC PARTY; MOSCOW AGREEMENT.

SOUTH KOREA-JAPAN NORMALIZATION TREATY. Several series of talks to establish normal relations between South Korea and Japan which were held between the representatives of the two governments eventually brought about the signing of this treaty on June 22, 1965 in Tokyo, settling several thorny issues which the two countries had faced.

The main aspects of the Normalization Treaty included: establishment of diplomatic and commercial relations between the two countries; nullification of all treaties which had been signed prior to August 22, 1910, between Korea and Japan; and Japan's reaffirmation of the government of the Republic of Korea as the only lawful government in the Korean Peninsula. With the conclusion of this treaty, Japan tactfully recognized the legitimacy of the Rhee (Peace) Line, and made property compensation (reparation) in the amount of $300 million, and agreed to make government and commercial loans to South Korea amounting to $300 million. Such thorny issues as the status of Koreans residing in Japan and the ownership of an island named Tokto in the Sea of Japan were left unsettled.

The long series of talks began in October 1951, but full meetings of the representatives of both governments were not held until April 15–21, 1952. The second full meeting was held between April 15 and July 23, 1953, and the third full meeting began on October 6, 1953. However, the talks were broken off when on October 21 Japan's chief delegate, Kuboda Kan'ichiro, made a statement regarding "beneficial Japanese rule in Korea," inflaming anti-Japanese sentiment.

Only after Kuboda withdrew his statement were the talks resumed in April, 1958, but they were interrupted by the April Student Uprising in Korea in 1960. After some preliminary meetings, the fifth full meeting began on October 25, 1960, but it too was cut short by the military revolution in May 1961.

Those who brought about the May Military Revolution were anxious to solve the pending problems between South Korea and Japan, and to secure financial and technical assistance from Japan for South Korea's economic reconstruction. Therefore, in October 1961 the military junta took the initiative, reopening the talks with the Japanese. During the period of the sixth series of talks, General Park Chung-hee met Japanese Prime Minister Ikeda Hayato on November 12, 1961 in Tokyo on the way to the United States, and special meetings of the foreign ministers of South Korea and Japan were held in March 1962 and March 1963, followed by an exclusive meeting between Kim Jong-pil and Japanese Foreign Minister Ōhira Masayoshi in Tokyo from October 20 to November 12, 1962 which resulted in the issuance of the Kim-Ōhira Memorandum. These top-level special meetings brought about the final stage leading toward the culmination of a long series of talks.

The seventh talks which began on December 3, 1964 saw the initialing on February 20, 1965 of the Normalization Treaty in Seoul. The treaty was officially concluded in Tokyo on June 22. *See also:* FOREIGN AFFAIRS; RHEE (PEACE) LINE, THE.

SOUTH KOREA-U.S. MUTUAL DEFENSE TREATY. Recognizing that "an armed attack in the Pacific Area on either of the Parties . . . would be dangerous to its own peace and safety . . ." the Republic of Korea and the United States signed a mutual defense treaty on October 1, 1953. Under the treaty, the United States provided defense assistance to South Korea and maintained its troops there as a deterrent to North Korea's new armed invasion.

SOUTH KOREAN INTERIM GOVERNMENT. With the appointment of An Chae-hong as Civil Administrator in February 1947, the Korean element of the American military government which actually handled administration was named the South Korean Interim Government (SKIG, or Nam Chosŏn Kwado Chŏngbu). However, the U.S. Army Military Government in Korea was not abolished, and South Korea was ruled by a military governor who headed that government. The SKIG had no independent power.

SOUTH KOREAN INTERIM LEGISLATIVE ASSEMBLY. Following the announcement on October 3, 1946 by Gen. John R. Hodge, commander of U.S. forces in South Korea, the South Korean Interim Legislative Assembly (SKILA, or Nam Chosŏn Kwado Ippŏp Ŭiwŏn) was established as a branch of the SKIG, replacing the Representative Democratic Council. However, it legislated no laws as such for the SKIG; only certain laws requested by the USAMGIK were written.

Composed of 90 members, 45 of them were appointed by the American military government, and the other members were elected by the people. More than half of them were right-wing nationalists, 16 were moderates, and 14 were leftists.

SOUTH KOREAN WORKERS' PARTY. *See:* KOREAN COMMUNIST PARTY.

SPECIAL COMMITTEE FOR NATIONAL SECURITY MEASURES (SCNSM). On May 31, 1980, in the wake of the Kwangju incident, the government established this committee, granting it extraordinary power. General Chun Doo-hwan, commander of the Defense Security Command, was named by President Ch'oe Kyu-ha as head of the Standing Committee of the SCNSM. Composed of some 30 high-ranking army officers, the SCNSM replaced the National Assembly and decreed many laws. In addition, it adopted several amendments to the Constitution, dissolved all existing political parties, and it put a total of 835 persons on a political blacklist, depriving them of any rights to engage in political activity. The SCNSM was abolished in October 1981 following the establishment of the Fifth Republic in March. *See also:* CONSTITUTIONAL AMENDMENTS; KWANGJU UPRISING.

SPECIAL COMMITTEE FOR THE INVESTIGATION OF ILLEGAL ACTIVITIES OF THE FIFTH REPUBLIC. A special committee of the National Assembly formed in June 1988 to investigate wrongdoings of the ex-president Chun and top leaders of the Fifth Republic. Although it was unable to bring former president Ch'oe Kyu-ha to testify before the National Assembly, it was able to make former president Chun testify before the National Assembly in December 1989. Although the Special Committee could not expose most of the serious wrongdoings of the Chun administration, in February 1989 the Prosecutor-General's Office arrested some 47 persons, most of whom had been high government officials and close relatives of the ex-president Chun. *See also:* CH'OE KYU-HA; CHUN DOO-HWAN.

SPECIAL COMMITTEE ON CONSTITUTIONAL AMENDMENT. An ad hoc 24-member committee of the National Assembly established in November 1979 for the purpose of drafting a new constitution, abolishing the *Yushin* Constitution. *See also:* CONSTITUTIONAL AMENDMENTS.

SPECIAL MEASURES LAW FOR NATIONAL SECURITY AND DEFENSE. On December 26, 1971 following the proclamation of a state of national emergency by the president on December 6, the National Assembly passed this law without the presence of the opposition party lawmakers. The law empowered the president to exercise, whenever the need arose, the same power which he would otherwise be able to invoke only under martial law. The law, which was immediately proclaimed, authorized the president to curb press freedom, freeze wages and prices, restrict outdoor assemblage and demonstrations, and forbid labor strikes. *See also:* NATIONAL SECURITY LAWS.

SPECIAL PARLIAMENTARY COUNCIL ON REUNIFICATION ISSUES. A committee of the National Assembly set up in June 1988 to deal with all matters related to reunification of Korea.

STATE AFFAIRS COUNCIL. The cabinet of the Republic of Korea which was known as the State Council until 1962. Up to August 1960, it was a consultative administrative council of ministers controlled by the president. During the Second Republic period (August 1960–May 1961), it was a cabinet responsible to the National Assembly. After the fall of the Second Republic, the State Council was renamed the State Affairs Council, becoming a consultative body to the president. The prime ministers were appointed by the president, and all cabinet ministers were appointed by the prime minister with the approval of the president.

STUDENT MOVEMENT. Korean students had been politically active during the Japanese colonial period, engaged in various anti-Japanese activities and national independence as well as cultural and social movements. This legacy was inherited by students of the post-liberation periods, and from time to time they demonstrated their student power.

The student movement of the 1948–60 period was involved mainly in the struggle against the autocratic rule of President Rhee and the corruptive political practices of his administration and the Liberal Party, culminating in the April 1960 Student Uprising which overthrew the First Republic. After the May 16 Military Revolution of 1961, the student movement continued to grow in strength as students increased their demand for democracy. They demonstrated in 1964 against the conclusion of a "humiliating treaty" with Japan and the dispatch of South Korean troops to South Vietnam, bringing about the declaration of a state of emergency in the Seoul area in June. When President Park adopted the *Yushin* Constitution in October 1972, Korean students, who formed the Federation of Democratic Youth and Students in 1974, became the most active protesters, critics, and advocates for the revision of the constitution and the restoration of democracy, resulting in the Pusan-Masan revolt in October 1979 which led to the assassination of President Park. Along with their struggle for democracy, they were also protesting against compulsory student military training, pro-government professors, and economic and social injustices. Although the students initiated their antiestablishment and unification movements in 1960, creating many problems for the government of the Second Republic, the main purpose of the student movement of the period before the 1980s was to bring about the establishment of democratic government.

Following the death of President Park, the student movement was directed toward the adoption of a new constitution to replace the *Yushin* Constitution, the lifting of Emergency Martial Law issued on October 27, 1979, and the establishment of campus autonomy. Their movement escalated into more violent and frequent on-campus demonstrations.

When Gen. Chun Doo-hwan carried out his December 12th coup of 1979 and became acting director of the KCIA in April 1980, "a great march for democracy" of the students began, accompanied by widespread street demonstrations and violence in May. On May 17, some 90 representatives of the student associations in Seoul met and discussed their plans of action.

When the Kwangju Uprising broke out on May 18, hundreds of students in that city led the citizens in a bloody confrontation with troops, resulting in the "Kwangju massacre." After the Kwangju Uprising, the student movement not only struggled for democracy, but also for economic and social justice. Also apparent was their growing anti-U.S. sentiments as well as their desire for early Korean unification. There were many violent clashes with the riot police and deaths among the students. Some 2,900, or 85.2% of 3,400 political prisoners were students as of December 16, 1986. Between 1980 and 1987, a total of 124,600 students were expelled from colleges and universities.

Following the Kwangju Uprising, students put their efforts into broadening the basis of their movements by pursuing intercampus cooperation and a variety of forms of solidarity movements with the working people. At the same time, the movement expanded into a force of 2,000 students who were radicalized and imbued with a militant political ideology. Thus, in April 1985 the radical students from 23 colleges and universities formed a new National Federation of Student Associations (Chŏnhakyŏn), and its political arm called the Committee for the Three People's Struggle (Sammint'uwi) whose ideologies are characterized by three basic goals—the liberation of the masses (*minjung haebang*), the attainment of democracy (*minju chaengch'wi*), and the unification of the Korean people (*minzok t'ongil*). The leadership of the Sammint'uwi disintegrated with the arrest of its leaders, but in the spring of 1986 two more militant, antistate organizations called Minmint'u (People's Struggle for Democracy) and Chamint'u (Self-oriented Struggle for Democracy) emerged with distinctive ideologies.

Many college students who belonged to these radical groups left their schools, securing employment at various industrial establishments disguised as laborers, and aroused a new social consciousness among the workers as they organized them for the labor struggle.

Whereas the Minmint'u theorized that the current problems of the Korean society were created by internal forces, its class structure, and its inherent contradictions, and believed that by overthrowing the "military facist regime" it was possible to eliminate the influence of foreign powers, achieve people's democracy, and bring about the unification of the country, the Chamint'u argued that the existing contradictions of Korean society developed because of the external forces which influenced the internal workings of Korean society. The Chamint'u saw South Korea as a neocolonial society, advocating the so-called *chuch'e* (self-oriented) ideology of Kim Il-sung of North Korea. Thus, known as the *chusap'a* (the *chuch'e* faction), it focused its efforts on the elimination of foreign imperialist influences, pursuing antiforeignism, anti-imperialism, and anti-neocolonialism. On the whole, the Minmint'u sought to bring about "anti-imperialist people's democratic revolution," while the Chamint'u pursued its goal to bring about a "national liberation people's democratic revolution."

In June 1988, following the crackdown on radical groups, the national liberation movement of the Chamint'u formed the National Council of University Student Representatives (Chŏndaehyŏp) of some 115 colleges, pursuing three goals of democratization with socialism, the anti-U.S. reunification movement, and North-South student talks, and it sent a coed to North Korea's World Youth Festival held in Pyongyang in July 1989.

The radical student activism brought about the May 3rd Inch'ŏn Incident of 1986, the Kŏnguk University Incident of 1987, the June 10th Myŏngdong Cathedral Incident of 1987, the June 28th Peace March Movement of 1987, the Tongŭi University Incident of May 1989, and the invasion of the residence of the American ambassador in October 1989, as well as many violent demonstrations on campuses and in the streets in 1988 and 1989.

The sending of a coed to Pyongyang's festival and the disclosure of the killing by torture of a student, suspected of being a spy for intelligence agencies, in October 1989 by a few radical members of the Chŏndaehyŏp brought about the split in the college student activism between the radical faction, advocating national liberation with the *chuch'e* ideology, and the moderate faction, preaching the people's democracy without the *chuch'e* ideology. It was at this time that the people's democracy group formed a separate National Federation of Students for People's Democracy (Chŏnminhakyŏn). Meanwhile, an increasing number of college students deserted both Chŏndaehyŏp and Chŏnminhakyŏn.

STUDENT NATIONAL DEFENSE CORPS. Established in March 1949, the corps was aimed at providing spiritual and military training to college students, as well as enhancing national security. All college students were required to take a certain number of hours in military training. When the Korean War broke out, in July 1950, student volunteer units were organized and they were sent to the battlefields to augment the regular army. The corps and compulsory military training were abolished in 1988.

SUPREME COUNCIL FOR NATIONAL RECONSTRUCTION. On May 16, 1961, when the military revolutionaries carried out their coup, the Military Revolutionary Committee (MRC) consisting of five generals was established. It immediately exercised executive, legislative, and judicial functions of the government, and its first three decrees froze all bank assets, closed airports and harbors, placed publications under strict censorship, and forbade assembly. The committee headed by Lt. Gen. Chang To-yŏng, issued its six revolutionary pledges on May 18.

On May 20, the committee was renamed the Supreme Council for National Reconstruction (SCNR) following the proclamation of the Law Concerning Extraordinary Measures for National Reconstruction on May 19. It became the supreme organ of the state, consisting of thirty Supreme Councilors and two advisers. Three Supreme Councilors were Marine Corps generals, one each from the Air Force and the Navy, and the rest from the Army. The two advisers were retired military officers. Nineteen out of the thirty members were generals, and about a third of them were lieutenant colonels and colonels.

Lt. Gen. Chang served as its chairman until July, when he was replaced by Maj. Gen. Park Chung-hee. Its chairman was the head of the cabinet, or the prime minister. The Supreme Council adopted the following: Law Concerning Temporary Measures aimed at the Settlement of Critical Situations; the Revolutionary Court and Prosecution Law; the Political Activities Purification Law; the Political Party Law; the Anti-Communism Law. In June it established the Korean Central Intelligence Agency. With the restoration of a civilian government in December 1963 the Supreme Council completed its revolutionary task and went out of existence. *See also:* MILITARY REVOLUTION OF MAY 16, 1961; CHANG TO-YŎNG; PARK CHUNG-HEE.

-T-

TAEDŎK INDUSTRIAL RESEARCH TOWN. This new science town was established in 1977 by the government on the outskirts of Taejŏn, South Ch'ungch'ŏng Province, to ensure cooperative research among the various fields of science and joint utilization of facilities and equipment by bringing various research institutes together in one area. Among some of the major research institutes which were relocated at Taedŏk Industrial Research Town are the Korea Research Institute of Ships and Oceanography, the Korea Standard Research Institute, the Nuclear Fuel Development Institute, the Korea Research Institute of Geoscience and Mineral Resources, the Korea Telecommunications Institute, and the Korea Chemical Research Institute.

TAEDONG YOUTH CORPS. An ultrarightist youth organization established in September 1947 by Gen. Yi Ch'ŏng-ch'ŏn, a military leader who returned to Korea from China in 1945. With Dr. Syngman Rhee as its president, it combatted the leftists, particularly the Communists. In the 1948 general elections for the Constituent Assembly, its members won twelve seats and it gave strong support to President Rhee after 1948. At one point, it had over a million members.

TAEHAN YOUTH CORPS. *See:* KOREAN NATIONAL YOUTH CORPS.

TAEJONGGYO. A native religious cult which regards the divinity called Hanul as the supreme god. Hanul is a trinity—creator, teacher, and temporal king. It believes that this god took human form in the person of Tan'gun, and as father, teacher, and king of the Korean people, he founded the first Korean nation in 2333 B.C. By the 15th century, this cult had practically disappeared, but with the resurgence of Korean nationalism in recent times there emerged several sects within the cult. On October 3 of each year, the founding of the Korean nation by Tan'gun is celebrated. *See also:* RELIGIONS.

THIRTY-EIGHTH PARALLEL LINE. The parallel 38° N cuts through farms, villages, and long-existing administrative units of Korea in the 150-mile-long belt zone of the peninsula. When Soviet troops moved down swiftly southward following their invasion of Korea that began on August 10, 1945, (two days after the Soviet Union declared war on Japan), and as it seemed that the entire Korean Peninsula might be occupied by

Soviet troops before the arrival of U.S. troops, on August 13 the United States government proposed to the Soviet government the division of Korea into two military operational zones along this parallel line. Stalin requested minor changes in the American proposal, but accepted the provision of the 38th parallel without objection. The line of demarcation was "intended to be temporary and only to fix responsibility" between the United States and the Soviet Union for carrying out the Japanese surrender.

The 38th parallel line eventually became the boundary between North and South Korea in 1948.

TONGHAK. *See:* CH'ŎNDOGYO.

T'ONGILGYO. This most successful new Christian sect was organized as the Olive Tree Society by a former elder of the Presbyterian church, Moon Sun-myong, shortly after Korea's liberation from Japan. It was reorganized as T'ongilgyo, or the Holy Spirit Association for the Unification of World Christianity, and therefore became known as the Unification Church. When Rev. Moon was persecuted in South Korea, he relocated his base to the United States, expanding the activities of the sect. *See also:* RELIGIONS.

TRANSPORTATION AND COMMUNICATIONS. South Korea's transportation system was modernized, accompanying the expansion of railway mileage from 2,318 miles in 1945 to 3,987 miles by 1987. Of this, 503 miles were double-track railways while 292 miles were electric railways. All railways were nationally owned as before.

The mileage of highways also increased as four-lane expressways were constructed and the highway projects were launched in the 1960s. The Seoul-Inch'ŏn Expressway was opened in 1960, followed in 1970 by the 270-mile-long Seoul-Pusan Expressway. The latter runs the whole length of the country from Seoul, passing through such industrial and urban centers as Suwŏn, Ch'ŏnan, Taejŏn, and Taegu. Following the completion of these projects, additional expressways were built, bringing the total mileage of expressways close to

1,200 miles in 1987. Meanwhile, the subways completed between 1974 and 1987 vastly reduced traffic problems in the capital city, and construction of subways in Pusan began in 1987.

The government-owned and operated Korean Air Lines was turned over to a private company in 1963, and by the end of 1987 it had established 39 air routes connecting 24 foreign cities in 15 nations. In 1987, the number of domestic air routes reached 15. Another Korean airline company (Asiana) received a charter in 1988, beginning its domestic and foreign air traffic.

The communication system was also modernized with the introduction of a new telegraph and telephone system. In 1987, the number of telephone circuits grew to 10 million, and the number of telephone subscribers grew to 8.6 million with 20 out of every 100 homes having telephones. The newly established Korean Telecommunication Authority adopted a plan to add one million telephones each year during the sixth Five-Year Economic and Social Development Plan period from 1987 to 1991. In 1987, South Korea established its international facsimile services with 20 foreign countries, and the number continued to grow after that.

-U-

UNIFICATION CHURCH. *See:* T'ONGILGYO.

UNIFICATION NATIONAL PARTY. This party whose Korean name is T'ongil Kungmindang, is also known as United People's Party. It was formed in January 1992 by Chŏng Chu-yŏng, founder and chairman of the Hyundai Group. In February, it merged with the New Korea Party of Kim Tong-gil (formed in January 1992). A little over a month after its formation, its candidates won 24 district seats in the 14th National Assembly elections held in March. When the new National Assembly was formed, the Unification National Party was allocated seven at-large seats, making it a viable opposition party. *See also:* NEW KOREA PARTY.

UNIFICATION REVOLUTIONARY PARTY, THE CASE OF. An underground "party" said to have been established in South Korea by the North Korean Communists. In August 1968, the Korean CIA arrested some 73 of its members as antistate, espionage terrorists, and imprisoned them.

U.N. CIVIL ASSISTANCE COMMAND. *See:* CIVIL RELIEF IN KOREA.

U.N. COMMAND. After condemning North Korea as an aggressor, the United Nations Security Council resolved in July 1950 to establish the U.N. forces and the U.N. Command headquarters. A U.S. General, Douglas MacArthur, was named commander of the U.N. Command, and its troops, contributed by sixteen U.N. member nations and South Korea, countered the North Korean and the Chinese forces in the Korean War. *See also:* U.N. FORCES; U.N. SECURITY COUNCIL RESOLUTIONS.

U.N. COMMISSION FOR UNIFICATION AND REHABILITATION OF KOREA (UNCURK). In October 1950, the General Assembly of the United Nations established this commission, replacing the U.N. Commission of Korea. However, two months later, it was replaced by the United Nations Korean Reconstruction Agency (UNKRA). It was set up to be engaged in long-run reconstruction projects at the end of the Korean War. It actually provided only $150 million for the purpose up to June 1960. *See also:* U.N. TEMPORARY COMMISSION ON KOREA.

U.N. FORCES. After condemning North Korea as an aggressor, the Security Council of the United Nations, on June 27, 1950 asked the member nations of the U.N. to donate their troops to aid South Korea to repel the aggressors. A total of 16 nations provided ground forces, eight nations provided naval forces, and five nations donated air forces.

On July 10, the U.N. Command was established and U.S. General Douglas MacArthur was named its commander. Those nations which provided ground forces were: Australia, Belgium, Canada, Colombia, Cuba, Ethiopia, France, Greece,

Luxemburg, the Netherlands, New Zealand, the Philippines, Thailand, Turkey, the United Kingdom, and the United States. Those nations which provided naval forces were: Australia, Canada, Colombia, France, the Netherlands, Thailand, the United Kingdom, and the United States. Australia, Canada, the Union of South Africa, the United Kingdom and the United States also provided air forces.

Several other U.N. member nations provided medical services. They were: Denmark, India, Italy, Norway, Sweden, and the United Kingdom. Bolivia, China (Taiwan), Costa Rica, El Salvador and Panama offered their troops, but acceptance of their offer was deferred.

All armed forces provided by these nations, plus those of South Korea, were put under the United Nations Command. *See also:* KOREAN WAR; U.N. COMMAND.

U.N. KOREAN RECONSTRUCTION AGENCY (UNKRA). *See:* U.N. COMMISSION FOR UNIFICATION AND REHABILITATION OF KOREA.

U.N. RESOLUTION ON KOREA. On November 14, 1947, the United Nations General Assembly adopted a resolution to establish a unified government of Korea through general elections under the supervision of the U.N. This resolution was adopted following the presentation of the Korean question by the U.S. government to the U.N. General Assembly in September. The United States saw the futility of attempting to solve the Korean question with the Soviet Union through the Joint U.S.-Soviet Commission. *See also:* KOREAN WAR; U.N. COMMISSION FOR UNIFICATION AND REHABILITATION OF KOREA (UNCURK); U.N. TEMPORARY COMMISSION ON KOREA.

U.N. TEMPORARY COMMISSION ON KOREA. After the adoption of the resolution on Korea on November 14, 1947, the General Assembly of the United Nations created the U.N. Temporary Commission on Korea, consisting of representatives of Australia, Canada, China, El Salvador, France, India, the Philippines, Syria, and the Ukrainian Socialist Soviet Republic, for the purpose of fulfilling the program outlined in the resolution, namely to establish a unified government through general elections.

After conducting the May 10, 1948 general elections only in South Korea, the U.N. General Assembly, under a U.S. proposal, adopted a resolution on December 12 to replace the U.N. Temporary Commission on Korea with a new U.N. Commission on Korea, and authorized it to travel, consult, and observe throughout Korea for the purpose of fulfilling the original aims of the U.N. resolution of November 14, 1947. During the Korean War, it was replaced by other U.N. agencies. *See also:* U.N. COMMISSION FOR UNIFICATION AND REHABILITATION OF KOREA; U.N. RESOLUTION ON KOREA.

UNITED PEOPLE'S PARTY. *See:* UNIFICATION NATIONAL PARTY.

U.S. MILITARY ADVISORY GROUP. *See:* U.S. TROOPS IN KOREA.

U.S.-SOUTH KOREA COMBINED FORCES. On November 7, 1978, the United States and the South Korean Combined Forces Command was formally activated for the purpose of strengthening South Korea's defense posture. Under the agreement, the commander of the U.S. Forces in Korea and of the U.N. Command was to be commander of the Combined Forces with a Korean general as deputy commander. Under this system nearly all South Korean combat troops were put under the control of the joint U.S.-South Korea Military Commission.

U.S.-SOUTH KOREA MUTUAL DEFENSE TREATY. The Mutual Defense Treaty between the United States and the Republic of Korea was signed on October 1, 1953 in Washington D.C. The most crucial aspect of the six-article treaty is found in Article III which stated: "Each Party recognizes that an armed attack in the Pacific area on either of the Parties in territories now under their respective administrative control, or hereafter recognized by one of the Parties as lawfully brought under the administrative control of the other, would be dangerous to its own peace and safety and declares that it would act to meet the common danger in accordance with its constitutional processes."

The United States Senate gave its advice and consent to the ratification of the treaty with the understanding "that neither party is obligated, under Article III of the [Treaty], to come to the aid of the other except in case of an external armed attack against such party; nor shall anything in the present Treaty be construed as requiring the United States to give assistance to Korea except in the event of an armed attack against territory which has been recognized by the United States . . .".

The treaty was for an indefinite period, and either party could terminate it one year after giving notice to the other party. *See also:* KOREAN WAR.

U.S.-SOUTH KOREA STATUS-OF-FORCES AGREEMENT. The Agreement on the Status of American Forces in Korea was signed on July 9, 1966 with South Korea, as a supplement agreement to Article IV of the U.S.-South Korea Mutual Defense Treaty. Until the Status-of-Forces Agreement was signed, the legal status of the visiting forces of the United States in South Korea had been determined by individual *ad hoc* agreements and others which were initially agreed upon during the Korean War.

Along with agreements on facilities and areas used by the U.S. armed forces, this agreement provides a device for resolving the critical problems of legal jurisdiction when crimes are committed, property is damaged or destroyed, and/or local inhabitants are injured by the visiting forces. In 1990, the U.S.-South Korea Status-of-Forces Agreement was modified to give the Korean side more latitude in the arrest and prosecution of American military personnel charged with crimes in South Korea. *See also:* KOREAN WAR; U.S.-SOUTH KOREA MUTUAL DEFENSE TREATY; U.S. TROOPS IN SOUTH KOREA.

U.S. TROOPS IN SOUTH KOREA. The presence of U.S. troops in Korea, officially called United States Armed Forces in Korea (USAFIK), began with the arrival of an advance team of the XXIVth Corps on September 4, 1945, followed by the landing of 72,000 men of the Seventh, the Fortieth, and the Sixth infantry divisions of the XXIV Corps of the U.S. Eighth Army between September 8 and October 8. The commander of the U.S. Forces in Korea was Lt. Gen. John R. Hodge, a seasoned soldier who was assigned to accept the surrender of the Japanese governor-general in Korea, disarm Japanese troops and repatriate them, and maintain law and order. He was also instructed to establish an effective government along democratic lines and rebuild a sound economy as a basis for Korean independence, and train Koreans in handling their own affairs so as to prepare them to govern themselves as a free and independent nation. The American occupation forces established their main base in South Korea at Yongsan in Seoul, which had been the main military base of the Japanese in Korea, Gen. Hodge established his headquarters at Bando Hotel in downtown Seoul, and after outlawing the Korean People's Republic, in mid-September, he established the United States Army Military Government in Korea (USAMGIK) as a political arm of the U.S. occupation forces with Major General A.V. Arnold as first military governor. The USAMGIK ruled South Korea until August 15, 1948.

Following the establishment of the Republic of Korea in August 1948, the American occupation of Korea ended, the USAMGIK was abolished, and the evacuation of U.S. troops began in September, and in January 1949 the Headquarters of the XXIV Corps itself left Korea, leaving behind the 7,500-men Fifth Regimental Combat Team and a U.S. Military Advisory Group of 500 officers and enlisted men to train South Korean troops. In May and June, the Fifth Regimental Combat Team also withdrew from South Korea, completing the evacuation of all U.S. troops on June 29, 1949.

The outbreak of the Korean War in June 1950 brought back U.S. troops to Korea, first from Japan, spearheaded by the Twenty-Fourth Infantry Division commanded by Maj. Gen. William Dean, and then from mainland United States. The U.S. forces in South Korea during the war consisted of three army corps, one marine division, three naval groups, four air force groups and other supporting groups, totalling some 360,000 men at the end of the war. During the war, the headquarters of the U.N. Command and that of the Eighth Army were relocated to Seoul from Tokyo. The war produced some 147,262 American casualties (33,625 dead, 105,785 wounded, and 7,852 missing).

Following the signing of the Korean armistice in July 1953, U.S. troops withdrawal began in March 1954. However, under the U.S.-South Korea Mutual Defense Treaty, signed in October 1953, more than 40,000 U.S. troops remained in Korea. Most of the U.S. troops were stationed along, or near, the DMZ and in the vicinity of Seoul as a deterrent against renewed North Korean aggression. In July 1966, the U.S.-South Korea Status-of-Forces Agreement was signed, and the Headquarters of the U.N. Command and that of the Eighth Army, which had moved back to Tokyo in November 1954, returned to Seoul in July 1967, making Yongsan their new home.

As of 1970, there were some 40,000 U.S. troops in South Korea. But, with the withdrawal of the Seventh Infantry Division from South Korea under President Richard Nixon's new Asian policy, the number of U.S. troops in Korea was reduced to about 30,000. President Jimmy Carter's plan to withdraw all U.S. ground troops from South Korea (announced in March 1976) was not carried out, but some 3,400 U.S. troops were withdrawn from South Korea in December 1978. Meanwhile, in order to enhance mutual cooperation between the U.S. and South Korean military establishments, in November 1978 the U.S.-South Korean Combined Command Forces were created as the strength of the U.S.-Air Force in South Korea was greatly increased.

In 1989, the U.S. and South Korea agreed to relocate the U.S. military base from Yongsan to near Taejŏn, the South Korean government defraying the cost. As of late 1989, there were some 32,000 U.S. troops in South Korea, augmenting South Korea's national defense. *See also:* KOREAN WAR; U.S.-SOUTH KOREA COMBINED FORCES; U.S.-SOUTH KOREA MUTUAL DEFENSE TREATY; U.S.-SOUTH KOREA STATUS-OF-FORCES AGREEMENT.

UNITED STATES ARMY MILITARY GOVERNMENT IN KOREA (USAMGIK). *See:* U.S. TROOPS IN KOREA.

***USS PUEBLO*, CAPTURE OF.** On January 23, 1968, a U.S. intelligence ship, *Pueblo,* under Commander Lloyd M. Bucher and with a crew of 83 aboard, was seized by North Korean naval ships on the high seas some 15 miles east of the north Korean port of Wŏnsan on the east coast. Commander Bucher and 82 surviving crew members (one was killed during the capture) were returned to South Korea at Panmunjom on December 23, but the ship was not.

-W-

WHITE SKELETON CORPS. A terroristic youth group known as Paekkoltan in Korean emerged in 1952 in Pusan, actively supporting President Rhee and intimidating all those who opposed him.

WOMEN'S LEAGUE FOR THE CONSTRUCTION OF THE NATION. *See:* WOMEN'S MOVEMENT.

WOMEN'S MOVEMENT. The movement of Korean women, which had been curtailed by the Japanese after 1931, revived with the liberation of Korea as two women's organizations emerged. The first to emerge was a leftist Women's League for the Construction of the Nation (Kŏnguk Puin Tongmaeng), which was established in August 1945. Its three goals were: political, economic and social liberation of Korean women; promotion of the solidarity of Korean women to contribute to the establishment of a completely independent nation; and development of a new consciousness among Korean women and the advancement of their quality.

The second Korean women's organization formed was the Korean Women's Nationalist Society (Taehan Yŏja Kungminhoe) of the rightists, which was organized for the establishment of political, economic, and social rights of women, as well as for the elevation of their capacities. Its particular aims were to bring about the construction of a democratic society with women's strength, improve the standard of living, construct a healthy economy, and promote national culture. Among other women's organizations formed in 1945 were the Korean Patriotic Women's Society (Taehan Aeguk Puinhoe), the Patriotic Women's Society for the Rapid Realization of Independence (Tongnip Ch'oksŏng Aeguk Puinhoe), and the League for the Protection of Women's Rights (Yŏgwŏn Poho Tongmaeng).

Due to ideological differences, the women's movement was split, the rightists following the lead of the newly emerged National Federation of Women's Organizations (Chŏnguk Yŏsŏng Tanch'e Ch'ongyŏnmaeng) and the General League of Korean Women (Chosŏn Punyŏ Ch'ongdonemaeng) leading the left-wing faction. However, both of these women's national organizations and the YWCA took the initiative to bring about social reform. Thus, they launched a movement to abolish public prostitution and the so-called "*kisaeng* house" (large Korean-style restaurants called *yojŏng,* where female entertainers entertained men guests), and the petitions they submitted to the American military government brought about its publication of Ordinance No. 70 of May 17, 1946, banning the sale of women. Meanwhile, the opposing camps were engaged in a bitter struggle in connection with the Moscow Agreement and the Allies' plan to impose its trusteeship in Korea.

Shortly after the establishment of the South Korean Interim Legislative Assembly (SKILA) in late 1946, to which four women were appointed, these women's organizations and the newly emerged Democratic Women's League (Minju Yŏsŏng Tongmaeng) of the progressive (moderate leftist) women, presented a petition to SKILA for the enactment of a law guaranteeing equality of the sexes in political, economic, social, and cultural fields. Specifically, they sought equal voting rights, equal educational opportunity, equality in marriage and divorce, and equality in property inheritance, and their campaign for the abolition of public prostitution brought about the promulgation by the American military government on February 14, 1948, of the law abolishing public prostitution. Meanwhile, the left-wing women's movement declined after the fall of 1947 as many Communist leaders escaped to the north.

The Korean women gained their voting rights without any struggle as these were granted by the UNTCOK, and guaranteed by the Constitution of 1948. However, their struggle for equal rights had to be continued because, although the Constitution of 1948 established democratic principles and equality of the sexes, there were many laws and social traditions which stood against them.

In July 1948, several right-wing organizations merged to form the Korean Women's Society (Taehan Puinhoe). However, it became an ally to the autocratic Rhee administration first, and then to his Liberal Party after 1952. As a result, the development of the women's movement for social and economic equality suffered.

The Korean War had a decisive impact on the "inner revolution" of Korean women as they experienced an awakening of a new self in a tragic situation. Some 600,000 Korean women became war widows and breadwinners during and after the war, and as heads of households they took care of over one million war orphans, gaining self-confidence. As the traditional dependency on men weakened, the desire for freedom from bondage of the old order grew stronger while traditional ethical values and morality deteriorated.

While making a contribution toward economic recovery and restoration of social stability, the leaders of Korean women's associations, along with the newly emerged Institute for the Study of Women's Problems, fought for the adoption by the government of a democratic civil code and a new family law that would establish equal rights for women in many areas.

Not satisfied with the new civil code and a family law of 1957, since it failed to allow women to be legal heads of households, prohibited marriages between men and women of the same clan origin, and did not establish women's property rights, the leaders launched a new struggle for the revision of these laws, and in 1959 some 64 women's societies formed a united front by the creation of the National Council of Women's Organizations (NCWO), in order to strengthen their drive.

In August 1962, the NCWO along with other women's societies, petitioned the government to revise the family and inheritance laws, as well as to establish family courts. The government was favorably disposed to the latter, and in October 1963 the Family Court (Kajŏng Pŏpwŏn) was created to handle civil matters involving family members, but it was unwilling to take any steps to revise the civil code and the family law. Meanwhile, as a part of their social reconstruction movement, in 1968 Korean women leaders formed some 500 mother's clubs and launched their drive to popularize family planning. Their slogan was "Stop at Two and Raise Them Well." This movement gained momentum as Korean women took steps to reduce pregnancies.

In April 1972, the National Council of Women's Organizations and the YWCA cosponsored a lecture series on the need for the revision of the family law. In June, some 1,200 women, representing 61 women's associations, formed the Pan-Women's Association for the Accleration of Revision of the Family Law, and adopted a ten-point resolution which demanded, among other things: the abolition of the system of male household head; the abolition of the law against marriage between men and women of the same clan origin; the establishment of equal rights of father and mother; a woman's right to property upon divorce; and the rationalization of the system of property inheritance. Meanwhile, conservative women leaders received government support and established an institute called Hanguk Yejiwŏn in 1974, for the preservation of what they called Korea's "beautiful manners and good customs."

The progressive reform-minded women did not give up their struggle in the face of growing conservative opposition led by a society of Confucianists called Yudohoe. Holding a series of seminars on women at Christian Academy House in Seoul from 1973, Korean women leaders expressed a particular interest in promoting the status of women. In September 1974 as they prepared to celebrate 1975 as the Year of Women, some 2,000 representatives of 64 women's societies and 28 university women's groups held a national conference and adopted a resolution calling for the presidential declaration of 1975 as the Year of Women, the establishment of a presidential commission on promotion of the status of women, and the revision of the family law. Meanwhile, they proclaimed the "Women's Human Declaration," emphasizing the rights of women and their equality with men. In 1976, they formed the Council of Consumers as a lobbying organ of Korean women consumers.

In the 1970s, Korean women and female college students joined the struggle to end the *Yushin* rule and establish a democratic and egalitarian society. At the same time, they showed their concerns for working women as South Korea's economy developed with rapid industrialization and the multiplication of women workers. They were resolved also to establish equal employment opportunities and equal wages for women. Their efforts brought about some results when, in 1987, the government adopted a minimum wage system, and in early 1988, the National Assembly passed the Equality Law of Male and Female Employees.

Academic institutions for women became actively involved in the promotion of women's studies, paying particular attention to legal, economic and social problems. Thus the Research Center for Asian Women emerged at Sookmyung Women's University in 1960, followed by the Korean Women's Institute at Ewha Woman's University in 1977, and the establishment of both undergraduate and graduate programs in women's studies. The Korean Association of Women's Studies, which was established in October 1984, was joined by several other academically oriented women's societies, publishing journals and promoting new women's movements.

While educated Korean women were engaged in various activities to improve their status, Korean women in rural areas enthusiastically participated in the New Community Movement, forming the new community clubs of women of ages between 20 and 60. They did so because it stressed reforming the way of life of men as well as women, and it promoted new habits among rural people. These clubs were engaged in family planning, promotion of various money-making projects, and increase of the knowledge about how to improve living conditions, increase savings, and develop a cooperative spirit. Some three million women joined these clubs.

The family law which was revised in 1977 was disappointing because it made only a token concession to women. Consequently, the leaders renewed their efforts to bring about a complete change in the family law to satisfy their demands. To this end, in 1988, the representatives of 54 women's societies formed the Korean National Council of Women (KNCW) of 1.7 million members.

-Y-

YI KI-PUNG (1896–1960). Born in Seoul, he studied in the United States. While in New York, he participated in the nationalist movement of the Koreans as one of the publishers of a Korean-language newspaper, *Samil Shinmun*. He returned to Korea in 1934. In 1945, he became secretary to Dr. Syngman Rhee, and in 1949 he was appointed Mayor of Seoul. While serving as the minister of defense in 1951, he and others founded the Liberal Party, becoming one of its key leading members. Elected to the National Assembly in 1954, he became the speaker, closely allied with Dr. Rhee.

Yi ran as the vice-presidential candidate of the Liberal Party in 1956, but was defeated. He ran again in the March 1960 presidential elections, and was elected vice-president. However, when the April Student Uprising of 1960 overthrew the First Republic, he, his wife, and their son committed suicide.

YI PŎM-SŎK (1900–1972). Born in Seoul, he fled to China in 1915. After graduating from a Chinese military school in 1919, he joined the Korean army in Manchuria, participating in the anti-Japanese Ch'ŏngsan-ri battle of 1920. In 1933, he became commander of the Korean military unit at Loyang Military Academy of the Chinese Nationalists, and in 1941 he became chief of staff of the Korean Restoration Army in China, engaged in the anti-Japanese war on the side of the Chinese Nationalists.

Yi returned to Korea in August 1945, and in October, 1946 he formed the National Youth Corps (Minjok Ch'ŏngnyŏndan, or Chokch'ŏng for short). In 1948, he was appointed prime minister, concurrently the minister of defense. After serving as ambassador to Nationalist China in 1950, he became vice-president of the Liberal Party and was named the minister of home affairs in April 1952. He was nominated by the Liberal Party as its vice-presidential candidate, but was betrayed by Dr. Rhee and was defeated. After forming the Civil Rule Party in 1956, he ran for the vice-presidency, but again lost.

When the House of Councillors was established in 1960, he ran for office and was elected. In 1963, he formed the Party of the People, but thereafter played only a minor role in politics.

YI SI-YŎNG (1868–1953). A former high-ranking official in the government of the Yi dynasty who fled to Manchuria in 1910 and established a military school to train Korean youths. After serving as the minister of justice and the minister of finance of the Provisional Government in Korea in exile in China from 1919, in 1930 he and Kim Ku formed the Korean Independence Party, playing an important role in the Korean government in exile. On returning to Korea in 1945, he played a leading role in the National Council for Rapid Realization of Korean Independence as its chairman. He was elected vice-president of the Republic of Korea in 1948, but in 1951 he resigned the vice-presidency in protest against the undemocratic rule of Dr. Rhee. In 1952, he ran unsuccessfully for the presidency in opposition to Dr. Rhee.

YI SŬNG-MAN. *See:* RHEE, SYNGMAN.

YŎ UN-HYŎNG (1885–1947). Born in Yanp'yŏng, Kyŏnggi Province, he became an educator as he founded private schools in 1907 and 1908. When his schools were closed by the Japanese following Japanese annexation of Korea in 1910, he entered the Presbyterian Theological Seminary in Pyongyang, but in 1914 he went to China to fight for Korea's liberation. In 1918, after attending a college in Nanjing for a brief period, he organized the New Korean Youth Party in China, becoming a nationalist activist.

When the Provisional Government of Korea in exile was established, Yŏ became a member of its legislative assembly. Joining the Korean Communist Party, which was established in China in 1919, he attended the Conference of Oppressed Peoples of the Far East which was held in Moscow in 1921. Returning to Korea some time in late 1920s, he was imprisoned for three years by the Japanese.

In 1933, when he was released from prison, he became president of the Korean Central Daily News (Chosŏn Chung'ang Ilbo) Press, continuing his nationalist activities until the press was closed down by the Japanese in 1936. In 1944, he organized a secret society named the Alliance for Restoration of the Korean Nation, but he was again imprisoned.

Released from prison in August 1945, he organized the

Committee for the Preparation of National Reconstruction, and in September he brought about the establishment of the Korean People's Republic, becoming its vice-chairman. When the Korean People's Republic was outlawed by the American military government, he established the Korean People's Party (Chosŏn Inmindang) in November 1945, and in February 1946 his party joined the Korean National Democratic Front (Chosŏn Minjujuŭi Minjok Chŏnsŏn, or Minjŏn for short) of the leftists, supporting the implementation of the Moscow Agreement of the Allies.

Yŏ collaborated with radical Communists of the Korean Communist Party for a while, but in September 1946 he severed his ties with them, and joined the moderate right-wing nationalists in forming in May 1946 the Coalition Committee for Co-operation Between the Rightists and the Leftists (Chwau Hapchak Wiwŏnhoe) for the purpose of establishing "a democratic transitional government" of Korea in cooperation with the Allies under the Moscow Plan. Meanwhile, he brought about the unity of three other moderate leftist parties, forming a new party named Socialist Labor Party (Sahoe Nodongdang), which was renamed as the Working People's Party (Kŭllo Inmindang) in May 1947. For some unknown reasons, Yŏ left the Coalition Committee for Co-operation Between the Rightists and Leftists in December 1946, but he stated that he did not withdraw his support for its aims.

Yŏ's opposition to the rightists and the radical leftists made him the target of bitter criticism and attack of both groups. In the end, having endeavored in vain to unite the middle groups for the solution of the Korean question, he was assassinated in July 19, 1947 by a right-wing nationalist youth. *See also:* COALITION COMMITTEE OF THE RIGHTISTS AND THE LEFTISTS; COMMITTEE FOR THE PREPARATION OF NATIONAL RECONSTRUCTION; KOREAN NATIONAL DEMOCRATIC FRONT; KOREAN PEOPLE'S PARTY; KOREAN PEOPLE'S REPUBLIC.

YŎSU-SUNCH'ŎN REBELLION. This Communist-inspired rebellion began on October 19, 1948, when the Communist-infiltrated 14th Regiment of the Army, based in Yŏsu, South Chŏlla Province, carried out an insurrection by refusing to go to Cheju Island as ordered to subjugate the rebels there. When the military insurrection began, local inhabitants (Communists and Communist sympathizers) in the Yŏsu and Sunch'ŏn areas joined in, resulting in a large-scale rebellion. At this juncture, the Communist-infiltrated 4th Regiment which was based in Kwangju also carried out an abortive rebellion.

The rebels in the Yŏsu-Sunch'ŏn area seized government buildings, police stations, and set up people's committees and tribunals which tried local officials and civilian leaders, killing some 1,200 local officials, police and their family members, and destroyed several hundreds of homes and public buildings. In the wake of the rebellion, the government proclaimed martial law in the area and arrested some 23,000 rebels and civilian collaborators, over 80 per cent of whom were found guilty and several hundreds of them were executed.

The rebellion was crushed by early November, but many rebels fled into mountainous areas, especially in the Mt. Chiri area, in the southern regions of the country, and harassed the local officials and inhabitants, causing such tragic events as the Hamp'yŏng and Kŏch'ang incidents.

During and after the Yŏsu-Sunch'ŏn Rebellion, some troops of the 6th Regiment stationed at Taegu, who had been members of the underground South Korean Workers' Party, attempted to take over the regiment in November and December 1948. *See also:* CHEJU REBELLION; HAMP'YŎNG-KŎCH'ANG INCIDENTS.

YU CHIN-O (1906–1988). Graduate of Keijo Imperial University (in Seoul) in 1929, Yu joined the nationalist society named Suyang Tong'uhoe that was formed in 1922. Becoming one of its active members, he edited its organ, *Tonggwang (The Eastern Light)* from 1932 until the society was abolished by the Japanese colonial government in 1939. Being forced by the Japanese, Yu joined the Korean Society of Literary Persons that was established by the Japanese in 1939, collaborating with the Japanese.

In 1946, Yu became professor of law at Korea University, and then served as director of the Office of Government Legislative Affairs from August 1948 to June 1949. After being elected as a member of the National Academy of Science in 1954, he served as president of Korea University until 1966. He became a key member of the new Masses (Minjung) Party formed in May 1965, and was elected to the National Assembly in 1966. He was nominated by his party to run in the 1967 presidential race, but he brought about the merger of his party with the New Democratic Party of Yun Po-sŏn in February 1967, making Yun the sole presidential candidate of the major opposition party. With the emergence of the Fourth Republic in 1972, Yu retired from politics, playing the role of an elder statesman and adviser to the New Democratic Party (1970–79) and the National Unification Board (1980–84).

YUJŎNGHOE. *See:* POLITICAL FRATERNAL SOCIETY FOR REVITALIZING REFORM.

YUN PO-SŎN (1897–1990). Born into a former *yangban* family, he graduated from Edinburgh University in Scotland in 1930. He played no political role before 1945, but in November 1945, he joined the Korean Independence Party which had returned from China. He was appointed Mayor of Seoul in 1948, and served as the minister of trade and industry (1949–50). Elected to the National Assembly in 1954, he gained political importance, playing the leadership role in the opposition camp.

In August 1960, when the First Republic fell, he was elected by the National Assembly as the president of the Second Republic, encountering the Military Revolution of May 16, 1961. He remained in the office until March 1962 when he resigned the presidency protesting the Political Purification Law and the activities of the Political Purification Committee.

Yun ran for the presidency twice thereafter: first in 1963 as the candidate of the Civil Rule Party, and the second time in 1967 as the candidate of the New Democratic Party. He was founder of the Civil Rule Party (1963), the New Korea Party (1966), and helped found the New Democratic Party (1967). On leaving party politics in the mid-1980s, after serving as adviser to the president of the New Democratic Party, he played the role of an elder statesman.

***YUSHIN* RULE.** Shortly after his reelection for the third time in April 1971 under the revised Constitution of 1969, and his inauguration on July 1, President Park Chung-hee proceeded to tighten the control of the government over the nation in view of the rapidly changing domestic and international situations, particularly in view of new developments in North-South relations. Then on October 17, 1972, he proclaimed a nationwide martial law, suspending some provisions of the constitution, dissolving the National Assembly, and banning all political activities. The action taken by the government on October 17, 1972 brought about what is known as the October *Yushin* ("Revitalizing Reform"), ending the Third Republic and preparing for the coming of the Fourth Republic. His reasons for doing so was "to have unity in order to have a dialogue with the North," and to deal with the "great changes" which occurred on the international scene. The October *Yushin* was designed to remove politics from the vagaries of the politicians and electorate and at the same time, to completely centralize policy-making and the execution of functions in the hands of the president.

Under the *Yushin* program, a series of constitutional amendments were proposed by the government, and on November 21, the amended constitution was approved in a national referendum. With this, the new electoral college, named the National Conference for Unification, was established, with its 2,359 members being elected by popular vote on December 15. The new electoral college elected the incumbent president as the president of the Fourth Republic, without the limit of the term of office. The *Yushin* Constitution was proclaimed on December 12, 1972 as President Park took the oath of office as the eighth president. His death in October 1979 ended the *Yushin* rule. *See also:* NATIONAL CONFERENCE FOR UNIFICATION; PARK CHUNG-HEE; POLITICAL FRATERNAL SOCIETY FOR REVITALIZING REFORM.

BIBLIOGRAPHY

INTRODUCTION

Korean studies had long been underdeveloped and virtually ignored in the West, and were generally treated as an appendage to Chinese or Japanese studies due to Korea's peculiar historical circumstances. Politically and culturally, Korea had been a part of the Chinese world up to 1894, and after that date she fell under Japanese domination, and eventually became a colony. Only after Korea's liberation from Japanese rule in 1945 did Korean studies as such begin to emerge in the West.

The first book written by a Westerner on Korea was that of Hendrick Hamel's *An Account of the Ship Wreck of a Dutch Vessel on the Coast of the Isle of Quelpart, Together with a Description of the Kingdom of Corea,* published in Amsterdam and Rotterdam in 1668. In 1704, an English version of Hamel's book, edited by John Churchill, was published in London, but Korea remained a *terra incognita* as far as the Western people were concerned.

Some two hundred years after the publication of Hamel's book, a Frenchman, Charles Dallet, published *Historie de l'Églese de Corée* in Paris in 1874, followed by the publication of Captain Basil Hall's *Voyage to Corea and the Island of Loo-choo* (London: 1820), Leon de Rosny's *Les Coréens, apercu ethnologique et historique* (Paris: 1886) and Ernest Oppert's *A Forbidden Land: Voyages to Corea* (London: 1880), increasing the knowledge about Korea in the West. The first book about Korea published in the United States was that of Percival Powell entitled *Choson: The Land of Morning Calm—A Sketch of Korea* (Boston: 1888). In the late 1890s and in the early 1900s more books about Korea were published by American missionaries and diplomats, promoting some knowledge about the "hermit kingdom" of Korea in the United States.

After the Japanese annexation of Korea in 1910, only a handful of books about Korea were published in the West. One of them was by a Briton, published in 1920; two by Koreans in the 1920s, and three by Americans in 1944. Korea, in fact, became a "forgotten nation," and no Korean studies program as such existed either in Europe or in America. On the other hand, the Japanese government, as well as the Japanese colonial government called Government-General in Korea, published numerous English-language publications for propaganda purposes, misleading public opinion about Japanese rule in Korea.

Since the liberation, the interest in Korean studies grew as more books authored by Western writers and Koreans in the United States were published. The English-language publications of the government of the Republic of Korea also contributed to the promotion of Korean studies in the West. A new field such as Korean studies lacked balance in its development and was accompanied by certain weaknesses. However, Korean studies in the West, particularly in the United States, developed rather rapidly in recent decades, filling the gap which existed in certain areas, making available more English-language books and articles which are included in this bibliography.

The purpose of this bibliography is to assist further research and reading. Only English-language materials are included as they are likely to be the most useful to the majority of readers. When books on certain subjects or topics are unavailable, journal articles and doctoral dissertations have been substituted.

The following three bibliographies would provide further information on source materials in Korean studies. They are:

1. Institute of Asian Studies, Seoul National University. *Korean Studies Today—Development and State of the Field.* Seoul: 1970

This is an English-language publication, which includes bibliographical essays on the following subjects: ancient arts, dramatic arts, classical literature, modern literature, customs and folklore, history, economy, science, sociology, traditional music, traditional political and legal systems, linguistics, philosophy, and religion. Each section has a bibliography which, unfortunately, includes works for the most part of Korean and Japanese authors.

2. Korean National Committee of Historical Science. *Historical Studies in Korea: Recent Trends and Bibliography* (1945–1973). Seoul: National History Compilation Committee, Ministry of Education, Republic of Korea, 1975.

This is an English-language guide, which includes works by Koreans living in Korea. It provides authors' names and titles of books in Chinese. It is divided into three parts: Korean history, Eastern history, and Western history.

3. Han-kyo Kim ed. *Studies on Korea: A Scholar's Guide.* Honolulu: The University Press of Hawaii, 1980.

This most up-to-date guide includes English, French, German and other European-language materials such as books, journal articles, doctoral dissertations, and master's theses. It is divided into the following sections: bibliographies, handbooks, journals, and other publications; archaeology; history (up to 1945, including the history of science); philosophy and religion; language and linguistics; literature and folklore; art, music, and dance; education; geography and natural environment; people, family, and society; the economic system; government and politics; the legal system; international relations and national reunification; North Korea; and Russian-language materials. Each section, edited by one or more editors, has a brief bibliographical essay.

The organization of this bibliography is as follows:

1. Bibliographies and Korean Studies Guides
2. Periodicals and Newspapers
3. General
    - A. Travel/Guide Books
    - B. Map Collection
    - C. Handbooks/Statistical Abstracts
4. Culture
    - A. General
    - B. Archeology
    - C. Architecture
    - D. Arts

- E. Drama/Theater
- F. Language/Linguistics
- G. Literature
- H. Music/Dance
- I. Philosophy/Religion
- J. Press

5. Economy
   - A. General
   - B. Agriculture
   - C. Development
   - D. Finance
   - E. Trade
   - F. Industry
   - G. Labor
   - H. Transportation/Communications

6. History
   - A. Autobiography/Biography
   - B. General
   - C. Ancient/Pre-Modern
   - D. Colonial Period
   - E. Post-Independence Period
   - F. The Korean War

1. Bibliographies and Korean Studies Guides

Blanchard, Carroll H. *Korean War Bibliography and Maps of Korea.* Albany, NY: Korean Conflict Research Foundation, [1964?]

Chung, Yong Sun. *Korea: A Selected Bibliography, 1959–1963.* Kalamazoo, MI: Korea Research and Publications, 1965.

Gompertz, G. St. G. M. "Bibliography of Western Literature on Korean from the Earliest Times Until 1950." *Transactions of Korea Branch of the Royal Asiatic Society,* 15 (1963), 1–263.

Henthorn, William E. *A Guide to Reference and Research Materials on Korean History: An Annotated Bibliography.* Honolulu: East-West Center, 1968.

Institute of Asian Studies, Seoul National University. *Korean Studies Today—Development and State of Field.* Seoul: 1970.

Jones, Helen D. and Robin L. Winkler, comp. *Korea: An Annotated Bibliography of Publications in Western Languages.* Washington, DC: Library of Congress, 1950.

Kang, Kil-su. *A Short Bibliography in the English Language Material on Korea and Its Evaluation.* Pittsburgh: IDEP, University of Pittsburgh, 1968.

Kang, Sangwoon. *List of Articles on Korea in the Western Languages, 1800–1964.* Seoul: Tamgudang, 1967.

Kenz, Eugene and Chang-su Swanson. *A Selected and Annotated Bibliography of Korean Anthropology.* Seoul: The National Library of the Republic of Korea, 1968.

Kim, Han-kyo, ed. *Studies on Korea: A Scholar's Guide.* Honolulu: University of Hawaii Press, 1980.

Koh, Hesung Chun. *Korea: An Analytical Guide to Bibliographies.* New Haven: Human Relations Area Files, 1971.

———. *Social Science Resources on Korea: A Preliminary Computerized Bibliography.* New Haven: Human Relations Area Files, 1968.

Korean National Committee for Historical Science. *Historical Studies in Korea: Recent Trends and Bibliography (1946–1973).* Seoul: National History Compilation Committee, Ministry of Education, Republic of Korea, 1975.

Marcus, Richard, ed. *Korean Studies Guide.* Compiled by Benjamin H. Hazard Jr. and others. Berkeley: University of California Press, 1954.

Nahm, Andrew C., comp. *Japanese Penetration of Korea, 1894–1910: A Checklist of Archives in the Hoover Institution.* Stanford: Hoover Institution, 1959.

Shulman, Frank J. *Doctoral Dissertations on Asia: An Annotated Bibliographical Journal of Current International Research*. Vol. I. Ann Arbor: Xerox University Microfilms, 1975–. Vol. II Nos. 1 & 2, 1988.

———. *Doctoral Dissertations on Japan and Korea, 1969–1974: A Classified Bibliographical Listing of International Research*. Ann Arbor: University Microfilms International, 1976.

———. *Japan and Korea: An Annotated Bibliography of Doctoral Dissertations in Western Languages, 1877–1969*. Chicago: American Library Association, 1970.

Silberman, Bernard S. *Japan and Korea: A Critical Bibliography*. Tucson: University of Arizona Press, 1962.

2. Periodicals and Newspapers

Journal of Korean Affairs. Silver Spring, MD.: The Research Institute on Korean Affairs. Quarterly. 1971–76.

Journal of Korean Studies. Seattle: The Society for Korean Studies. Annual. 1979–.

Journal of Modern Korean Studies. Fredericksburg, VA.: Mary Washington College. Annual. 1984.

Journal of Social Science and Humanities. (Formerly *Bulletin of the Korean Research Center)*. Seoul: The Korean Research Center. Semiannual. 1960–.

Korea and World Affairs: A Quarterly Review. Seoul: Research Center for Peace and Unification. 1977–.

Korea Herald. Daily. Seoul.

Korea Journal. Seoul: Korean National Commission for UNESCO. Monthly. 1961–.

Korea Newsreview. Seoul: International Cultural Society of Korea. Weekly. 1961–.

Korea Observer. Seoul: The Academy of Korean Studies. Quarterly. 1968–.

Korea Review. Philadelphia. Monthly. 1919–22.

Korea Review. Seoul: The Methodist Publ. House. Monthly. 1901–06.

Korea Times. Seoul. Daily.

Korean Culture. Los Angeles: The Korean Cultural Society. Quarterly, 1979–.

Korean Quarterly. Seoul: International Research Center, 1974–. *Seoul: The Monthly Magazine of Korea Illustrated.* Seoul: HEK Communications, 1985–.

Korean Repository. Seoul: Trilingual Press. Monthly. 1892, 1895–98.

Korean Social Science Journal. Seoul: Korean Social Science Research Council, Korean National Commission for UNESCO. Annual. 1981–.

Korean Studies. Honolulu: Center for Korean Studies, University of Hawaii. Annual. 1976–.

Korean Survey. Washington, DC: Korean Pacific Press. Bimonthly, 1952–61.

Social Science Journal. Seoul: Korean National Commission for UNESCO. Annual. 1973–80.

Transactions of the Korea Branch of the Royal Asiatic Society. Annual. 1900–41, 1948–.

Voice of Korea. Washington, DC Korean Affairs Institute. Bimonthly. 1943–61.

3. General

A. Travel/Guide Books

Adams, Edward B. *Korea Guide.* Seoul: Taewon Publ. Co., 1976.

———. *Kyongju Guide: Cultural Spirit of Silla in Korea.* Seoul: Seoul International Tourist Co., 1979.

———. *Through Gates of Seoul.* Seoul: Seoul International Tourist Co., 1971.

———. *Palaces of Seoul.* Seoul: Taewon Pub. Co., 1982.

Chung, Kyung Cho et al. *The Korea Guidebook.* Boston: Houghton Mifflin, 1988.

Clark, Allen D. and Donald N. Clark. *Seoul: Past and Present: A Guide to Yi T'aijo's Capital.* Seoul: Royal Asiatic Society, Korea Branch, 1969.

Fodor's 89 Korea. New York: Fodor's Travel Publications, Inc. 1988.

Grayson, James H. and Donald N. Clark. *Discovering Seoul: A Historical Guide.* Seoul: Royal Asiatic Society, Korea Branch, 1986.

Han, Suzanne C. *Korea: A Pictorial Guide Book.* Seoul: Hollym Corp., 1988.

Hoefer, J. et al. *Insight Guides: Korea* APA Production 1988.

Hollym Corp. *Compact Guide to Korea.* Seoul: 1988.

———. *Seoul: A Pictorial Guide Book.* Seoul: 1985.

Kikbride, Wayne A. *Panmunjom: Facts About a Korean DMZ.* Seoul: Hollym Corp., 1988.

Middleton, Dorothy and William D. *Some Korean Journeys.* Seoul: Royal Asiatic Society, Korea Branch, 1975.

Popham, Peter. *The Insider's Guide to Korea.* Seoul: Seoul International Publishing House, 1987.

Price, David. *Between Two Seas: A Journey Into South Korea.* Seoul: Seoul International Publishing House, 1988.

Rucci, Richard B. ed. *Living in Korea.* Seoul: Seoul International Tourist Co., 1984.

B. Map Collection

Korea, Rep. of. Office of Rural Development. Institute of Plant Environment. Korean Soil Survey. *Reconnaissance Soil Map of Korea.* 9 vols. Seoul: 1971.

Lee, Ch'an. *Korean Old World Maps.* Seoul: Seoul National University Press, 1971.

———. *Old Maps of Korea.* Seoul: Korean Library Science Research Institute, 1977.

National Construction Research Institute. *The History of Mapping in Korea.* Seoul: 1972.

U.S. Army Map Service. Far East. *Korea.* AMS Series L 551, 651, 751, and 1052. Washington, DC: 1952–76.

C. Handbooks/Statistical Abstracts

American University. Foreign Areas Studies Division. *U.S. Army Handbook for Korea.* Washington, DC: Government Printing Office, 1964.

Bank of Korea. *Economic Statistics Yearbook.* Seoul: 1960–.

———. *Monthly Economic Statistics.* Seoul, 1960–.

Clare, Kenneth D., *et al. Area Handbook for the Republic of Korea.* Washington, DC: Government Printing Office.

Hapdong News Agency, Korea. *Korea Annual.* Seoul: 1962–80.

Korea, Rep. of. Ministry of Agriculture and Fisheries. *Yearbook of Agriculture and Fisheries Statistics.* Seoul: 1963–.

———. Ministry of Health and Social Welfare. Office of Labor Affairs. *Yearbook of Labor Statistics.* 1953–.

———. Overseas Information Service. Ministry of Culture and Information. *Facts About Korea.* Seoul: 1960–.

———. *A Handbook of Korea*. Seoul: 1978–.

Korean National Commission for UNESCO. *Review of Educational Statistics in Korea.* Annual. Seoul: 1972–.

Nilsen, Robert. *South Korea Handbook.* Chico, CA: Moon Publishing Co., 1988.

Vreeland, Nena et al. *Area Handbook for South Korea.* Washington, DC: Government Printing Office, 1975.

Yonhap News Agency, Korea. *Korea Annual.* Seoul: 1981–.

4. Culture

A. General

Covell, Jon C. *Korea's Cultural Root.* Salt Lake: Moth House and Seoul: Hollym Corp., 1981.

Ha, Tae-hung. *Folk Culture and Family Life.* Seoul: Korean International Society, 1958.

———. *Guide to Korean Culture.* Seoul: Yonsei University Press, 1979.

———. *Korean Cultural Series.* 12 vols. Seoul: Yonsei University Press, 1978.

Hakwon-sa. *Korea: Its Land, People and Culture of All Ages.* Seoul: 1963.

International Cultural Foundation. *Buddhist Culture of Korea.* Korean Culture Series, No. 3. Seoul: 1960.

———. *Folk Culture in Korea.* Korean Culture Series, No. 4. Seoul: 1974.

———. *Thought and Culture in Korea.* Korean Culture Series, No. 10. Seoul: 1979.

———. *Upper-class Culture in Yi-dynasty Korea.* Korean Culture Series, No. 2. Seoul: 1973.

Jeon, Kyu-tae. *Korean Heritage.* Seoul: Jeong Eum Sa, 1975.

Kang, Hugh W., ed. *The Traditional Culture and Society of Korea: Thought and Institutions.* Occasional Paper, No. 5. Center for Korean Studies, University of Hawaii, 1975.

Lee, Hugh W., ed. *The Traditional Culture and Society of Korea: Art and Literature.* Occasional Paper, No. 4. Center for Korean Studies, University of Hawaii, 1975.

Morse, Ronald A. *Wild Asters: Explorations in Korean Thought, Culture and Society.* Lanham, MD: University Press of America, 1987.

Pearson, Richard J., ed. *The Traditional Culture and Society of Korea: Prehistory.* Occasional Paper, No. 3. Center for Korean Studies, University of Hawaii, 1975.

Yu, Eui-young and Earl H. Phillips. *Traditional Thoughts and Practices in Korea.* Los Angeles: Center for Korean-American and Korean Studies. California State University, Los Angeles, 1983.

B. Archeology

Gardiner, J.H.H. *The Early History of Korea: The Historical Development of the Peninsula Up to the Introduction of Buddhism in the Fourth Century A.D.* Honolulu: University of Hawaii Press, 1969.

Ham, Pyong-sam. "Neolithic Culture of Korea," *Korea Journal* 14:4 (April 1974), 12–17.

Kim, Chewon and Moo-byong Young, *Studies of Dolmens in Korea.* 6 vols. Seoul: National Museum of Korea, 1967.

Kim, Jeong-hak. *The Prehistory of Korea.* Tr. by Richard J. Pearson and Kazue Pearson. Honolulu: University of Hawaii Press, 1979.

Kim, Won-yong. *Art and Archeology of Ancient Korea.* Seoul: Tawgwang Pub. Col, 1986.

Pearson, Richard J. "Archeology in Korea," *Antiquity,* 46:183 (1972), 227–230.

Sohn, Pow-key. "Palaeolithic Culture of Korea," *Korea Journal.* 14:4 (April 1974), 4–12.

———. *The Upper Palaeolithic Habitation Sokchang-ni, Korea: A Summary Report.* Seoul: Yonsei University Press, 1973.

C. Architecture

Adams, Edward B. *Palaces of Seoul.* Seoul: Taewon Pub. Co., 1972.

Bacon, Wilbur. "Tombs of the Yi Dynasty Kings and Queens," *Transactions of the Korea Branch of the Royal Asiatic Society.* Vol. 33 (1957), 1–40.

Chapin, Helen B. "A Little Known Temple in South Korea and Its Treasures," *Artibus Asiae,* 11:3 (1948), 189–195.

———. "Kyongju, Ancient Capital of Silla," *Transactions of the Korea Branch of the Royal Asiatic Society.* Vol. 32 (1951), 55–72.

———. "Palaces in Seoul," *Transactions of the Korean Branch of the Royal Asiatic Society.* Vol 32 (1951), 3–50.

Chong, In-kook. "Two Styles of Korean Wooden Architecture," *Korea Journal,* 15:2 (Feb. 1975), 4–15.

Kwang Jang Press. *Korean Architecture Series.* Seoul: 1984.

Lee, Kyu. "Aspects of Korean Architecture," *Apollo,* No. 88 (Aug. 1968), 94–107.

D. Arts

Adams, Edward B. *Art Treasures of Seoul With Walking Tour.* Seoul: International Tourist Pub. Co., 1980.

———. *Korean Folk Art and Craft.* Seoul: International Publishing House, 1987.

———. *Korea's Pottery Heritage.* Seoul: International Publishing House, 1986.

Barinka, J. *The Art of Ancient Korea.* Translated from German by Iris Urwin. London: Peter Nevill Ltd., 1962.

Covell, Alan Carter. *Folk Art and Magic: Shamanism in Korea.* Seoul: Hollym Corp., 1988.

———. *Shamanistic Folk Paintings: Korean Eternal Spirits.* Seoul: Hollym Corp. 1984.

Eckardt, P. Andreas. *A History of Korean Art.* Translated from German by J. M. Kindersley. London: E. Goldston, 1929.

The Folkist Society. *Folkism.* 2 vols. Seoul: Emille Museum, 1922–73.

Gompertz, G. St. G. M. *Korean Celadon and Other Wares of the Koryo Period.* London: Faber and Faber, 1963.

———. *Korean Pottery and Porcelain of the Yi Period.* London: Faber and Faber, 1968 and New York: Praeger, 1968.

Hak Dang Pub. Co. *Cultural Treasures of Korea.* 8 vols. Seoul: 1986.

Honey, William B. *Corean Pottery.* London: Faber and Faber, 1947.

Huh, Dong-hwa. *Crafts of the Inner Court: The Artistry of Korean Women.* Seoul: The Museum of Korean Embroidery, 1987.

Hyung-mi Pub. Co. *Korean Folk Painting.* Seoul: 1980.

Janata, Alfred. *Korean Painting.* Translated by M. Shenfield. New York: Crown, 1964.

Kim, Chewon and G. St. G.M. Gompertz. *The Ceramic Art of Korea.* London: Faber and Faber, 1961.

Kim, Chewon and Lena Kim Lee. *Arts of Korea.* Tokyo: Kodansha International, 1974.

Kim, Chewon and Won-yong Kim. *Treasures of Korean Art: 2000 Years of Ceramics, Sculpture and Jeweled Arts.* New York: Abrams, 1966.

Kim, Won-yong. *The Art and Archaeology of Ancient Korea.* Seoul: Taegwang Pub. Co., 1986.

Kim, Won-yong, *et al,* ed. *The Arts of Korea.* 6 vols. Seoul: Tong Hwa Pub. Co., 1986.

Kim, Yong-joon. *Dan Won: Kim Hong-do.* Pyongyang: Foreign Language Publishing House, 1956.

Korea, Rep. of. Ministry of Culture and Information, *The Ancient Arts of Korea.* Seoul: 1975.

———. *Survey of Korean Art.* 2 vols. Seoul: 1972.

———. National Academy of Fine Arts. *Survey of Korean Arts: Fine Arts.* 2 vols. Seoul: 1974.

Korean National Commission for UNESCO. *Modern Korean Painting.* Seoul: 1971.

Kyemyong-sa. *The Folk Crafts of Korea.* Seoul: 1980.

McCune, Evelyn G. *The Arts of Korea: An Illustrated History.* Rutland, VT: Tuttle, 1962.

———. *The Inner Art: Korean Screens.* New York: Asian Humanities Press, 1983.

Paine, Robert R. Jr., ed. *Masterpieces of Korean Art.* Boston: 1957.

Si-sa-yong-o-sa Pub. Co. *Traditional Korean Art.* Seoul: 1984.

Soper, Alexander. *Chinese, Korean and Japanese Bronzes.* Series Orientale Roma, No. 35. Rome: ISMEO, 1966.

Swan, Peter. *Art in China, Korea and Japan.* New York: Praeger, 1965.

Togchun Pub. Co. *Masterpieces of 500 Years of Korean Painting.* Seoul, 1978.

Yoo, Yushin. *Korea the Beautiful: Treasures of the Hermit Kingdom.* New York: Condall Publishers, 1987.

Zo, Zayong, ed. *The Humor of Korean Tiger.* Seoul: Emille Museum, 1970.

———. *Introduction to Korean Folk Painting.* Seoul: Emille Museum, 1977.

E. Drama/Theater

Cho, Oh-kon. *Traditional Korean Theatre.* New York: Asian Humanities Press, 1988.

Choe, Sang-su. *A Study of a Korean Puppet Play.* Seoul: Korea Book Pub. Co., 1960.

———. *A Study of a Mask Play of Hahoe.* Seoul: Korea Book Pub. Co., 1959.

Kardose, John. *An Outline History of Korean Drama.* Greenville, NY: Long Island University Press, 1966.

Korea, Rep. of. National Academy of Arts. *Survey of Korea Arts: Folk Arts.* Seoul: 1974.

Korean National Commission for UNESCO, *Traditional Performing Arts of Korea.* Seoul: 1975.

F. Language/Linguistics

Chang, Namgui and Yong-chol Kim. *Functional Korean: A Communicative Approach.* Seoul: Hollym Corp., 1988.

Chang, Suk-jin. *A Generative Study of Discourse: Pragmatic Aspects of Korea with Reference to English.* Seoul: Language Research Institute, Seoul National University, 1973.

Cho, S.B. *A Phonological Study of Korea: Acta Universitatis Upsaliensis.* Uppsala: Almqvist & Wiksells, 1967.

Gale, James S. *Korean Grammatical Forms.* Seoul: Trilingard Press, 1984.

Grant, Bruce K. *A Guide to Korean Characters: Reading and Writing Hangul and Hanja.* Seoul: Hollym Corp., 1988.

Kanazawa, Shosaburo. *The Common Origin of the Japanese and Korean Languages.* Tokyo: 1910.

Kim, Soon-ham Park. *A Transformational Analysis of Negation in Korean.* Seoul: Paekhap Pub. Co., 1967.

Lee, Chung-min. Abstract Syntax and Korea with Reference to English. Seoul: Pan Korea Book Corp. 1974.

Lee, Jeong-ho. *Explanation and Translation of Huminchŏng'ŭm.* Seoul: Korean Library Science Research Institute, 1973.

Lee, Sang-baek. *The Origins of the Korean Alphabet Hangul According to New Historical Evidence.* Seoul: National Museum, 1957.

Martin, Samuel E. *Korean Morphophonemics.* Baltimore: Linguistics Society of America, 1954.

Park, Byung-soo. *Complement Structure in Korean: A Systematic Study of the Verb "ha."* Seoul: Kwangmun-sa, 1974.

Phil, Marshall R. Jr. *A Study on Non-conclusives in Modern Korean.* Seoul: T'ongmungwan, 1965.

Ramsteedt, G.J. *Studies in Korean Etymology.* Helsinki: Suomalais Ugrilainen senra, 1949–1953.

Rogers, M.C. *Outline of Korean Grammar.* Berkeley and Los Angeles: University of California Press, 1953.

Sohn, Ho-min, ed. *The Korean Language: Its Structure and Social Projection.* Occasional Papers, no. 6. Honolulu: Center for Korean Studies, University of Hawaii, 1975.

Song, Seok Choong. *Explorations in Korean Syntax and Semantics.* Berkeley: Institute of East Asian Studies, University of California, 1988.

Sunoo, Hag-won. *A Korean Grammar.* Prague: Statni pedagoicke nakladateristivi, 1952.

Yang, In-seok. *A Korean Syntax: Case Markers, Delimiters, Complementation, and Relativization.* Seoul: Paekhap-sa, 1972.

G. Literature

Buck, Pearl S. *The Living Reed: A Novel of Korea.* New York: John Day, 1963.

Carpenter, Frances. *Tales of a Korean Grandmother.* Garden City: Doubleday, 1947.

Chang, Tok-sun, comp. *The Folk Treasury of Korea: Sources of Myth, Legend and Folktale.* Tr. by Tae-wung Kim. Seoul: Society for Korean Oral Literature, 1970.

Griffis, William E. *The Unmannerly Tiger and Other Koran Tales.* New York: Crowell, 1918.

Hong, Myong-hee, tr. *Korean Short Stories.* Seoul: Ilchi-sa, 1975.

International Cultural Foundation. *Humour in Korean Literature.* Korean Culture Series, No. 1, Seoul: 1977.

———. *Korean Folk Tales.* Korean Culture Series, No. 7. Seoul: 1979.

Kim, Chong-un, tr. *Postwar Korean Short Stories.* Seoul: Seoul National University Press, 1974.

Kim, Jaihiun. *The Immortal Voice: An Anthology of Modern Korean Poetry.* Seoul: Inmun Pub. Co., 1974.

Kim, So-an. *The Story Bag.* Rutland, VT: Tuttle, 1957.

Ko, Won, comp. and tr. *Contemporary Korean Poetry.* Iowa City: University of Iowa Press, 1970.

Koh, Chang-woo. *Anthology of Contemporary Korean Poetry.* Seoul: International Pub. House, 1987.

Korean National Commission for UNESCO. *Modern Korean Short Stories: 109 Best Korean Short Stories.* Seoul: Si-sa-yong-o-sa Pub. Co., 1983.

———. *Synopses of Korean Novels: Reader's Guide to Korean Literature.* Seoul: 1972.

Lee, Peter H. *Anthology of Korean Literature From Early Times to the Nineteenth Century.* Honolulu: University of Hawaii Press, 1981.

———. *Anthology of Korean Poetry From the Earliest Era to the Present.* New York: John Day, 1964.

———., ed. *Flowers of Fire: Twentieth Century Korean Stories.* Honolulu: University of Hawaii Press, 1974.

———. *Korean Literature: Topic and Themes.* Tucson: University of Arizona Press, 1965.

———., tr. *A Korean Storyteller's Miscellany: The P'aegwan chapki of O Sukkwon.* Princeton: Princeton University Press, 1989.

———. tr. with an Introduction. *Pine River and Lone Peak: An Anthology of Three Chosŏn Dynasty Poets.* Honolulu: University of Hawaii Press, 1991.

———. *Studies in the Saenaenorae: Old Korean Poetry.* Rome: Istituto Italian per il Medio ed Estremo Oriente, 1959.

McCann, David R. *Form and Freedom in Korean Poetry.* Leiden: E.J. Brill, 1988.

Metzger, Berta. *Tales Told in Korea.* New York: Frederick S. Stokes, 1932.

O'Rourke, Kevin. *Ten Korean Short Stories.* Seoul: Yonsei University Press, 1973.

Phil, Marshall R. *Listening to Korea: A Korean Anthology.* New York: Praeger, 1973.

Rutt, Richard. *An Anthology of Korean Sijo.* Taejon: Ch'ongja Sijo Society, 1970.

———. *The Bamboo Grove: An Introduction to Sijo.* Berkeley: University of California Press, 1971.

——— and Chong-un Kim, tr. *Virtuous Women: Three Masterpieces of Traditional Korean Fiction.* Seoul: Korean National Commission for UNESCO, 1974.

Skilled, W.E. *Kodae Sosol: A Survey of Traditional Korean Style Popular Novels.* London: School of Oriental and African Studies, University of London, 1968.

Sym, Myung-ho. *The Making of Modern Poetry: Foreign Influence and Native Creativity.* Seoul: Seoul National University Press, 1982.

Zong, In-sob. *Folk Tales from Korea.* London: Routledge and Kegan Paul, 1952.

———. *A Guide to Korean Literature.* Seoul: Hollym Corp., 1986.

H. Music/Dance

Chang, Sa-hun. *Glossary of Korean Music.* Seoul: Korean Musicological Society, 1972.

Cho, Won-kyung. *Dances of Korea.* New York: Norman J. Seaman, 1962.

Heyman, Alan. *Dances of the Three Thousand Leagues Land.* Seoul: Myungju University, 1966.

Howard, Keith. *Bands, Songs and Shamanistic Rituals.* Seoul: Royal Asiatic Society, Korea Branch, 1989.

Lee, Hey-ku. *An Introduction to Korean Music and Dance.* Seoul: Royal Asiatic Society, Korea Branch, 1977.

———. *Essays on Korean Traditional Music,* tr. by Robert C. Provine, Seoul: Royal Asiatic Society, Korea Branch, 1980.

Pratt, Keith. *Korean Music: Its History and its Performance.* Seoul: Jeong Eum Sa, 1987.

Si-sa-yong-o-sa Pub. Co. *Traditional Korean Music.* Seoul: 1984.

Song, Bang-song. *Source Readings in Korean Music.* Seoul: Korean National Commission for UNESCO, 1980.

I. Philosophy/Religion

Ahn, In-sik. *Ri Yul-kok, His Life and Works.* Seoul: Sungkyungwan University, 1958.

Buswell, Robert E. Jr. *The Formation of Ch'an Ideology in China and Korea: the Vajrasamadhi-Sutra, A Buddhist Apocraphon.* Princeton: Princeton University Press, 1989.

———., tr. *The Korean Approach to Zen: the Collected Works of Chinul.* Honolulu: University of Hawaii Press, 1983.

Choi, Min-hong, *A Modern History of Korean Philosophy.* Seoul: Songmunsa, 1980.

Chon, Sin-yong, ed. *Buddhistic Culture in Korea.* Korean Culture Series, No. 3. Seoul: International Cultural Foundation. 1974.

Clark, Allen D. *History of the Korean Church.* Seoul: Christian Literature Society, 1961.

Clark, Charles A. *Religions of Old Korea.* New York: Revell, 1932, and Seoul: Christian Literature Society of Korea, 1961.

Clark, Donald N. *Christianity in Modern Korea.* Lanham, MD.: University Press of America, 1986.

Covell, Alan C. *Folk Art and Magic: Shamanism in Korea.* Seoul: Hollym Corp., 1986.

de Bary, William T. and Jahyun Kim Haboush. *The Rise of Neo-Confucianism in Korea.* New York: Columbia University Press, 1985.

Grayson, J.H. *Early Buddhism and Christianity in Korea: A History in the Emplantation of Religion.* Leiden, Netherlands: E. J. Brill, 1985.

Huhm, Halla Pai. *Kut: Korean Shamanist Rituals.* Seoul: Hollym Corp., 1980.

Hunt, Everett H. *Protestant Pioneers in Korea.* New York: Orbis Books, 1980.

Janelli, Roger. *Ancestor Worship in Korean Society.* Stanford: Stanford University Press, 1982.

Kang, Wi Jo. *Religion and Politics in Korea Under the Japanese Rule.* Lewiston, NY: The Edwin Mellen Press, 1988.

Kendall, Laurel. *The Life and Hard Times of a Korean Shaman: Of Tales and the Telling of Tales.* Honolulu: University of Hawaii Press, 1988.

———. *Shamans, Housewives and Other Restless Spirits.* Honolulu: University of Hawaii Press, 1985.

Kendall, Laurel and Griffin Dix. *Religion and Ritual in Korean Society.* Berkeley: Institute of East Asian Studies, University of California, 1987.

Kim, Hai-jin. *Buddhism and Korean Culture.* New Delhi: The International Academy of Indian Culture, 1958.

Kim, Yong-choon. *The Ch'ondogyo Concepts of Man: An Essence of Korean Thought.* Seoul: Pan Korea Books, 1978.

Kusan Sunim. *The Way of Korean Zen.* New York: John Weatherhill, 1985.

Lee, Jung Young, ed. *Ancestor Worship and Christianity in Korea.* Lewiston, NY: The Edwin Mellen Press, 1988.

Paik, L. George. *The History of Protestant Mission in Korea, (1832–1910).* Pyonsyang: Union Christian College Press, 1929. Reprinted Seoul: Yonsei University Press, 1971.

Palmer, Spencer J. *Confucian Rituals in Korea.* New York: Asian Humanities Press, 1984.

———. *Korea and Christianity: The Problems of Identification with Tradition.* Seoul: Hollym Corp. n.d.

Phillips, Earl H. and Eui-young Yu, ed. *Religions in Korea: Beliefs and Cultural Values.* Los Angeles: Center for Korean-American and Korean Studies, California State University, Los Angeles, 1982.

Starr, Frederick. *Korean Buddhism.* Boston: Marshall Jones, 1918.

Weems, Benjamin. *Reform, Rebellion and the Heavenly Way.* Tucson: University Press of Arizona, 1964.

Yang, Key P. and Gregory Henderson. "An Outline of History of Korean Confucianism," *Journal of Asian Studies,* 17:11 (1958), 81–101 and 18:2 (1959), 259–276.

Ye, Yun Ho. *A New Cult in Postwar Korea.* Princeton: Princeton Theological Seminary, 1959.

Yu, Chai-shin and R. Guisso, ed. *Shamanism: The Spirit World of Korea.* New York: Asian Humanities Press, 1988.

J. Press

Kim, Bong-gi. *Brief History of the Korean Press.* Seoul: The Korean Information Service, 1963.

5. Economy

A. General

Cho, Lee-jay and Yoon Hyung Kim, ed. *Economic Development in the Republic of Korea.* Honolulu: East West Center, 1991.

Choi, Ho-chin. *The Economic History of Korea: From the Earliest Times to 1945.* Seoul: Freedom Library, 1971.

Chung, Kae H. and Hak Chong Lee, ed. *Korean Managerial Dynamics.* Westport, CT: Praeger Publishers, 1989.

Eckert, Carter Jr. *Offspring of Empire: The Koch'ang Kims and the Colonial Origins of Korean Capitalism, 1867–1945.* Seattle and London: University of Washington Press, 1991.

Hansan, Paryez. *Korea: Problems and Issues in a Rapidly Growing Economy.* Baltimore: Johns Hopkins University Press, 1976.

International Cultural Foundation. *Economic Life in Korea.* Korean Culture Series, No. 8. Seoul: 1978.

Keon, Michael. *Korean Phoenix: A Nation from the Ashes.* Englewood Cliffs, NJ: 1977.

Korea Development Institute: *Korea's Economy: Past and Present.* Seoul: 1975.

Kwon, Jene J. ed. *Korean Economic Development.* New York: Greenwood Press, 1990.

Sorensen, Clark. *Over the Mountains Are Mountains.* Seattle: The University of Washington Press, 1983.

Suh, Sang-chul. *Growth and Structural Changes in the Korean Economy, 1910–1940.* Cambridge: Council on East Asian Studies, Harvard University, 1978.

Woronoff, Jon. *Asia's "Miracle" Economies.* Armonk, NY: M.E. Sharpe, 1986.

———. *Korea's Economy: Man-made Miracle.* Seoul: The Si-sa-yong-o-sa Publishers and Arch Cape, OR: Pace International Research, Inc., 1983.

B. Agriculture

Chang, Oh-hyun. *Land Reform in Korea: A Historical Review.* Madison, WI: University of Wisconsin Press, 1973.

Korea Land Economics Research Center. *A Study of Land Tenure System of Korea.* Seoul: 1966.

Korea University. College of Agriculture. *A Study of the Regional Characteristics of Korean Agriculture.* Seoul: 1967.

Lee, Hoon Koo. *Land Utilization and Rural Economy in Korea.* Shanghai and Hong Kong: Kelly and Walsh, and Chicago: University of Chicago Press, 1936.

Pitts, Forrest R. *Mechanization of Agriculture in the Republic of Korea.* n.p. 1960.

United Nations. Food and Agricultural Organization. *Agricultural Survey* and *Demonstration in Selected Watersheds: Republic of Korea.* New York: 1969.

———. *Rehabilitation and Development of Agriculture, Forestry and Fisheries in South Korea.* New York: Columbia University Press, 1954.

Wade, Robert. *Irrigation and Agricultural Politics in South Korea.* Boulder, CO: Westview Press, 1982.

C. Development

Adelman, Irma, ed. *Practical Approaches to Development Planning in Korea: Second Five-Year Plan.* Baltimore: Johns Hopkins University Press, 1969.

Brown, Gilbert T. *Korean Price Policies and Economic Development in the 1960s.* Baltimore: Johns Hopkins University Press, 1973.

Burmeister, Larry L. *Research, Realpolitik and Development in Korea: The State of the Green Revolution.* Boulder, CO: Westview Press, 1988.

Cho, Lee-jay and Yoon Hyung Kim, ed. *Economic Development in the Republic of Korea: A Policy Perspective.* Boulder, CO: Westview Press, 1990.

Chung, Joseph S.H., ed. *Patterns of Economic Development: Korea.* Kalamazoo, MI: Korea Research and Publications, 1966.

Cole, Davis C. and Princeton N. Lyman. *Korean Development: The Interplay of Politics and Economics.* Cambridge: Harvard University Press, 1971.

Huer, Jon. *Marching Orders: The Role of the Military in South Korea's Economic Miracle, 1961–1971.* Westport, CT: Greenwood Press, 1989.

Kim, Kyong-dong, ed. *Dependency Issues in Korean Development.* Korean Studies Series of the Institute of Social Science, Seoul National University, No. 11. Seoul: 1987.

Kim, Seung-hee. "Economic Development of South Korea" in Se-jin Kim and Chang-gyun Cho, ed. *Government and Politics of Korea.* Silver Spring, MD: Research Institute on Korean Affairs, 1972.

Korea, Rep. of. Economic Planning Board. *The Korean Economy: Present and Future.* Seoul: 1973.

———. *Major Economic Indicators of the Korean Economy, 1953–61.* Seoul: 1977.

———. *Major Indicators of the Korean Economy, 1962–73.* Seoul: 1973.

———. *Major Indicators of the Korean Economy, 1974–79.* Seoul: 1979.

———. *A Summary of the First Five-Year Economic Plan, 1962–66.* Seoul: 1962.

———. *A Summary of the Second Five-Year Economic Plan, 1967–71.* Seoul: 1966.

———. *A Summary of the Third Five-Year Economic Plan, 1972–76.* Seoul: 1971.

———. *A Summary of the Fourth Five-Year Economic and Social Development Plan, 1977–81.* Seoul: 1981.

Kuznets, Paul W. *Economic Growth and Structure in the Republic of Korea.* New Haven: Yale University Press, 1977.

Lewis, J.P. *Reconstruction and Development in South Korea.* Washington, DC: National Planning Association, 1955.

Mason, Edward *et al. The Economic and Social Modernization of the Republic of Korea: Studies in the Modernization of the Republic of Korea, 1945–1975.* Cambridge: Harvard University Press, 1980.

Steinberg, David I. *The Republic of Korea: Economic Transformation and Social Change.* Boulder, CO: Westview Press, 1988.

Wang, In-keun. *Rural Development Studies.* Cambridge: Harvard University Press, 1986.

Whang, In-jong. *Management of Rural Change in Korea: The Saemaul Undong.* Seoul: Seoul National University Press, 1981.

D. Finance

Ahn, Seung Chul. "A Monetary Analysis of the Korean Economy, 1953–1966, on the Basis of Demand and Supply Functions of Money." Ph.D. Dissertation, University of California, Berkeley, 1968.

Gurley, John G. *et al. The Financial Structure of Korea.* Seoul: Bank of Korea, 1965.

Kim, Jung-sae. *The Evaluation of the Financial Structure for Industrialization.* ILCORK Working Paper, 13. Seoul: 1971.

Kim, Seung-hee. *Foreign Capital for Economic Development: A Korean Case.* New York: Praeger, 1970.

Kim, Young-chin and Jane K. Kwon. *Capital Utilization in Korean Manufacturing, 1962–1971: Its Level, Trend and Structure.* Seoul: Korean Industrial Development Research Institute, 1973.

Korea, Rep. of. Ministry of Finance. *An Introduction to Korean Taxation.* Seoul: 1968.

———. *Outline of Banking System and Policy of Korea.* Seoul: 1966.

Kwak, Yoon Chick et al. *Credit and Security in Korea: The Legal Problems of Development Finance.* Manila: Asian Development Bank, 1973.

Lee, Seung Yun and Byong Kuk Kim. *Determinants of Money Supply and the Scope of Monetary Policy, 1954–64.* Seoul: Research Institute for Economic and Business, Sogang University, 1968.

Lyong, Gene. *Military Policy and Economic Aid: The Korean Case.* Columbus: Ohio State University Press, 1961.

Park, Chin Keun. "The Role of the Exchange Rate in a Developing Economy: A Case Study of Korea," Ph.D. Dissertation, University of California, Los Angeles, 1972.

U.S. Comptroller General of the United States. *U.S. Assistance for the Economic Development of the Republic of Korea.* Series B 164264. Washington, DC: General Accounting Office, 1973.

E. Trade

Lee, Dae Sung. "International Trade and the Economic Development of the Korean Economy." Ph.D. Dissertation, University of Massachusetts, 1970.

Lee, Hy Sang. "International Trade of South Korea," in Young C. Kim, ed., *Foreign Policies of Korea.* Washington, DC: Institute for Asian Studies, George Washington University, 1973.

Luedde-Neurath, Richard. *Import Controls and Export-Oriented Development: A Reassessment of the South Korean Case.* Boulder, CO: Westview Press, 1986.

Most, Amicus. *Expanding Exporters: A Case Study of the Korean Experience.* Washington, DC, U.S. Agency for International Development, 1969.

Park, Seong Ho. "Export Expansion and Import Substitution in the Economic Development of Korea, 1955–1965." Ph.D. Dissertation, American University, 1969.

Reubens, Edwin P. "Commodity Trade, Export Taxes and Economic Development: The Korean Experience," *Political Science Quarterly* 7 (March 1965), 55–62.

Voivodas, Constantin. "Exports, Foreign Capital Inflow, and South Korean Economic Growth," *Economic Development and Cultural Change* (April 1974), 480–484.

F. Industry

Amsden, Alice H. *South Korea and Late Industrialization.* New York: Oxford University Press, 1989.

Byun, Hyung-yoon. "Industrial Structure in Korea with Reference to Secondary Industry," *Seoul National University Economic Review* 1 (December 1967), 31–69.

Hamilton, Clive. *Capitalist Industrialization in Korea.* Boulder, CO: Westview Press, 1986.

Korea, Rep. of. Heavy and Chemical Industry Promotion Council. *Heavy and Chemical Industry Development Plan.* Seoul: 1973.

———. *Heavy and Chemical Industry Development Policy of Korea.* Seoul: 1973.

Korea Development Bank. *Industry in Korea.* Seoul: 1976.

Kuznets, Paul W. "Korea's Emerging Industrial Structure." *ILCORK Working Paper,* 6. Seoul: 1971.

Lim, Youngil. *Gains and Costs of Postwar Industrialization in South Korea.* Occasional Paper, No. 2. Center for Korean Studies, University of Hawaii, 1973.

Medium Industry Bank of Korea. *An Introduction to Small Industries in Korea.* Seoul: 1966.

U.S. Dept. of Interior. Bureau of Mines. *The Mineral Industry of the Republic of Korea.* Washington, DC: Government Printing Office, 1974.

G. Labor

Cho, Yong Sam. *Disguised Unemployment in Underdeveloped Areas with Special Reference to South Korean Agriculture.* Berkeley: University of California Press, 1963.

Choe, Ehn-hyun. *Population Distribution and Internal Migration in Korea. 1960 Census Monograph Series.* Seoul: Bureau of Statistics, Economic Planning Board, Republic of Korea, 1966.

Kim, Kyong-dong. "Industrialization and Industrialism: A Comparative Perspective in Values of Korean Workers and Managers." *ILCORK Working Paper,* 1. Honolulu: University of Hawaii Press, 1971.

McVoy, Edgar C. *Manpower Development and Utilization in Korea.* Washington, DC: U.S. Dept. of Labor, 1965.

U.S. Dept. of Labor. *Labor Law and Practices in the Republic of Korea.* BLS Series No. 361. Washington, DC: Government Printing Office, 1969.

Watanabe, Susumu, "Exports and Employment: The Case of the Republic of Korea," *International Labor Review* (Geneva), 106:6 (December 1972), 445–526.

H. Transportation/Communications

No books exclusively dealing with these subjects are available. *A Handbook of Korea* has sizeable portions on transportation and communications. (See Handbooks/Statistical Abstracts, pages 216–17). See also books on economy, geography, and history.

6. History

A. Autobiography/Biography

Allen, Richard C. *Korea's Syngman Rhee: An Unauthorized Portrait.* Rutland, VT: Tuttle, 1960.

Chong, Key Ray. "Ch'oe Che-u's Thonghak Doctrine: Its Sources and Meanings," *Journal of Korean Studies,* 1:2 (1971), 71–84.

Clark, Donald N. "Yun Ch'i-ho (1864–1945): Portrait of a Korean Intellectual in an Era of Transition." *Occasional Papers on Korea,* No. 4 (Sept. 1975), 36–76. Seattle: Society for Korean Studies.

Cook, Harold, "Pak Yong-hyo: Background and Early Years," *Journal of Social Science and Humanities,* The Korean Research Center, No. 31 (Dec. 1965), 1–24.

Jaisohn, Muriel. "Philip Jaisohn, B.S., M.D. (1869–1951), *Medical Annals of the District of Columbia,* 21 (1952), 250–353.

Jho, Sung-do. *Yi Sun-shin: A National Hero of Korea.* Chinhae, Korea: Choongmu-kong Society, 1970.

Kang, Young-hill. *The Grass Roof.* New York: Scribner's 1931.

Kim, Agnes Davis. *I Married a Korean, with Sketches of the Author.* New York: John Day, 1953.

Kim, Richard G. *Lost Names: Scenes from a Korean Boyhood.* New York: Praeger, 1970.

Kim, Yong-dok. "A Life and Thought of Pak Che-ga," *Korea Journal,* 12:7 (July 1972), 40–43.

King Seijong Memorial Society. *King Seijong the Great: A Biography of Korea's Most Famous King.* Seoul: 1970.

Ko, Byung-ik. "Chung Yak-yong's Version of Progress as Expressed in His Kiye-ron (Essays on Art and Technique), *Journal of Social Science and Humanities,* the Korean Research Center, 23 (1965), 29–36.

Lee, Peter H., Tr. *Lives of Eminent Korean Monks: The Haedong kosung chon.* Harvard-Yenching Institute Studies, No. 25. Cambridge: Harvard University Press, 1969.

Li, Mirok. *The Yalu Flows: A Korean Childhood.* Tr. by H.A. Hammelmann. East Lansing: Michigan State University, 1956.

New, Ilhan. *When I Was a Boy in Korea.* Boston: Lothrop, Lee and Shepard, 1928.

Oliver, Robert T. *Syngman Rhee: The Man Behind the Myth.* New York: Dodd Mead, 1954.

Pahk, Induk. *September Monkey.* New York: Harper, 1954.

Pak, No-ch'un. "Pak Chi-won, Satirist of the Aristocratic Society," *Korea Journal,* 13:3 (March 1973), 48–53.

Song, Chu-yong. "Yu Hyung-won," *Korea Journal,* 13:7 (July 1, 1972), 33–39.

Yi, Pangja. *The World is One: Princess Yi Pangja's Autobiography.* Seoul: Taewan Pub. Co., 1973.

Yim, Louise. *My Forty Years Fight for Korea.* Seoul: International Cultural Research Center, Chungang University, 1951.

B. General

Allen, Horace, N. *Korea, Fact and Fancy.* Seoul: The Methodist Publishing House, 1904.

———. *Things Korean: A Collection of Sketches and Anecdotes, Missionary and Diplomatic.* New York: Revell, 1908.

Center for East Asian Cultural Studies, comp. and revised. *A Short History of Korea.* Tokyo, 1963. (Originally published as *Korean History Handbook* by the Government-General of Korea in 1937).

Choy, Bong-youn. *Korea: A History.* Rutland, VT: Tuttle, 1971.

Chung, Kyung Cho. *New Korea: New Land of the Morning Calm.* New York: Macmillan, 1962.

Gale, James S. *The History of the Korean People.* Seoul: Christian Literature Society, 1927.

Ha, Tae Hung. *Korea—Forty Three Centuries.* Korean Cultural Series, 1. Seoul: Yonsei University Press, 1962.

Han, Woo-keun. *The History of Korea.* Tr. and edited by Kyun-shik Lee and Grafton K. Mintz. Seoul: Ulyu, 1969 and Honolulu: University of Hawaii Press, 1971.

Hatada, Takashi. *A History of Korea.* Tr. by Warren S. Smith, Jr. and Benjamin H. Hazard. Santa Barbara: CLIO, 1969.

Henderson, George. "Chŏng Ta-san: A Study of Korea's Intellectual History," *Journal of Asian Studies* 16 (May 1957), 377–386.

Henthorn, William E. *A History of Korea.* New York: The Free Press, 1971.

History Research Institute. Academy of Social Science, Democratic People's Republic of Korea, comp. *The Outline of Korean History.* Pyongyang: Foreign Languages Publishing House, 1977.

Hulbert, Homer B. *The History of Korea.* 2 vols. Seoul: The Methodist Publishing House, 1905.

———. *The Passing of Korea.* New York: Doubleday, Page, 1916.

Ilyon. *Samguk yusa: Legends and History of the Three Kingdoms of Ancient Korea.* Tr. by Tae Hung Ha and Grafton K. Mintz. Seoul: Yonsei University Press, 1972.

Ireland, Alleyne. *The New Korea.* New York: E.P. Dutton, 1929.

Joe, Wanne J. *Traditional Korea: A Cultural History.* Seoul: Chungang University Press, 1972.

Korea, Rep. of. Office of Public Information. *Korea: Her History and Culture.* Seoul: 1954.

Lee, Ki-baek. *A New History of Korea.* Tr. and expanded by Edward W. Wagner and Edward J. Schultz. Cambridge: Harvard University Press and Seoul: Ulyu, 1984.

Longford, Joseph, H. *The Story of Korea.* New York: C. Scribner's, 1911.

Lowell, Percival. *Choson: The Land of the Morning Calm—A Sketch of Korea.* Boston: Ticknor, 1888.

MacDonald, Donald S. *The Koreans: Contemporary Politics and Society.* Boulder, CO: Westview Press, 1988.

Nahm, Andrew C. *A Panorama of 5000 Years: Korean History.* Seoul and Elizabeth, NJ: Hollym International, 1983.

———. *Korea: Tradition and Transformation—A History of the Korean People.* Seoul and Elizabeth, NJ: Hollym International, 1987.

Ross, John. *History of Corea, Ancient and Modern: With Description of Manners, Customs, Language and Geography.* London: Elliot Stock, 1891.

Rutt, Richard. *James Scrath Gale and His History of the Korean People.* Seoul: Royal Asiatic Society, Korea Branch, 1972.

Sohn, Pow-key et al. *The History of Korea.* Seoul: Korean National Commission for UNESCO, 1970.

Wagner, Ellasue. *Korea: The Old and the New.* New York, Revell, 1931.

Weems, Clarence Norwood, ed. *Hulbert's History of Korea.* 2 vols. New York: Hillary House, 1962.

C. Ancient/Pre-Modern

Choe, Chin-young. *The Rule of the Taewŏn'gun, 1864–1873, Reconstruction in Yi Korea.* Cambridge: East Asian Research Center, Harvard University, 1972.

Choi, Woon Sang. *The Fall of the Hermit Kingdom.* Dobbs Ferry, NY: Oceana Publications, 1963.

Conroy, Hillary. *The Japanese Seizure of Korea, 1868–1910—A Study of Realism and Idealism in International Relations.* Philadelphia: University of Pennsylvania Press, 1960.

Cook, Harold F. *Korea's 1884 Incident: Its Background and Kim Ok-kyun's Elusive Dream.* Seoul: Royal Asiatic Society, Korea Branch, 1972.

Gale, James S. *Korea in Transition.* Cincinnati: Jennings and Graham, and New York: Eaton and Maines, 1909.

Gardiner, K.J.H. *The Early History of Korea: The Historical Development of the Peninsula Up to the Introduction of Buddhism in the Fourth Century A.D.* Honolulu: University of Hawaii Press, 1969.

Haboush, JaHyun Kim. *A Heritage of Kings: One Man's Monarchy in the Confucian World.* New York: College University Press, 1988.

Henthorn, William F. *Korea: The Mongol Invasions.* Leiden: Brill, 1963.

Jo, Yung-hwan, ed. *Korea's Response to the West.* Kalamazoo, MI: Korea Research and Publications, 1971.

Kim, C.I. Eugene and Han-kyo Kim. *Korea and the Politics of Imperialism, 1876–1910.* Berkeley: University of California Press, 1967.

Ledyard, Gari. *The Dutch Come to Korea: An Account of the Life of the First Westerners in Korea (1653–1666).* Seoul: Royal Asiatic Society, Korea Branch, 1971.

Lee, Chang-soo. *Modernization of Korea and the Impact of the West.* Los Angeles: East Asian Studies Center, University of Southern California, 1981.

McCrane, George A. *Korea's Tragic Hours: The Closing Years of the Yi Dynasty.* Ed. by Harold F. Cook and Alan M. MacDougall. Seoul: Taewon Pub. Co., 1973.

McCune, Shannon. *Korea: The Land of Broken Calm.* New York: Van Nostrand, 1961.

McKenzie, Frederick A. *The Tragedy of Korea.* London: Hodder and Stoughton, 1908. Reprinted Seoul: Yonsei University Press, 1969.

Oppert, Ernest. *A Forbidden Land: Voyages to Corea.* London: Sampson, Low, Marston, Searle and Revington, 1880.

Palais, James B. *Politics and Policy in Traditional Korea.* Harvard East Asian Series, No. 82. Cambridge: Harvard University Press, 1974.

Pearson, Richard J. *The Traditional Culture and Society of Korea: Prehistory.* Occasional Paper No. 3. Center for Korean Studies, University of Hawaii, 1975.

Wagner, Edward W. *The Literati Purges: Political Conflict in Early Yi Korea.* Cambridge: East Asian Research Center, Harvard University, 1974.

Weems, Benjamin B. *Reform, Rebellion, and the Heavenly Way.* Tucson: University of Arizona Press, 1964.

Wilkinson, W.H. *The Corean Government: Constitutional Change, July 1894–October 1895, with an Appendix on Subsequent Enactment to June 3rd 1896.* Shanghai: The Statistical Department of Inspectorate General of Customs, 1897.

Yi, Kyu-tae. *Modern Transformation of Korea.* Tr. by Sung Tongmahn *et al.* Seoul: Sejong Pub. Co., 1970.

D. Colonial Period

Chung, Henry. *The Case of Korea: A Collection of Evidence on the Japanese Domination of Korea, and on the Development of the Korean Independence Movement.* New York: Revell, 1921.

Grajdanzev, Andrew J. *Korea Looks Ahead.* IPR Pamphlet 15. New York: American Council, Institute of Pacific Relations, 1944.

———. *Modern Korea.* New York: Institute of Pacific Relations, 1944.

Japan. Government-General of Korea. *Annual Report on Administration of Chosen.* Keijo (Seoul), 1907–1937.

———. *Thriving Chosen: A Survey of Twenty-five Years' Administration.* Keijo (Seoul): 1935.

Kim, C.I. Eugene and Doretha E. Mortimore, ed. *Korea's Response to Japan: The Colonial Period, 1910–1945.* Kalamazoo, MI: Center for Korean Studies, Western Michigan University, 1975.

Kim, Richard E. *Lost Names: Scenes from a Korean Boyhood.* New York: Praeger. 1970.

Ku, Dae-yeol. *Korea Under Colonialism: The March First Movement and Anglo-Japanese Relations.* Seoul: Royal Asiatic Society, Korea Branch, 1985.

Lee, Chong-sik. *The Politics of Korean Nationalism.* Berkeley: University of California Press, 1965.

McKenzie, Frederick A. *Korea's Fight for Freedom.* New York: Revell, 1920. Reprinted Seoul: Yonsei University Press, 1969.

Nahm, Andrew C., ed. *Korea Under Japanese Colonial Rule—Studies of the Policy and Techniques of Japanese Colonialism.* Kalamazoo, MI: Center for Korean Studies, Western Michigan University, 1973.

Oliver, Robert. *Korea: Forgotten Nation.* Washington, DC, Public Affairs Press, 1944.

Rhee, Syngman. *Japan Inside Out: The Challenge of Today.* New York: Revell, 1941.

Robinson, Michael Edwin. *Cultural Nationalism in Colonial Korea, 1920–1925.* Seattle: University of Washington Press, 1988.

Scalapino, Robert A. and Chong-sik Lee. *Communism in Korea.* 2 vols. Berkeley: University of California Press, 1972.

Suh, Dae-sook, *The Korean Communist Movement, 1918–1948.* Princeton: Princeton University Press, 1967.

E. Post-Independence Period

Caldwell, John C. *The Korea Story.* New York: Henry Regnery, 1952.

Cho, Soon-sung. *Korea in World Politics, 1940–1950: An Evaluation of American Responsibility.* Berkeley: University of California Press, 1967.

Chung, Henry. *The Russians Came to Korea.* Seoul and Washington, DC: Korean Pacific Press, 1947.

Chung, Kyung Cho. *Korea: The Third Republic.* New York: Macmillan, 1971.

Clark, Donald N., ed. *The Kwangju Uprising: Shadow Over the Regime in South Korea.* Boulder, CO: Westview Press, 1987.

Clough, Ralph N. *Balancing Act: The Republic of Korea Approaches 1988.* FPI Policy Brief 5. Lanham, MD: University Press of America, 1987.

Cumings, Bruce. *The Origins of the Korean War: Liberation and the Emergence of Separate Regimes, 1945–1947.* Princeton: Princeton University Press, 1981.

Goodrich, Leland M. *Korea: A Story of U.S. Policy in the United Nations.* New York: Council on Foreign Relations, 1956.

Han, Sungjoo. *The Failure of Democracy in South Korea.* Berkeley: University of California Press, 1974.

Hurst, E. Cameron, III. *Korea 1988: A Nation at the Crossroad.* Lanham, MD: University Press of America, 1988.

Kim, Se-jin. *The Politics of Military Revolution in Korea.* Chapel Hill: University of North Carolina Press, 1971.

Korea, Rep. of. Supreme Council for National Reconstruction. *The Military Revolution in Korea.* Seoul: 1961.

Mason, Edward S. *et al. The Economic and Social Modernization of the Republic of Korea: Studies in the Modernization of the Republic of*

Korea, 1945–1975. Cambridge: Harvard University Press, 1980.

McCune, George M. and Arthur Grey Jr. *Korea Today.* Cambridge: Harvard University Press, 1951.

Meade, Grant. *American Military Government in Korea.* New York: Columbia University Press, 1951.

Nahm, Andrew C., ed. *Korea and the New Order in East Asia.* Kalamazoo, MI: Center for Korean Studies, Western Michigan University, 1975.

———., ed. *Studies in the Developmental Aspects of Korea.* Kalamazoo, MI: Graduate College and Institute of International and Area Studies, Western Michigan University, 1969.

Oh, John K.C. *Democracy on Trial.* Ithaca: Cornell University Press, 1968.

Reeve, W.D. *The Republic of Korea: A Political and Economic History.* London: Oxford University Press, 1963.

Sawyer, Robert. *Military Advisors in Korea: KMAG in Peace and War.* Washington, DC: Office of the Chief of Military History, 1962.

F. The Korean War

Berger, Carl. *The Korean Knot: A Military-Political History.* Philadelphia: University of Pennsylvania Press, 1957.

Clark, Mark W. *From The Danbue to the Yalu.* New York: Harper, 1954.

Gardner, Lloyd C., ed. *The Korean War.* New York: Quadrangle Books, 1977.

Hastings, Max. *The Korean War.* New York: Simon & Schuster, 1987.

Kaufman, Burton I. *The Korean War: Challenge in Crisis, Credibility and Command.* New York: Alfred A. Knopf, 1986.

Kim, Chun-kon. *The Korean War, 1950–53.* Seoul: Kwangmyong Pub. Co., 1973.

Lowe, Peter. *The Origins of the Korean War.* London: Longman, 1986.

Merrill, John. *Korea: The Peninsula Origins of the War.* Newark, DE: University of Delaware Press, 1989.

Noble, Harold J. *Embassy at War.* Edited with an introduction by Frank Baldwin. Seattle: University of Washington Press, 1975.

Oliver, Robert T. *Verdict in Korea.* State College, PA: Bald Eagle Press, 1952.

Paige, Glenn D. *The Korean Decision—June 24–30.* New York: The Free Press, 1968.

Reese, David. *Korea: The Limited War.* New York: St. Martin's Press, 1964.

Ridgway, Matthew B. *The Korean War.* New York: Popular Library, 1967.

Riley, John W. and Wilbur Schramm. *The Reds Take a City: The Communist Occupation of Seoul, with Eyewitness Accounts.* New Brunswick, NJ: Rutgers University Press, 1954.

Stone, Isidor F. *The Hidden History of the Korean War.* New York: Monthly Review Press, 1952.

Vatcher, William H. *Panmunjom: The Story of the Korean Military Armistice Negotiations.* New York: Praeger, 1958.

Whiting, Allen A. *China Crosses the Yalu: The Decision to Enter the Korean War.* New York: Macmillan, 1960.

G. Diplomatic History/Foreign Relations

Baldwin, Frank, ed. *Without Parallel: The American-Korean Relationship Since 1945*. New York: Pantheon Book, 1974.

Baynard, Thomas O. and Soo-gil Young, ed. *Economic Relations Between the United States and Korea: Conflict or Cooperation?* Washington, DC: Institute for International Economics, 1989.

Bishop, Isabella L.B. *Korea and Her Neighbors: A Narrative of Travel with an Account of the Recent Vicissitudes and Present Condition.* 2 vols. London: John Murray, 1897. A single-volume London: KPI, 1985.

Burnett, Scott, S., ed. *Korean-American Relations: Documents Pertaining to the Far Eastern Diplomacy of the United States.* Vol. III: The Period of Diminishing Influence, 1896–1905. Honolulu: University of Hawaii Press, 1989.

Buss, Claude A. *The United States and the Republic of Korea: Background for Policy.* Stanford: Hoover Institution Press, 1982.

Chien, Frederick Foo. *The Opening of Korea: A Study of Chinese Diplomacy, 1876–1885.* Hamden, CT: Shoe String Press, 1967.

Choi, Woon Sang. *The Fall of the Hermit Kingdom.* Dobbs Ferry, NY: Oceana Publications, 1967.

Chung, Chong-wha and J.E. Hoare, ed. *Korean-British Relations: Yesterday, Today, and Tomorrow.* Cho'ongju: Ch'ongju University, 1984.

Clough, Ralph N. *Embattled Korea: The Rivalry for International Support.* Boulder, CO: Westview Press, 1987.

Conroy, Hillary, *The Japanese Seizure of Korea, 1868–1910: A Study of Realism and Idealism in International Relations.* Philadelphia: University of Pennsylvania Press, 1960.

Cumings, Bruce, ed. *Child of Conflict: The Korean-American Relationship, 1943–1953.* Seattle: University of Washington Press, 1983.

Curzon, George N. *Problems of the Far East: Japan-Korea-China.* London: Longmans, Green, 1894.

Dennet, Tyler. *Americans in East Asia: A Critical Study of the Policy of the United States with Reference to China, Japan and Korea in the Nineteenth Century.* New York: Macmillan, 1922.

Denny, Owen N. *China and Korea.* Shanghai: Kelly and Walsh, 1888.

Deuchler, Martina. *Confucian Gentlemen and Barbarian Envoys: The Opening of Korea, 1875–1885.* Seattle: University of Washington Press, 1983.

Drake, H.B. *Korea and the Japanese.* London: John Lane/the Bodley Head Ltd., and New York: Dodd, Mead, 1930.

Frazer, Everett. *Korea and Her Relations with China, Japan and the United States.* Orange, NJ: Chronicle Book, 1884.

Gregor, A. James. *Land of the Morning Calm: Korea and American Security.* Washington, DC: Ethics and Public Policy Center, 1990.

Han, Sung-joo, ed. *U.S.-Korea Security Cooperation: Retrospects and Prospects.* ARC Foreign Policy Studies No. 4. Seoul: Asiatic Research Center, Korea University 1983.

Harrington, Fred H. *God, Mammon and the Japanese: Dr. Horace N. Allen and Korean-American Relations, 1884–1905.* Madison: University of Wisconsin Press, 1944.

Kim, Young C., ed. *Foreign Policies of Korea.* Washington, DC: Institute for Asian Studies, George Washington University, 1973.

———. *Major Powers and Korea.* Silver Spring, MD: Research Institute on Korean Affairs, 1973.

Koo, Young-nok and Dae-sook Suh, ed. *Korea and the United States: A Century of Cooperation.* Honolulu: University of Hawaii Press, 1984.

Koo, Young-nok and Sung-joo Han, ed. *The Foreign Policy of the Republic of Korea.* New York: Columbia University Press, 1985.

Kwak, Tae-hwan *et al,* ed. *The Two Koreas in World Politics.* Seoul: Institute for Far Eastern Studies, Kyungnam University, 1983.

———. *U.S.-Korean Relations, 1882–1982.* Boulder, CO: Westview Press, 1983.

Ladd, George T. *In Korea with Marquis Ito.* New York: C. Scribner's, 1908.

Lee, Manwoo *et al,* ed. *Alliance Under Tension: The Evolution of South Korean-U.S. Relations.* Boulder CO: Westview Press, 1989.

Lee, Yul-bok. *Diplomatic Relations Between the United States and Korea, 1866–1887.* New York: Humanities Press, 1970.

———. *West Goes East: Paul Georg von Mollendorff and Great Power Imperialism in Late Yi Korea.* Honolulu: University of Hawaii Press, 1988.

Lee, Yul-bok and Wayne Patterson, ed. *One Hundred Years of Korean-American Relations, 1882–1982.* University, AL: University of Alabama Press, 1986.

Lensen, George A. *Balance of Intrigue; International Rivalry in Korea and Manchuria, 1884–1899.* Tallahassee: University Presses of Florida, 1982.

———, ed. *Korea and Manchuria Between Russia and Japan, 1895–1904: The Observations of Sir Ernest Satow.* Tallahassee: Diplomatic Press, 1966.

Malozemoff, Andrew. *Russian Far Eastern Policy, 1881–1904: With Special Emphasis on the Causes of the Russo-Japanese War.* Berkeley: University of California Press, 1958.

Matray, James I. *The Reluctant Crusader: American Foreign Policy in Korea, 1941–1950.* Honolulu: University of Hawaii Press, 1985.

Mazarr, Michael J. *et al,* ed. *Korea 1991: The Road to Peace.* Boulder, CO: Westview Press, 1991.

McCune, George M. "The Exchange of Envoys Between Korea and Japan During the Tokugawa Period," *Far Eastern Quarterly,* 5 (May 1946), 308–325.

McCune, George M. and John A. Harrison, ed. *Korean-American Relations: Documents Pertaining to the Far Eastern Diplomacy of the United States.* Vol. I: The Initial Period, 1883–1886. Berkeley: University of California Press, 1951.

Morse, Ronald, ed. *Reflections on a Century of United States-Korean Relations.* Lanham, MD: University Press of America, 1983.

Nahm, Andrew C., ed. *Korea and the New Order in East Asia.* Kalamazoo, MI: Center for Korean Studies, Western Michigan University, 1975.

———, ed. *The United States and Korea: American-Korean Relations, 1866–1976.* Kalamazoo, MI: Center for Korean Studies, Western Michigan University, 1979.

Nelson, Melvin F. *Korea and the Old Order in Eastern Asia.* Baton Rouge: Louisiana State University, 1945. Reprinted New York: Russel and Russel, 1967.

Noble, Harold J. *Embassy at War.* Edited with an introduction by Frank Baldwin. Seattle: University of Washington Press, 1975.

Oliver, Robert T. *Syngman Rhee and American Involvement in Korea, 1942–1960: A Personal Narrative.* Seoul: Panmun Book Co., 1978.

Olsen, Edward A. *U.S. Policy and the Two Koreas.* Boulder, CO: Westview Press, 1988.

Palmer, Spencer J. *Korean-American Relations: Documents Pertaining to the Far Eastern Diplomacy of the United States.* Vol. I: *The Period of Growing Influence, 1887–1895.* Berkeley: University of California Press, 1963.

Rockhill, William. *China's Intercourse with Korea from the XVth Century to 1895.* London: Luzac, 1950.

Sands, William J. *Undiplomatic Memoirs: The Far East, 1896–1905.* New York: McGraw-Hill, 1930.

Sanford, Dan C. *South Korea and the Socialist Countries: The Politics of Trade.* New York: St. Martin's Press, 1990.

Steinberg, David I. *Korea: Nexus of East Asia.* New York: American-Asian Educational Exchange, 1970.

Swartout, Robert R.J. *Mandarins, Gunboats, and Power Politics: Owen Nickerson Denny and the International Rivalries in Korea.* Honolulu: University of Hawaii Press, 1980.

Taylor, William J. Jr. *et al,* ed. *The Future of South Korean-U.S. Security Relations.* Boulder, CO: Westview Press, 1989.

White, Nathan N. *U.S. Policy Toward Korea: Analysis, Alternatives, and Recommendations.* Boulder, CO: Westview Press, 1978.

7. Politics

A. General

Cole, David G. and Princeton N. Lyman. *Korean Development: The Interplay of Politics and Economics.* Cambridge: Harvard University Press, 1971.

Han, Sungjoo. *The Failure of Democracy in South Korea.* Berkeley: University of California Press, 1974.

Henderson, Gregory. *The Politics of the Vortex.* Cambridge: Harvard University Press, 1968.

Kihl, Young Whan. *Politics and Policies in Divided Korea: Regimes in Contest.* Boulder, CO: Westview Press, 1984.

Kim, C.I. Eugene, ed. *A Pattern of Political Development: Korea.* Kalamazoo: Korea Research and Publications, 1964.

Kim, Ilpyung and Young Whan Kihl, ed. *Political Change in South Korea.* New York: Korean PWPA, 1988.

Kim, Joungwon Alexander. *Divided Korea: The Politics of Development, 1945–1972.* Cambridge: East Asia Research Center, Harvard University, 1975.

Lee, Chong-sik. *Japan and Korea: The Political Dimension.* Stanford: Hoover Institution, 1985.

Lee, Manwoo. *The Odyssey of Korean Democracy: The Korean Politics, 1987–1990.* New York: Praeger, 1990.

Nam, Koon Woo. *South Korean Politics: The Search for Political Consensus and Stability.* Lanham, MD: University Press of America, 1989.

Oh, John K.C. *Democracy on Trial.* Ithaca: Cornell University Press, 1968.

Pak, Chi-young. *Political Opposition in Korea, 1945–1963.* The Institute of Social Science. Korean Studies Series No. 2. Honolulu: University of Hawaii Press, 1980.

Palais, James B. *Politics and Policy in Traditional Korea.* Cambridge: Harvard University Press, 1975.

Suh, Dae-sook and Chae-jin Lee, ed. *Political Leadership in Korea.* Seattle: University of Washington Press, 1975.

Tewksburg, Donald G., comp. *Source Materials on Korean Politics and Ideologies.* New York: Institute of Pacific Relations, 1950.

Wright, Edward, ed. *Korean Politics in Transition.* Seoul: Royal Asiatic Society, Korea Branch, 1974.

Yang, Sung Chul. *Korea and Two Regimes: Kim Il Sung and Park Chung Hee.* Cambridge, MA: Schenkman Pub. Co., 1981.

Yoon, Woo-kon. "Korean Bureaucrats' Behavior": An Analysis of Personality and Its Effect," *Korea Journal,* 14:7 (July 1974), 22–29.

B. Government

Ch'oe, Young-ho. *The Civil Examinations and the Social Structure in Early Yi Dynasty Korea, 1392–1600.* Seoul: Korean Research Center, 1987.

Haboush, JaHyun Kim. *A Heritage of Kings: One Man's Monarchy in the Confucian World.* New York: Columbia University Press, 1988.

Kihl, Young Whan. *Local Elections, Power Structure and the Legislative Process in Korea.* Occasional Paper, No. 8. Comparative Legislative Research Center, Iowa University, 1975.

Kim, Bum-woong and Joon Rho, ed. *Korean Public Bureaucracy.* Seoul: Kyobo Publishing, 1982.

Kim, Kwan Bong. *The Korean-Japanese Treaty Crisis and the Instability of the Korean Political System.* New York: Praeger, 1971.

Kim, Se-jin and Chang-hyun Cho, ed. *Government and Politics of Korea.* Silver Spring, MD: Research Institute on Korean Affairs, 1972.

Koh, Byung Chul, ed. *Aspects of Administrative Development in South Korea.* Kalamazoo: Korea Research and Publications, 1967.

Lee, Hahn-been. *Korea: Time, Change, and Administration.* Honolulu: East-West Center Press, 1968.

Oh, Chung Hwan. "The Civil Service of the Republic of Korea." Ph.D. Dissertation, New York University, 1961.

Paik, Wanki. "Modernization of Korean Bureaucracy," Ph.D. Dissertation, Florida State University, 1972.

Rhee, Yong-pil. *The Breakdown of Authority Structure in Korea in 1960.* Honolulu: University of Hawaii Press, 1982.

Wagner, Edward W. *The Literati Purges: Political Conflict in Early Yi Korea.* Cambridge: East Asian Research Center, Harvard University, 1974.

Yoo, Hoon. "Social Background of Higher Civil Servants in Korea," *Korea Quarterly,* 10:1 (1968), 35–55.

C. Law

Chun, Bong Duck. "The Commercial Laws in Korea," *Digest of Commercial Laws of the World.* Vol. 2. Dodds Ferry, NY: Oceana Publications, 1966.

Dull, Paul S. "South Korean Constitution." *Far Eastern Survey,* 17:17 (Sept. 1948), 205–207.

Hahm, Pyong-choon. *The Korean Political Tradition and Law: Essays in Korean Law and Legal History.* Seoul: Royal Asiatic Society, Korea Branch, 1967.

International Cultural Foundation. *Legal System of Korea.* Korean Culture Series No. 5. Seoul: 1975.

Korea, Rep. of. Central Election Management Committee. *Korean Constitution, Election and Political Party Law,* Seoul: 1964 and 1987.

———. Office of Labor Affairs. *Labor Law of Korea.* Seoul: 1969.

Korean Legal Center. *Laws of the Republic of Korea.* Seoul: 1975.

Kwack, Yoon-chick. "The Korean New Civil Code," *Bulletin of the Korean Research Center,* 17 (1962), 11–23.

Pak, C.Y. "Third Republic Constitution of Korea," *Western Political Quarterly,* 21 (March 1968), 110–122.

Park, Byong Ho. "Characteristics of Traditional Korean Law," *Korea Journal,* 16:7 (July 1970), 4–16.

Ryu, Paul Kichyon. *The Korean Criminal Code.* American Series of Foreign Penal Code No. 2. South Hackensack, NJ: Fred B. Rothmann, 1960.

Shaw, William. "Traditional Korea Law: A New Look," *Korea Journal,* 13:9 (Sept. 1973), 40–53.

U.S. Dept. of Labor. *Labor Law and Practices in the Republic of Korea.* BLS Series No. 361. Washington, DC. Government Printing Office, 1969.

Wilkinson, W.H. *The Corean Government: Constitutional Changes, July 1894–October 1895, with an Appendix on Subsequent Enactment to June 3rd 1896.* Shanghai: The Statistical Department of Inspectorate General of Customs, 1897.

World Peace Through Law Center. *Law and Judicial Systems of Nations: Korea.* Washington, DC, 1968.

Yoon, Dae-kyu. *Law and Political Authority in South Korea.* Boulder, CO: Westview Press and Masan: Kyungnam University Press, 1990.

D. Political Parties

Chu, Shao-hsien. "Past and Present of the Political Parties in the Republic of Korea," *Issues and Studies,* 1:10 (July 1965), 20–30.

Han, Ki-shik. "Development of Parties and Politics in Korea," *Korea Journal,* 14:9 (Sept. 1974), 37–49.

Han, Tae-soo. "A Review of Political Party Activities in Korea (1945–1954)," *Korean Affairs* 1 (1962), 413–427.

Han, Y.C. "Political Parties and Political Development in South Korea," *Pacific Affairs,* 42:4 (Winter 1969–1970), 444–464.

Kihl, Young Whan. "Research on Party Politics in Korea: An Analytical Scheme." *Korean Political Science Review* 6 (June 1972), 279–296.

Kim, C.I. Eugene and Young Whan Kihl, ed. *Party Politics and Elections in Korea.* Silver Spring, MD: Research Institute on Korean Affairs, 1976.

Kim, Chulsu, "Parties and Factions in Korean Politics." Ph.D. Dissertation, University of Massachusetts, 1973.

8. Science

A. Geography/Geology

Bartz, Patricia M. *South Korea.* Oxford, Eng.: Clarendon Press, 1972.

Canada. Dept. of Mines and Technical Survey. *Korea: A Geographical Appreciation.* Foreign Geography Information Series No. 4. Ottawa: 1951.

Cavendish, Alfred E. and Henry E. Goold-Adams. *Korea and the Sacred Mountain.* London: G. Philip, 1894.

Chen, Cheng-siang. *Agricultural Geography of Korea.* Research Report No. 31. Hong Kong: University of Hong Kong, 1970.

Hall, Basil. *Account of Voyage of Discovery to the West Coast of Corea and the Great Loo-choo Island.* London: John Murray, 1818.

Korea, Rep. of. *Geological Survey of Korea: An Outline of the Geology of Korea.* Seoul: 1956.

———. *Geological Survey of Korea: Hydrogeologic Maps of Korea: Anseong River Basin.* Seoul: 1961.

Landor, Arnold H.S. *Corea: Or Chosen, the Land of the Morning Calm.* London: Heinemann, 1895.

Lee, Dai-sung, ed. *Geology of Korea.* Seoul: Kyobo-sa, 1987.

McCune, Shannon. *Korea's Heritage: A Regional and Social Geography.* Rutland, VT: Tuttle, 1956.

———. *Views of the Geography of Korea, 1935–1960.* Seoul: The Korean Research Center, 1980.

Reedman, Anthony J. and Sangho Um. *The Geography of Korea.* Seoul: Geological and Mineral Institute of Korea, 1975.

Zaichikov, V.T. *Geography of Korea.* Translated from Russian by Albert Parry with an introduction by Shannon McCune. New York: Institute of Pacific Relations, 1952.

B. Public Health/Medicine

Bowman, Newton H. "The History of Korean Medicine," *Transactions of the Korea Branch of the Royal Asiatic Society,* 6 (1915), 1–34.

No, Chong-u. "Chinese Medicine in Korea," *Korea Journal,* 11:2 (February 1971), 24–29.

Yeon, Ha-cheong. *Primary Health Care in Korea: An Approach to Evaluation.* Honolulu: University of Hawaii Press, 1981.

C. Science/Technology

Jeon, Sang-woon. *Science and Technology in Korea: Traditional Instruments and Techniques.* Cambridge: MIT Press, 1974.

Needham, Joseph *et al. The Hall of Heavenly Records: Korean Astronomical Instruments and Clocks, 1380–1780.* London: Cambridge University Press, 1959.

Sohn, Pow-key. *Early Korean Typography.* Seoul: Korean Library Science Research Institute, 1971.

9. Society

A. Anthropology

Allen, Horace N. *Things Korean: A Collection of Sketches and Anecdotes, Missionary and Diplomatic.* New York: Revell, 1908.

Bergman, Stan. *In Korean Wilds and Villages.* Trans. by Frederick Whyte. London: Travel Book Club, 1938.

Brandt, Vincent S.R. *A Korean Village Between Farm and Sea.* Cambridge: Harvard University Press, 1971.

Carles, William R. *Life in Corea.* London: Macmillan, 1888.

Choe, Sang-u. *Annual Customs of Korea.* Seoul: Seomun Dang, 1983.

Chun, Kyung-soo. *Reciprocity and Korean Society: An Ethnography of Hasami.* Seoul: Seoul National University Press, 1985.

Dallet, Charles. *Traditional Korea.* New Haven: Human Relations Area Files, 1964.

Gale, James S. *Korean Sketches.* Nashville: Publishing House of the Methodist Episcopal Church South, 1898.

Gifford, Daniel L. *Every-day Life in Korea: A Collection of Studies and Stories.* New York: Revell, 1898.

Lee, Ou Young. *In This Earth and in This Wind: This Is Korea.* Seoul: Hollym Corp., 1967.

Lowell, Percival. *Choson: The Land of the Morning Calm: A Sketch of Korea.* Boston: Ticknor and Co., 1885.

Moose, J. Robert. *Village Life in Korea.* Nashville: Publishing House of the Methodist Episcopal Church South, 1911.

Pak, Ki-hyuk and Sidney D. Gamble. *The Changing Korean Village.* Seoul: Royal Asiatic Society, Korea Branch, 1975.

Rutt, Richard. *Korean Works and Days: Notes from the Diary of a Country Priest.* Seoul: Royal Asiatic Society, Korea Branch, 1964.

Underwood, Lillian H. *Fifteen Years Among the Top-Knots, or Life in Korea.* New York: American Tract Society, 1908.

B. Education

Adams, Donald K. "Education in Korea 1945–1955." Ph.D. Dissertation, University of Connecticut, 1955.

Choo, Young-ha. *The Education in the Yi Dynasty.* Seoul: Soodo Women's Teachers College, 1961.

Dodge, Herbert W. "A History of the U.S. Assistance to Korean Education: 1953–1966." Ph.D. Dissertation, George Washington University, 1971.

Edman, Marion L. *Primary Teachers of Korea Look at Themselves.* Seoul: Central Educational Research Institute, 1962.

Fisher, James W. *Democracy and Mission Education in Korea.* New York: Columbia University Press, 1928. Reprinted Seoul: Yonsei University Press, 1970.

Kim, Chong-chol. "Higher Education in the Republic of Korea," *Bulletin of the UNESCO Regional Office of Education in Asia,* 7:1 (Sept. 1972), 89–99.

Kim, Hellen Kiteuk. *Rural Education for the Regeneration of Korea.* New York: Columbia University Press, 1931.

Kim, Hyun-chul. "History of Education in Korea." Ph.D. Dissertation, American University, 1931.

Korea, Rep. of. Ministry of Education. *Education in Korea.* Annual. Seoul: 1961–.

———. *Higher Educational Reform in the Republic of Korea.* Seoul: 1963.

———. *Summary of Education in Korea.* Annual. Seoul: 1963–.

Korean National Commission for UNESCO, *Review of Educational Studies in Korea.* Seoul: 1972.

Lee, Kyu-hwan. *The Equalization Policy of Middle Schools in the Republic of Korea.* Seoul: Ewha Woman's University, 1972–.

Lee, Yung Dug. *Educational Innovations in the Republic of Korea.* Geneva: International Bureau of Education, 1974.

McGinn, N.J. *et al. Educational Development in Korea.* Cambridge: Harvard University Press, 1980.

Meineske, Charlotte. *Education in Korea.* Seoul: Ministry of Education, Republic of Korea, 1958.

Morgan, Robert and C.B. Chadwick. *System Analysis for Educational Change: The Republic of Korea.* Tallahassee: Florida State University, 1971.

Nam, Byung-hun. "Educational Reorganization in South Korea under the United States Army Military Government, 1945–48." Ph.D. Dissertation, University of Pittsburgh, 1962.

Underwood, Horace H. *Modern Education in Korea.* New York: International Press, 1926.

UNESCO. "Republic of Korea," *World Survey of Education.* Vol. 2. Primary Education. Paris: 1958.

———. "Republic of Korea," *World Survey of Education.* Vol. 3. Secondary Education. Paris: 1961.

———. "Republic of Korea," *World Survey of Education.* Vol. 4. Higher Education. Paris: 1965.

———. "Republic of Korea," *World Survey of Education.* Vol. 5. Educational Policy, Legislation and Administration. Paris: 1971.

UNESCO. Regional Advisory Team for Educational Planning in Asia. *Long-Term Projections for Education in the Republic of Korea.* Bangkok: 1965.

Werk, Richard. "Educational Development under the South Korean Interim Government," *School and Society,* 69 (April 20, 1949), 305–309.

You, In-jong. "The Impact of the American Protestant Missions on Korean Education from 1885–1932." Ph.D. Dissertation, University of North Carolina, 1967.

Yu, Hyung-jin. "Educational Developments in the Republic of Korea: 1957–1967," *Bulletin of UNESCO, Regional Office of Education in Asia,* 2:1 (Sept. 1967), 37–43.

C. Sociology

Aqua, Ronald. *Local Institutions and Rural Development in South Korea.* Ithaca: Cornell University Press, 1974.

Ban, Sung Hwan. *The New Community Movement in Korea.* Seoul: Korean Development Institute, 1975.

Barringer, Herbert R. "Social Stratification and Industrialization in Korea." *ILCORK Working Paper,* No. 11. Seoul: 1971.

Brunner, Edward de S. *Rural Korea.* New York: International Missionary Council, 1942.

Chung, Sei-wha, ed., Shin Chang-hyun et al tr., *Challenge for Women: Women's Studies in Korea.* Seoul: Ewha Woman's University Press, 1986.

Crane, Paul. *Korean Patterns.* Seoul: Hollym Corp., 1967.

Gilmore, George W. *Korea from Its Capital with a Chapter on Missions.* Philadelphia: Presbyterian Board of Publication, 1892.

Hong, Sawon. *Community Development and Human Reproductive Behavior.* Seoul: Korea Development Institute, 1979.

International Cultural Foundation. *Korean Society.* Korean Culture Series, No. 6. Seoul: 1976.

Kendall, Laural and Mark Peterson, ed. *Korean Women: Views from the Inner Room.* New Haven: East Rock Press, 1983.

Kim, Agnes Davis. *I Married a Korean.* Seoul: Royal Asiatic Society, Korea Branch, 1953.

Kim, C.I. Eugene and Changboh Chee. *Aspects of Social Change in Korea.* Kalamazoo: Korea Research and Publications, 1963.

Kim, Yung-chung, ed. *Women of Korea: A History from Ancient Times to 1945.* Seoul: Ewha Woman's University Press, 1977.

Kwon, Tae Hwan. *Demography of Korea.* Seoul: Seoul National University, 1973.

Kwon, Tae Hwan *et al. The Population of Korea.* Seoul: Population and Development Studies Center, 1975.

Lee, Han Soon, *A Study on Korean Internal Migration in the 1960s.* Seoul: Kyunghee University, 1973.

Lee, Hyo-jae. "Changing Family in Korea," *Bulletin of the Korean Research Center,* 29 (Dec. 1968), 87–89.

———. "Industrialization and the Family in Korea." *ILCORK Working Paper.* Honolulu: University of Hawaii, 1971.

Lee, Man Gap. *The Social Structure in a Korean Village and Its Change.* Seoul: Seoul National University, 1973.

———. *Sociology and Social Change in Korea.* Seoul: Korea Development Institute, 1982.

Lee, Man Gap and Herbert R. Barringer, ed. *A City in Transition: Urbanization in Taegu, Korea.* Seoul: Hollym Corp., 1971.

Macdonald, Donald S. *The Koreans: Contemporary Politics and Society.* Boulder, CO: Westview Press, 1988.

Mason, Edward S. *et al. The Economic and Social Modernization of the Republic of Korea: Studies in the Modernization of the Republic of Korea, 1945–1975.* Cambridge: Harvard University Press, 1980.

Mattielli, Sandra, ed. *Virtues in Conflict: Tradition and the Korean Women Today.* Seoul: Royal Asiatic Society, Korea Branch, 1977.

Morse, Ronald. *Wild Asters: Explorations in Korean Thoughts, Culture and Society.* Lanham, MD: University Press of America, 1987.

Oppert, Ernest. *A Forbidden Land: Voyage to Corea.* London: Sampson Low, Marston, Searle and Rivington, 1880.

Pak, Ki-hyuk and Seung Yun Lee. *Three Clan Villages in Korea.* Seoul: Yonsei University Press, 1963.

Pak, Ki-hyuk and Sidney D. Gamble. *The Changing Korean Village.* Seoul: Royal Asiatic Society, Korea Branch, 1975.

Park, Chong Kee. *Social Security in Korea: An Approach to Socio-Economic Development.* Seoul: Korea Development Institute, 1979.

Park, Chung Hee. *Saemaul: Korea's New Community Movement.* Seoul: Korea Textbook Co., 1979.

Research Center for Korean Women, Sookmyung Women's University. *Women of the Yi Dynasty.* Studies on Korean Women Series, No. 1. Seoul: 1986.

Steinberg, David I. *The Republic of Korea: Economic Transformation and Social Change.* Boulder, CO: Westview Press, 1988.

Struyk, Raymond J. and Margery Austin Turner. *Finance and Housing Quality in Two Developing Countries: Korea and the Philippines.* Lanham, MD: University Press of America, 1986.

Trewartha, Glen T. and Wilbur Zelinsky. "Population Distribution and Change in Korea, 1925–1949," *Geographical Review,* 45:1 (January 1955), 1–26.

Wagner, Edward W. "The Korean Chokpo as a Historical Source," in Spencer J. Palmer, ed., *Studies in Asian Genealogy.* Provo, UT: Brigham Young University Press, 1972.

———. "The Ladder of Success in Yi Dynasty Korea," *Occasional Papers on Korea* 1 (April 1974), 1–8. Seattle: The Korean Studies Society.

———. "Social Structure in Seventeenth Century Korea: Some Observations from a 1663 Census Register," *Occasional Papers on Korea* 1 (April 1974), 36–54. Seattle: The Korean Studies Society.

Yoon, Jong-joo. *A Study on Rural Population.* Seoul: Seoul Women's College, 1974.

APPENDIX A
GOVERNMENT STRUCTURE OF THE REPUBLIC OF KOREA (DECEMBER 1991)

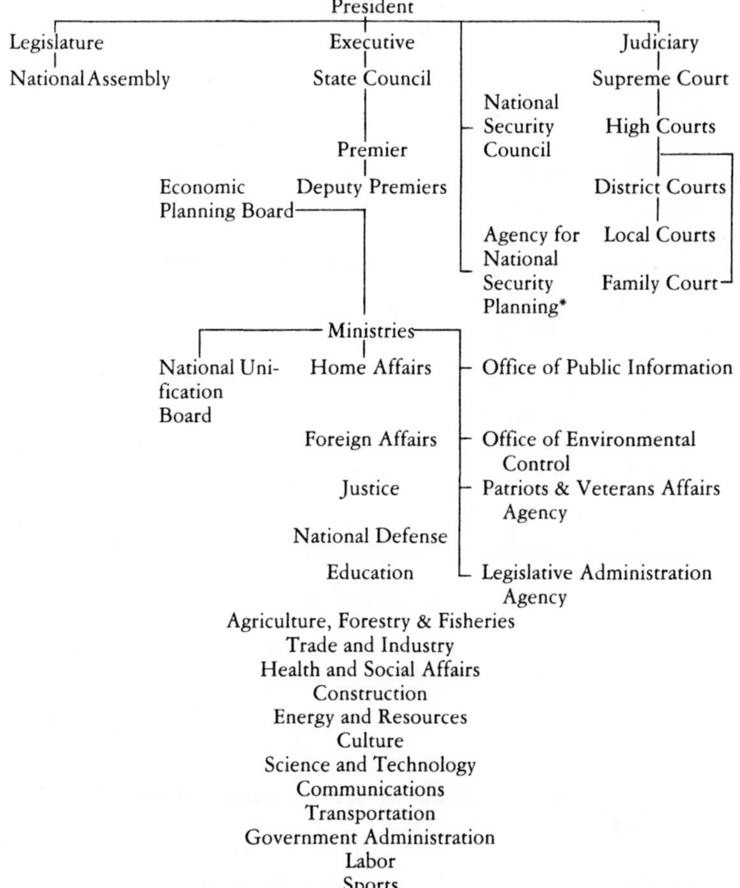

Independent Organs: Board of Audit and Inspection; Central Election Management Committee; Constitution Court

*Formerly the Central Intelligence Agency

APPENDIX B
PRESIDENTS, VICE-PRESIDENTS, AND PRIME MINISTERS

Presidents

Syngman Rhee	August 1948–April 1960
Hŏ Chŏng (Acting)	April–June 1960
Kwak Sang-hun (Acting)	June 1960
Hŏ Chŏng (Acting)	June–August 1960
Yun Po-Sŏn	August 1960–March 1962
Park Chung-hee (Acting)	March 1962–December 1963
Park Chung-hee	December 1963–October 1979
Ch'oe Kyu-ha (Acting)	October 1979
Ch'oe Kyu-ha	October 1979–August 1980
Park Choong-hoon (Acting)	August 1980
Chun Doo-hwan	September 1980–March 1981
Chun Doo-hwan	March 1981–February 1988
Roh Tae-woo	February 1988–

Vice-Presidents (This office was abolished in June 1960)

Yi Si-yŏng	August 1948–May 1951
Kim Sŏng-su	May 1951–May 1952
Ham Tae-yŏng	August 1952–August 1956
Change Myŏn	August 1956–April 1960

Prime Ministers (There was no premiership between November 1954 and August 1960)

Lee Pom-sŏk	August 1948–April 1950
Shin Sŏng-mo (Acting)	April–November 1950
Chang Myŏn	November 1950–April 1951
Hŏ Chŏng (Acting)	November 1951–April 1952
Lee Yun-yŏng (Acting)	April–May 1952

Chang T'aek-sang	May–October 1952
Paik Too-chin (Acting)	October 1952–April 1953
Paik Too-chin	April 1953–June 1954
Pyŏn Yŏng-t'ae	June–November 1954
Chang Myŏn	August 1960–May 1961
Chang To-yŏng	May–July 1961
Song Yo-ch'an	July 1961–June 1962
Kim Hyun-chul	June 1962–December 1963
Ch'oe Tu-sŏn	December 1963–May 1964
Chŏng Il-kwŏn	May 1964–December 1970
Paik Too-chin	December 1970–June 1971
Kim Jong-pil	June 1971–December 1975
Ch'oe Kyu-ha (Acting)	December 1975–March 1976
Ch'oe Kyu-ha	March 1976–December 1979
Shin Hyun-hwak	December 1979–May 1980
Park Choong-hoon (Acting)	May–September 1980
Nam Duck-woo	September 1980–January 1982
Yu Ch'ang-soon	January–June 1982
Kim Sang-hyŏp	June 1982–October 1983
Chin Iee-chong	October 1983–February 1985
Lho Shin-yŏng	February 1985–May 1987
Lee Han-key	May–June 1987
Kim Chung-yul	July 1987–February 1988
Lee Hyun-jae	February–December 1988
Kang Young-hoon	December 1988–December 1990
Ro Jae-bong	December 1990–February 1991
Chung Won-shik	February 1991–

Spelling of the names according to official records.

APPENDIX C
PRESIDENTIAL ELECTIONS

A total of fourteen presidential elections were held between July 20, 1948 and December 16, 1987. The dates, number of candidates, number of eligible voters, number of votes cast, and methods of elections were as follows:

	Dates	No. of Candidates	No. of Eligible Voters	No. of Votes Cast	Elected by
1st	Jul. 20, 1948	4	198	196	National Assembly
2nd	Aug. 5, 1952	4	8,259,428	7,275,883	Popular vote
3rd	May 15, 1956	3	9,606,870	9,067,063	Popular vote
4th	Mar. 15, 1960*	2	11,196,490	10,862,272	Popular vote
5th	Aug. 12, 1960	12	263	258	National Assembly
6th	Oct. 15, 1963	5	12,985,015	11,036,075	Popular vote
7th	May 3, 1967	6	13,035,093	11,645,215	Popular vote
8th	Apr. 27, 1971	7	15,552,236	12,147,824	Popular vote
9th	Dec. 23, 1972	1	2,359	2,359	National Conference for Unification**
10th	July 6, 1978	1	2,578	2,578	National Conference for Unification
11th	Dec. 6, 1979	1	2,560	2,549	National Conference for Unification
12th	Aug. 27, 1980	1	2,540	2,525	National Conference for Unification
13th	Feb. 25, 1981	4	5,277	5,274	Presidential *** Electoral College
14th	Dec. 16, 1987	5	25,873,624	23,070,748	Popular vote

*The results of the March 15, 1960 presidential and vice-presidential elections were nullified as a result of the April Student Uprising.

**The National Conference for Unification was established as an electoral college under the *Yushin* Constitution.

***The new Presidential Electoral College replaced the National Conference for Unification as an electoral college.

APPENDIX D
NATIONAL ASSEMBLY ELECTIONS

	Dates	Number of Seats	Number of Candidates	Number of Eligible Voters	Number of Votes Cast
1st	May 10, 1948	300*	942	7,840,871	7,497,649
2nd	May 30, 1950	210	2,227	8,434,737	7,752,076
3rd	May 20, 1954	203	1,207	8,446,509	7,698,380
4th	May 2, 1958	233	841	10,164,328	8,923,905
5th	July 29, 1960**				
	Lower House	233	1,518	13,344,149	9,778,921
	Upper House	58	210	13,344,149	9,747,688
6th	Nov. 26, 1963	175	976	13,344,149	9,622,183
7th	July 8, 1967	175	821	14,717,354	11,203,317
8th	May 25, 1971	204	696	16,616,258	11,430,202
9th	Feb. 27, 1973	219+	339	15,690,130	11,196,484
10th	Dec. 12, 1978	231++		19,489,490	15,029,387
	In October 1980, the National Assembly was dissolved, replaced by the Legislative Council for National Security of 81 members.				
11th	Mar. 25, 1981	276*+	634	20,909,210	15,403,151
12th	Feb. 12, 1985	276*+	440	23,987,830	20,290,867
13th	Feb. 26, 1988	299*+	1,045	26,198,205	19,853,890
14th	Mar. 24, 1992	299	1,052	29,003,828	20,844,403

*When the National (Constituent) Assembly was established in May 1948, 100 seats of the 200-seat assembly were reserved for the representatives from the north.

**Under a revised constitution adopted in 1960, a bicameral legislative assembly of the 58-member House of Councillors (upper house) and the 233-member House of Representatives (lower house) was established.

+Only 146 members were elected, and according to the *Yushin* Constitution of 1972, one-third (73 seats) of the members of the National Assembly was filled by the members of the Yujŏnghoe, who were nominated by the president and elected by the National Conference for Unification.

+ +Only 154 members were elected by the popular vote in the 1978 National Assembly elections, and 77 seats were filled by the members of the Yujŏnghoe as was in the case of 1973.

*+Under a revised constitution of 1980, certain number of seats were allotted to major political parties as "representatives at large," according to the number of seats won by each party by the popular vote. Thus, in the National Assembly elections of 1981 and 1985 only 184 members were popularly elected and 92 seats were distributed according to the formula. In the 1988 National Assembly elections, 224 were popularly elected and 75 seats were likewise distributed. In the 1992 National Assembly elections, 237 were popularly elected and 62 seats were distributed under a revised formula.

ABOUT THE AUTHOR

DR. ANDREW C. NAHM arrived in the United States in 1948 from South Korea as a college student, whereupon he went on to earn a B.A. from Andrews University and an M.A. from Northwestern University. After teaching Korean language and culture at the U.S. Defense Language School, he earned a Ph.D from Stanford University. He took up college teaching in 1960 at Western Michigan University where he taught various courses on East Asian history. While at the same institution, he founded and directed a Center for Korean Studies. Concurrently, he has also taught at the University of Nebraska and Michigan State University as a guest lecturer. At present, he is Professor of History Emeritus and consultant to the Office of International Affairs of Western Michigan University, and concurrently Adjunct Professor of History at Kalamazoo College.

Dr. Nahm has published numerous articles in academic and professional journals, including *American Heritage*, *Journal of Asian Studies*, *Journal of Social Sciences and Humanities*, and *Korea Journal*. He edited *Korea Under Japanese Colonial Rule—Studies of the Policy and Techniques of Japanese Colonialism* and *The United States and Korea: American-Korean Relations, 1866–1976*. He also contributed articles to the *Encyclopaedia Britannica*, *Collier's Year Book*, and the year book *The Far East and Australasia*. Among his major publications are: *North Korea: Her Past, Reality, and Impression; A Panorama of 5000 Years: Korean History; Korea: Tradition and Transformation—A History of the Korean People;* and *Introduction to Korean History and Culture*.

The author is recipient of an Honorary degree of Doctor of Laws and served as chairman of the Committee on Korean Studies of the Association of Asian Studies.